THE IMMORTAL

BOOK III

The Lost Key Of The Buddha

J. J. DEWEY

GREAT AD-VENTURES

P. O. Box 8011
Boise, Idaho 83707

Great AD-Ventures; P. O. Box 8011; Boise, Idaho 83707

ISBN: 0-9665053-3-6

First Printing: November, 2003

Printed in USA

FOREWORD

As Siddhartha Gautama, who became the Buddha, sat under the Bodhi Tree near starvation, seeking enlightenment, he heard some singing; the words he heard are said to be something like this:

If you tune the strings of a harp too tight,
the sound will not be right.

If the strings are too slack as they play,
a beautiful sound will not be made.

Neither too tight nor too limp shall be the strings,
If the player is to be worthy of kings.

The tension must be tuned by the ear
To fill the soul of all who hear.

When he heard these words, a light turned on in his mind. He realized that the first part of his life, where he dwelt in luxury, was likened unto a string too loose. The second part of his life, where he sought nirvana through starvation and austerity, was as a string too tight.

He now saw a Middle Way that was just right.

Unfortunately, that vision was lost and replaced in history by a watered-down idea that was already common knowledge and turns on no light. In this age it is assumed that the Middle Way is moderation. This assumption is not correct.

In this volume the true Middle Way is again revealed.

The Middle Way will turn on the light, and the principle of enlightenment will again have meaning.

Also Available by J J Dewey:

The Immortal, Books I and II

The Molecular Relationship

The Gathering of Lights

The Gods of the Bible

The Keys of Knowledge

Volumes 1-4

You have in your hands Book III, the long-awaited sequel to the Immortal series. Even though it is third in a series, it can be read as an independent entity with much enjoyment. We warn you, however, you will want to purchase the first two books (published as one volume) after reading this volume.

I have shared this book with numerous friends from my Keys of Knowledge discussion class on the internet, and wish to express my appreciation to them for their opinions and suggestions. If their comments are any indication, the reader is in for a great experience.

In particular, I owe Susan Carter a special thanks for her many hours of editing. Without her help, the printing of this book would not have occurred when it did.

Finally, I give as much appreciation as a man can give for the love and moral support of my wife. I couldn't ask for a more supportive partner, who is always the first to read and edit my chapters.

Are the other characters in the book fact or fiction? Did the events described really occur? I leave this for the reader to decide, with the caveat that the story portion of the book is a combination of true and fictional events. The mystery is… which is which?

THE LOST KEY OF THE BUDDHA

By

J. J. Dewey

CHAPTER ONE
Back from the Future

It was Sunday morning and I had just gotten up from sleeping in. For the first time in a long time Elizabeth and I had the whole day to just relax.

"It's great to have you cooking again," I said to her as I was eating some delicious bacon and eggs.

"Enjoy it while you can," she replied. "One good thing that came out of my illness was that I discovered that you are a great cook. I'm certainly not going to let your talents there go to waste."

"Whatever amount of cooking I get out of you from here on out will seem like a bonus," I smiled. "It's been a week now since you were healed and I must say it's been a great week. It's like a great burden has been lifted."

"You don't know the half if it," she said. "You have to remember the desperate shape I was in. I don't think there is a person alive that is happier to be alive and well than I am."

"I could argue with you on that. You don't know how good it is to see you back to normal."

"I'm glad you appreciate the new healthy me," she said. "By the way, you'll never guess what I heard on the radio this morning while you were having your beauty rest."

"What's that?"

"This local DJ is calling for a search for the Mad Streaker as they are calling him. Apparently everyone thinks it's a big joke, but that football player that tackled you called in, and *he* didn't think it was funny."

"Really!"

"He sounded very angry. He's not too happy about being punched out by a naked prankster."

"Did he say whether or not he got a good look at me?"

"He thinks he would recognize you if he saw you again, but when the DJ pressed him for a description he was kind of vague."

"Thank goodness it was dark. I'm not sure if I could get the best of him without the extra adrenaline and purpose I had that night."

She reached over and kissed me on the cheek, "What a knight in shining armor I have here. You cut your foot, got bit by a dog, beat up a football player and still made it home to rescue me."

She laughed, "You were a little rough-looking, but you made it!"

"Well, I didn't think I made it. My heart really sank when you seemed to die in my arms."

"But you still didn't give up on me, did you?"

"I just about did, but I so glad that I didn't."

"You could have waited a while longer before you brought me back though. I could have stayed on the other side forever if it wasn't for you."

"Based on my short visit to the New Jerusalem I can understand. I've been trying to piece together some of the details you have given me though. Part of the things you saw is different than what I saw. You say you saw a modern looking structure as you approached it and I saw a more ancient-looking one."

"Yes. My memory of the experience seems sketchy, but I do remember seeing a modern-looking structure. I didn't see the pillars or old fashion Greek architecture that you described."

"But you did see the pyramid?"

"Yes. I did see that inside a translucent wall of gold, but the wall seemed to be a modern surface like the Sears Tower or something like that."

"I definitely did not see anything like the Sears Tower," I said. "I wonder if there was some reason that we saw different things. Did you see the circular portals?"

"Yes. There were circular portals."

"How about the names of the tribes of Israel above the portals?"

"Yes, I think I did see the names, but it seems that there were two names on each portal instead of just one.

"So, did you enter through the one with the name of Joseph?"

"No. I don't think so. There were two unusual names, but neither one of them were Joseph."

"Really? I thought we would have both been in the same group vibration. Do you have any memory of the names you saw?"

She paused reflectively a moment. "I'm not sure, but the names were unusual. The first one was something like Zaphnapana."

"How about the second one?"

She closed her eyes for a few seconds and then opened them. "I think the second name was something like _ yes, I remember this one. It was Asenath. That was it, Asenath."

"Zaphnapana and Asenath, those *are* unusual names. I have never heard of them before. They don't sound like Bible names. Are you sure you aren't a closet Buddhist or something? John told me that we see the names that have meaning to our belief system. What kind of belief system could these strange names mean to you?"

"I'm not sure, but I did get the impression they represented something from the Bible. Why don't you see if you can find them in there?"

"Well, I could look, but I wouldn't bet on finding anything."

"Look anyway," she directed.

I went upstairs, got my Bible concordance, brought it to the dining room and opened it on the table. After a few minutes of research I said, "I think I've found something here. Hand me that Bible over there."

I then turned to Genesis Chapter 41 and read verse 45: "And Pharaoh called Joseph's name Zaphnathpaaneah; and he gave him to wife Asenath the daughter of Potipherah priest of On. And Joseph went out over all the land of Egypt."

I looked up at Elizabeth. "This is fascinating. Joseph, who was sold into Egypt, had an Egyptian name of Zaphnathpaaneah and his wife was named Asenath. Were these the two names you saw?"

Her eyes lit up, "Yes. Yes, those are the two names."

"That's just like you. You had to be different and see Joseph's name in Egyptian."

"But I saw more than that. I also saw his wife's name, the female name. That's just like you typical males. You overlook the female half so much that you were unaware that the female name also belongs on the entrance."

"Perhaps," I said reflectively. "I did see both male and female angels, but I did not see the female names. Maybe it was because the idea was not in my belief system."

"Then it's probably time you put it there," she said with firmness.

"Maybe so," I smiled, knowing there was no way to argue with her when she spoke in that tone of voice.

"I wish I could remember it all though. My memories are a little sketchy. I wonder if John would help me retrieve it."

"That may be a while," I said. "In our brief encounter last Thursday he said it would be a while before I saw him again, that this was a time for us to renew our relationship and for me to study and contemplate."

"So have you been studying the life and teachings of Buddha then?"

"Well, I got several books from the library and have been looking through them."

"I'm going to pick your brain on this second key soon. I'm not completely sure I will be permanently healed until you get through the third key. When that is reached we have John's word that I will be well. I take this to mean that after Key Three the disease cannot come back."

"So how do you feel now? Do you still have all of your strength?"

"To tell you the truth, I feel almost too good to be true," she smiled. "I feel better than I have in a long *long* time. Maybe the best I have felt in my entire life."

"But you know what they say?"

"What?"

"There is *nothing* too good to be true."

She exhaled a short laugh. "I guess I just need to have faith in all these wonderful things we have learned."

"I know how you feel," I said. "It's easier to believe that something bad is going to happen than something good. When you think of it, there are probably 100 people predicting negative things for the turn of the millennium compared to one predicting good things. The last time I was in the grocery store a tabloid had a glaring headline about the end of the world around the corner."

"I have an idea," she said, her eyes lighting up, reminding me of her countenance when she was ten years younger.

"What's that?"

"I was just remembering how you used to do guided meditations. Maybe you could take me back to my out-of-body experience and retrieve some of my lost memories. I remember some of it, but I feel a strong need to remember it all."

"I tried to regress you shortly after we first met, but you weren't a good subject, remember? You must be too independent or something," I said only half joking.

"But I remember seeing you do a number of successful guided meditations. Maybe it would work this time."

"I could try. It doesn't work with everyone, but if you're willing we could give it a shot."

After I finished my coffee we went in the living room to begin the experiment. She sat in an easy chair and I sat on a chair in front of her. I tried two different guided meditations and neither was successful.

In frustration I said, "Well I gave it my best shot."

"Try something else then," she said. "You can always find a way to do something when you set your mind to it."

"You seem to have more faith in me than I do," I said.

"Do it," she commanded.

I paused a few moments and formulated another guided meditation in my mind. I spent about a half-hour going through it with her, but she only seemed to remember sketchy details.

"So does anything new seem to be coming back?" I said.

"I don't think so," she said. "This is just the stuff that's been going through my mind all week, but I know there's more, much more! When I try to remember, it's like the whole experience is just hanging there before my consciousness, but just beyond my reach."

"Maybe John can help us. I'll ask him the next time I see him."

"But I feel a strong need to do this now. Can't you just connect with John somehow and get his help?"

"You mean through the Oneness Principle? Well, I can kind of sense his energy, but it's not quite like opening an encyclopedia."

"So what do you sense now?"

"I feel like he's involved in other things right at the moment. He said that this was a time for us to renew our relationship, but I think his absence is more than that. There are some things I don't have a right to know."

"I thought all knowledge is supposed to be available through this union of minds," she challenged.

"All spiritual laws, principles and pure knowledge *are* available after a period of contemplation and seeking, but there are many details we keep to ourselves. John even told me that he needed permission to see my private thoughts so I'm sure the principle works in reverse."

"If you can't get the knowledge through John, then can't you go the next level up to Jesus, the Ancient of Days, or the God of the Universe?"

"All levels seem to be always there," I said. "No matter how high your spirit aspires, there is some intelligence available to meet the need. I know that when I was given power to raise you from the dead that the being assisting me was higher up the ladder than John. I'm not sure who it was. I don't think it was the Ancient of Days, but I know it was a loving and powerful entity of great intelligence."

"Maybe you can contact him again." she said. "Somehow I feel that we are supposed to do this now."

"And where do you suppose that feeling comes from? Maybe you're getting messages yourself through the chain of higher lives."

"I never thought about it," she said. "The impulse I have

seems so natural, but now that you bring the idea up, I sense some presence is guiding me to retrieve my memories. Maybe if I do not retrieve them soon they'll be gone. I'm not sure."

"I've got an idea," I said. "If some entity is trying to guide you to retrieve the memories then maybe we can somehow use his assistance."

"Or *her* assistance," she insisted firmly.

I smiled in acquiescence. "OK. I'm not going to touch that one. Now sit back, close your eyes and relax. We'll give this a try again."

She closed her eyes, "I'm ready," she said.

"Now you said you remembered seeing the light at the end of a tunnel or blackness, but you can't remember what happened just after this?"

"Yes, that is correct."

"Now see yourself approaching this light. Reconstruct everything you can from your memory. You not only saw the light but you had feelings also. What did you feel?"

"I felt peaceful, curious, and hopeful. I don't know why I wasn't scared."

"OK. Put your attention on the approaching light and feel that peace you had as you drew near it. How do you feel?"

"I think I am sensing that peace again."

"Keep feeling that peace and looking at the light." I paused a moment, "Now see if you can sense a presence within you. Concentrate on this a moment and tell me what you feel."

She was quiet for about two minutes. I was just about to break the silence when she spoke. "Someone is here with me. A presence is here. It seems familiar, very familiar."

"What do you sense from it?"

"It wants to help, like it's a guardian angel or something."

"Can you communicate with it?"

"I think so, but I can't put it in words right now."

"Try to ask it how you are supposed to talk to it?"

She was silent again for a few long seconds, then stated, "You are to call it forth."

I paused a moment, not being exactly sure what to do, so I gave it my best shot. I tried to concentrate on what I thought was the presence and said, "Who are you?"

Suddenly, Elizabeth's body went limp. Just as I became a little nervous she sat up straight again and a whisper came out of her mouth. "I am Aluma-EL."

"What happened to Elizabeth?"

"I am Elizabeth."

"But you don't sound like Elizabeth and you say you are Aluma-EL. Who is Aluma-EL?"

"Elizabeth and Aluma-EL are one," she whispered.

"Then why do you call yourself Aluma-EL?"

"I am Elizabeth many of your years from now."

"Are you saying you are from the future?"

"Your future, yes."

"How far in the future are you?"

"Many years, many lifetimes. We are one with the formless worlds and time is not as you know it."

"But you are still Elizabeth?"

"Yes. But I cannot explain all because I am now a part of a *We*, a unity, and you are with me, Joseph.

"And you are Elizabeth or some composite in the future? In other words her future self?"

"I am a part of a unity but the part that was Elizabeth still is as Aluma-El.

Wow! I thought to myself. If I have found a time traveler this is about as fantastic as meeting John. I thought that I should test out this entity as much as possible. Who knows, it could be a Dark Brother or something in disguise.

"I've been in the presence of channeled entities before. How do I know you aren't just a tricky spirit from the spirit world, or worse? How do I know you are not a Dark Brother?"

"A disciple such as you can feel the presence of a Dark Brother. Do you feel any dark presence?"

I had to admit to myself that I did not, but maybe I did not know all their tricks yet. "OK. I feel no negative presence, but you could be masking your true self somehow."

"Then ask Elizabeth how she feels."

"How do I do that?"

"How do you usually do it?"

I took that to mean that I should just speak to her. I called her name, "Elizabeth. Elizabeth."

Her body went still for a moment and then she spoke in her regular voice. "Yes. I am here."

"How do you feel?"

"Fine. Tired, but very peaceful."

"Do you realize that I have just been speaking to someone who claims to be your future self?"

"I'm not sure, but that would explain why the presence seems so familiar. It's like it is a part of me."

"Do you think we can trust it to speak through you?"

"Yes. You need to call it forth again," she said as she closed her eyes again.

Since I could sense no evidence of negativity or the Dark Brothers, I called her future self by name, "Aluma-EL!"

"I am here," was whispered.

"Why are you here?"

"This was one of my most important lifetimes," the voice said. "I am nurturing and guiding this childlike life of mine so she will become as I am now becoming. I am also putting attention on this life. It is sweet unto me."

"You say you are guiding her. Does your guidance in the past change the future? What if she had given in to Philo? Would you not be as you are now?"

"From where we are, all lives and all things in time are before us in consciousness. This is why I can put attention on any past life I desire. If I had chosen the dark path as Elizabeth, I would still be where I am now. From your point of view it would have taken a much longer time period for me to arrive here, but from our point of view there is a part of Elizabeth that never left. This eternal part will wait for recovery from any setback for the union of souls. In the end, we all have the same destiny, but each has a different journey, and some take longer in time to learn lessons than others."

"Are you saying that in the end, choosing good or evil makes no difference?"

"Your choices make a good deal of difference in worlds governed by space and time, and even continue to make a difference in the eternal worlds."

"How could that be true if you say we all wind up in the same place?"

"Because in this world all the past is here before us as NOW. If Elizabeth had chosen the dark path she would have gone into such illusion that I would not want to put attention on such an unreal life. As it is, she is a joy to reflect upon. Her growth and reflection upon the Spirit brings a sense of eternal joy to me. Even though I have become and am still becoming so you hardly recognize me, this little life of becoming as Elizabeth made a great difference in the world of time. Have you heard a good story you like to reflect upon? It is a little like that, but not exactly."

I was beginning to have a little confidence that this person was really from the future as I said, "If you are who you say you are then I have a million questions for you."

"There is not time for that now," said Aluma-EL. "My vibration is too high for Elizabeth to hold for long. You must tell me what you want."

I noted the use of the word 'is' even though Elizabeth was past tense to Aluma-EL from our point of view. "When Elizabeth died she had some fascinating experiences but only has a sketchy memory. Is there anything you can do to bring them back?"

"Joseph...Joseph...Don't you realize that nothing is ever lost? The entire event is before me even now, just as you are."

"So if you see everything that will happen in Elizabeth's life, is the future set then? Could you tell me all the decisions she will make, how long she will live and so on?"

"When I put attention on this point in time and space I am then here in your reality and absorbing it. When I am here I can give you the general direction of your future from the overall picture that I see when in the NOW, but cannot predict it exactly because when I am here I am seeing what is, not what will be."

I found this quite fascinating and asked, "So can you move ahead to what will be and then come back and tell us?"

"I can move ahead, as you say, but when I come back to you I am then here and not there. In our world we do not have memory as you do because we do not need it, all things are before our eyes in the NOW. If all things are before me, then what do I need to remember?"

"So can't you just tell us about some coming future events?"

"I am not seeing all things now because I have focussed attention and I am here; the only memory available to me is that which lies with Elizabeth."

"So right now you cannot tell the future any better than Elizabeth can?"

"I can tell the future better than she only because I am closer to the soul of things, but I cannot be infallible. It is as it should be. No one in the universe is allowed to destroy the power of decision. DECISION will always BE."

"So how do you even know your name to be Aluma-El or that you are from the future?"

"Only because Elizabeth discovered it in her death experience and has the knowledge in her brain memory. This made this point in time and space ideal for me to visit. My time with you is short and you will find out when we proceed. Shall we?"

I had a lot more questions to ask, as this person seemed much wiser than any channeled entity I had ever witnessed, but I decided that if our time was indeed short, then we should just proceed.

"OK," I said. "Let's see what Elizabeth encountered in the afterlife."

"Very well," said Aluma-EL. "Now command me to go back."

"Back to where?"

"Where I died in your arms, when else?"

At this point I noticed a tear running down her cheek. I was surprised for some reason. It didn't occur to me that an entity beyond time and space could still cry.

"You're crying," I said.

She paused momentarily, gathered composure, wiped the tears from her eyes, and said, "Yes, Joseph, my love. I am filled with the joy of eternal love as I go back to this moment. The Apostle Paul was right when he said *Love endureth forever*. All the moments of divine love never die and are taken with us to eternity. I cannot go back to this moment and not weep with joy, even though for you it was a great sorrow. The faith you had, even in the face of death, will live forever with both of you."

At this moment we were both silent for a moment. As we looked in each other's eyes we shed more tears, embraced, and enjoyed a New Jerusalem moment in real time. I sensed that the *me* of the future would love the Elizabeth of the future even more than the Elizabeth of the present. But that is a good thing.

CHAPTER TWO
A Look Beyond

After finishing what I could only describe as a Vulcan Mind Meld with the future Elizabeth, I remembered her saying she could only be with us a short time, so I proceeded to direct her into the past.

"OK. Now I want you to go back to the time Elizabeth died in my arms and retrieve the experience and the memories and relate them to me. What is happening?"

Elizabeth, or should I say Aluma-EL, was silent with eyes closed for a moment; then she spoke:

"I am leaving my body and am standing beside you, looking at my lifeless body in your arms."

"Are you speaking as Elizabeth or Aluma-EL?"

"We are now one, but you can call me Elizabeth. I, as her future consciousness, will be with her to assist and bring the memories back."

"OK," I said. "Elizabeth, you are standing beside me. What are your thoughts?"

"I'm thinking of how light and peaceful I feel, but my thoughts are still with you. I seem to be aware that I am dead and must leave you, but do not want to go. I go to your side and try to comfort you. Then I become aware of a message inside my head telling me I must go a certain direction, but I resist. I do not want to leave you."

She paused a moment so I asked: "Then what?"

"A presence seemed to detect my determination to stay with you and suddenly a beautiful personage appeared to my side, angelic in appearance, in a glistening white robe. Somehow I felt it may be Jesus so I asked: *Are you Jesus or Joshua*?"

"'I am Christed, or anointed of the body of Christ, but I am not that entity who was Jesus, as you call him.'

"*What is your name then*?

"'I AM BECOMING, but you can decide what I AM at this point. Choose a name for me.'

"I found this odd and unexpected. I had read about a number of near- death experiences and never came across a messenger like this. So I said, *If I want to call you George, is that all right?*

"'If you sense George, that is fine. Is that what you receive?'

"*Well, no. I haven't received anything.*

"'Then receive something.'

"*I don't know how.*

"'You do know how. Please – receive a name.'

"I was taken back by this answer. How was I supposed to have some esoteric knowledge like that? Then the words y*ou do know* registered strongly in the core of my being. I reflected momentarily and felt I must name this angel, God or whoever he was.

"*I feel you are very ancient. How about calling you Elder? In a way it seems silly because you look so young, but I sense the word Elder or Ancient.*

"'You are close, think again,' he said.

"I thought again on his name and replied, *I pick up the word EL,* sounding a little like the word ALL.

"That is close enough,' he smiled.

"*What do most people call you*?"

"'It depends on their religion and background. Many Christians I meet want to think of me and others like me, as Jesus. They usually don't say it, but just think it. They sense I am of the body of Christ so this thought is not entirely incorrect.'

"*So this explains how Jesus can greet millions of people who die every day*?"

"'It is one of a number of explanations, if you are willing to receive them.'

"*I don't think I am willing. I can't leave my husband in this condition. Aren't we given some time to linger or something like that*?

"'In many cases yes, but there are things you must be shown

before your time runs out.'

"*What do you mean 'time runs out?' Isn't there all the time in the Universe here*?

"'You do not understand. You shall shortly return to your body. Even now John is sending your husband the message to bring you back.'

"*I'm going back*? I exclaimed. Suddenly I felt good and bad at the same time. It was great to feel the freedom and joyousness of being in the presence of the angel EL, but more than anything I wanted to rejoin my grieving husband.

"'Yes,' said EL, sensing my thoughts. 'You are going back and even now we will have to compress time to cover so much in such a small period.'

"*So if I go with you now, can I return to my husband*?

"'There is a good chance you can come back if Joseph listens to the voice speaking through the soul.' He paused and then spoke, 'It is supposed to be.'

"*What if I stay here for now*?

"'Then I cannot assist in your return.'

"*I was shaken with the realization that going back to my body and my husband was contingent on my cooperation. I instantly decided to cooperate.*

"*OK. You have my attention. What's next*?

"'You will have just enough time to receive some knowledge of the unseen worlds. Some you shall later recall and some you shall not, but you will have an inner sense of the mystery of being hereafter because of what you see.'

"*I've read that time was not even supposed to exist over here.*

"'If consciousness exists, then time exists in one form or another. Consciousness and time are different in the unseen worlds, but they both still exist. Time in the physical world is always passing, but disembodied entities do not have the sense of such passing as do those in physical bodies. Nevertheless, we must proceed here if I am to deliver to you all that are required.

"At this, he took my hand and said: 'You understand how, in human birth on the physical plane, you must first go through the dark birth canal. A correspondence to this happens after death. This is the dark tunnel with the approaching light that many have reported seeing after returning to earth. This is the birth canal leading to a new birth in a new world for the one who passes. Instead of calling the movement from one world to another death, it would be more accurate to call it a new birth. Many who are attuned to higher worlds make the transition so rapidly that the new birth is almost instantaneous and the tunnel is not even observed.'

"Then we proceeded to move into a blackness which I assumed was the much talked about tunnel. I didn't have a sense of speed like we do on earth, but somehow I felt that we were moving a great distance of some kind. I also sensed the motion of many other beings in the darkness. I assumed they were others who had just died and were finding their way to their new home. After what seemed like quite a few minutes I saw a light approaching, and seconds later a living light of some kind seemed to surround us. Then the next thing I knew, I saw a kindly old man in a white beard sitting on a glorious golden throne, surrounded by thousands of beings with harps singing praises or hymns of some kind.

"I was somewhat astounded to be visiting such a standard view of heaven when EL said, 'Would you like to be given a harp and join in the singing?'

"I felt rather nervous and a little guilty for not wanting to join in the singing and playing. I spoke to EL, *Are you telling me that Reverend Bill was right after all – that the good people go to heaven and sing praises all day to God*?

"'What do you think?' he asked.

"*This just doesn't seem right to me.*

"'Then just reject it,' said EL

"*What do you mean*?"

"'I mean feel within yourself that this is not what you want.'

"I gave this direction a try and thought within myself, *This is not the heaven I want.* Suddenly, the whole landscape before me disappeared and a new one emerged. This time I was horrified to see a vision of Reverend Bill's hell. There were lakes of fire as far as the eye could see with a landscape of flaming rocks and desert between the fiery lakes. There seemed to be millions of people boiling in the lakes or being burned by the flames in the rocks and sand. The flames themselves appeared to be living entities that enjoyed participating in the torment, and the stench of burning sulfur seemed to be present everywhere.

"'Would you rather join the residents of the Lake of Fire?' EL said.

"The thought of going to such a place caused a fear to surface that I hadn't known since my youth when I was forced to listen to the sermons of the good Reverend. *Please*, I said. *Take me away from here*.

"'Are you sure you do not feel the need to join these residents?' he said.

"*I do not mean to be disrespectful*, I answered, *but how could anyone feel the need to be in a place like this*?

"'All the people here feel such a need,' he sighed.

"*You can't be serious*!

"'There are numerous heavens and hells, similar to what you see before you, created not by God, but by the illusionary thoughts of humanity. Energy follows thought, and when the thoughts of people dwell on heaven or hell, as they have been taught through the traditions of men, the power of thought draws them to the place where they judge themselves worthy to dwell.'

"*So are you saying that if I was a believer in the standard heaven or hell and felt guilty and unworthy of heaven that I would go to hell*?

"'Yes,' he said. 'Fortunately, this illusionary belief is dissipating among humanity and is losing its hold on many.'

"*How long do people stay in heaven or hell*?

"An entity will stay there until he realizes that something is not right – that the situation could not be something from the mind of God."

"*What happens then*?

"'Then the illusion disappears and the entity has an encounter with his soul. This is sometimes referred to as the *judgment seat of Christ*.'

"*What if one is a Buddhist, Hindu or Moslem*? I asked.

"The temporary heaven or hell will then be adjusted according to their belief system. If the Moslem lives according to his conscience he will go to the heaven described in the Koran having lush gardens, flowing streams and perhaps have virgins or even Mohammed to attend to his desires.'

"*Will it be the real Mohammed*?

"'No,' said EL. 'Instead it will be a Mohammed composed of angelic life forms, called devas by some. These angelic forms are attracted to heavenly thought forms and build forms of desire. These forms of desire can manifest as Jesus, Buddha, Krishna, or God himself, herself, or itself.

"They can also build actuated forms of beautiful men and women who will seem to fulfill every whim of the devotee.'

"*What about hell*? I asked.

"'Various hells are built out of a lower order of angel or deva lives. In a strange way even these lives feel they are giving the entity what he wants or needs. There are many Christians and Moslems who have lived contrary to their conscience and their guilt attracts these lower devas who zealously deliver to them a horrific world based on their thought currents which the devas read. Because these lives build upon thought currents, as I said, they actually feel they are giving the deceived entities what they want'.

"*How is it that an illusionary Mohammed or Jesus is created from angel lives*?

"'All forms in all worlds are created from a multitude of smaller lives. On earth your bodies are created from billions of cells and atoms. Each of these units are a life unto themselves joining to make a greater life which is you. Even your liver, heart and kidneys are lives unto themselves, yet join to create the greater life which is your body.

"'Even so, in the various heavens and hells forms are created by a multitude of lesser lives. Each sphere has its order of building lives.'

"*Does all this have anything to do with the 'many mansions' spoken of by Jesus*?

"The many mansions spoken of by Jesus do not include these lower heavens and hells. A master such as Jesus does not build here, but in the higher realms. These lower heavens and hells form the closest thing to *purgatory* as taught by the church in that they purge a person of illusions which keep him from his soul, or the Christ part of himself.'

"*Do all people go through this purgatory experience*?

"'No,' said EL. 'This is only necessary for those who have held fast in their lifetimes to teachings of strong illusion. Those who live and let live and are open to all truth as it is presented, bypass this experience. They go directly to a temporary union with the soul and pass through the door of the *Hall of Memories, or the Book of Life.*'

"*What about those in Purgatory*?

"'When they realize through inner contact with the soul that God would not consign them to an eternal hell or milk toast heaven then they enter through the door of the soul into the Book of Life.'

"*Then what happens? Is it true that we have some type of life review*?

"'Yes, you encounter a Trinity of ELs such as me, sometimes called Elders or Ancient ones. Under their direction you will become aware of at-one-moment with every part of your life and the meaning of it all. You will also be aware of this life you recently left as it relates to both past and future lives and you will formulate, in connection with your counselors, your next life.'

"He continued, 'After this union with the soul, or judgment as some might call it, you take with you only a skeletal memory of your last life and enter a world which vibrates to a note similar to your own. If you are centered on the feeling nature you will enter one of the seven astral worlds, but if you have developed mind, love and higher thought you enter one of the seven spheres of the mind of God. If you have transcended mind, you will go to a sphere of fiery bliss which some call, the sphere beyond words, or Nirvana.'

"*And is this the highest then*?

"'It is the highest conception I can relate to you, but far from the highest.'

"I wondered at this and asked, *Am I ready to go to the Hall of Memories*?

"'You are not officially separated from earth life. Your silver cord is still connected and this is why you felt yourself going through a tunnel. You are yet between both worlds and will soon return to your body. You only have time for a view of the New Jerusalem and then you shall return. You shall not retrieve on earth all of the knowledge you shall be given hereafter, for there is much that is not to be written. You will, however, remember the feelings you shall experience.'

"*So will I remember what I have been given so far*?

"'Joseph will write it when the time is right, but there is much he cannot write. Tell him that he has New Jerusalem in his heart and he can write it through the Oneness Principle as the need arises.

"There is one more thing…' he said, pausing.

"*What is that*?

"'Light destroys darkness and thus do the dark forces seek first to put out the light. They will do all in their power to prevent the light of truth from coming to the world. These forces will work in many subtle ways to discourage and slow down or stop the mission. The way to victory was given to Joseph in a dream. Tell him to remember and reflect on this dream and he will be victorious.'

"*What dream is that*?

"'He will know when you ask him. Now I give you no more that can be written except this: Reflect on the words of Jesus wherein he said *In the Father's house there are many mansions.* All that you have seen and will see is only the beginning of the mansion worlds.'"

Elizabeth said no more, but her countenance had the most peaceful expression and her eyes moved back and forth as if she were dreaming. I felt that I should not disturb her, but wait to see what happened. She seemed to be going through this blissful dream state for about five minutes and then she opened her eyes and spoke one word.

"Wow!" she exclaimed.

"Wow what? What did you see?"

"Its not so much what I saw, but what I felt. I can barely remember any details, but the experience of New Jerusalem is embedded in my soul and it is *glorious.* I have a memory of the feeling and not the details, but it is enough. I wish I could go back there."

"I know what you mean," I said, remembering my experience there with John. "Now you know the meaning of the scripture that says the reward of Christ is with him. It is not some castle in the sky that he gives us, but unspeakable joy."

"Yes," she said. "That is it, unspeakable joy. I wish this moment could last forever."

"It will someday, my dear," I said. "When we are ready to receive it."

CHAPTER THREE
The Mystery of the Middle Way

"The messenger talked about a dream that you had," said Elizabeth. "He said you would know the one and that you should reflect on it."

"Yes," I said. "As soon as he mentioned it I knew which one it was."

"Have you told me about it before?"

"I think I might have mentioned it."

"I feel it is important you recall it in full and reflect on it as the angel suggested," she said. "Tell me about it again."

"Actually, I do think about it now and again, but now it takes on even greater meaning. I'll think about it more often now that I have the word of an angel. The dream was short, but had a profound affect on me. I dreamed I was climbing a mountain and was nearing the top. With each foot or so of progress I became weaker and it became increasingly difficult to move onward. I forced myself to struggle on and up because there seemed to be no retreat. I had to either reach the top or fall to my death. Using all of my strength I progressed close to the top and found myself hanging from the edge of a cliff. Now all I had to do was pull myself up over the edge and I would be at the top.

"Using the little strength I had left, I attempted to ascend, but my strength was gone. I was tired beyond belief. I was hanging there for a few minutes, becoming wearier until I felt so weak that falling to my death seemed sweet compared to the pain of trying to climb again when I had no strength. In a short time, I reached a point where I was so exhausted that I was losing my grip and seemed to have no hope of saving my life. I was about to let go and fall to my almost welcome death when a voice spoke to me."

"And what did that voice say?" Elizabeth asked, showing increased interest.

"As far as I recollect it said, 'You must try again to pull yourself up, but not for yourself. Many lives depend on you reaching the top. You must succeed for them.'

"After this it was like an impression was planted in my mind. It was as if my success at reaching the top was much more important than my life, for many would benefit from it – thousands, perhaps millions. It seemed to be a large number."

"So did you try again?"

"Yes. Yes, I did. But the trouble was I was so exhausted that I wasn't even sure I could try, but because the voice seemed like the voice of God, I decided I would try again. "Using all of my will, I seemed to find a little strength again, and using determination and faith I didn't know I had, I tried again to climb. As I did I found that the strength I applied seemed to be matched by an unseen hand, and with the assistance of this unseen power I pulled myself over the edge to the top of the mountain. I lay there for a moment in joyous bliss, knowing that I was not only safe, but had attained a power to serve that would help many people and somehow move the purpose of God forward."

"You know what that dream makes me think?" said Elizabeth.

"What's that?"

"It makes me think of the struggle you made to save my life. What other man would have run naked through the streets to save his wife? How many would have not given up even after she seemed to be dead? When you were faced with the impossible, you still had faith, just like you did in the dream when the voice told you to try again."

"That's very sweet of you to say" I said. "Yes, that incident did kind of correspond to the dream, but the impression I have is that ascending to the top of the mountain will be the successful completion of the mission of which John spoke. Apparently, it will be quite difficult to achieve, and there may be times that it will seem impossible to accomplish."

Elizabeth stood up and stretched. "Speaking of your mission, have you been thinking about the last question John gave you?"

"Yes, I have."

"Tell me again exactly what John told you about the second key," she said, sitting down again.

"Basically, he gave me a sketch of Buddha's life – how he went from extreme riches, and finally, to extreme poverty and degradation in search for enlightenment. He received a revelation that neither extreme is the path to God, but a principle called the Middle Way, a path between the two extremes."

"I can't really see any great mystery here," she said. "Most people have the common sense to realize that extremism is not a good way to go. Isn't the average person kind of moderate in his views? What do you suppose John really wants?"

"I'm not sure, but I'll tell you this. The Middle Way is bound to be more than simple moderation. John said the true knowledge of it has been lost, even to the Buddhists."

"And what do Buddhists say it is?"

"From what I can gather, their teaching is very similar to what you just summarized. Some claim the Middle Way is not moderation, but when they teach, it often sounds like they are telling us to take a moderate approach."

"What did Buddha actually say about it?"

"That's one of the problems," I said. "His words were passed down by memorization for hundreds of years before they were written down. Who knows how accurate a record we have of his teachings today? When he was seeking enlightenment through starving himself to death he heard a song that inspired him. The words he heard were something to the effect that if you tightened the strings of a harp too tight, they will break, but if you do not tighten them enough they will not make a good sound. They have to be tightened moderately to produce pleasing music.

"He then concluded that the mind is like a musical instrument that has to be tuned, not to the extreme, but in moderation to function well."

"It does sound like they teach moderation," she said.

"It seems that way," I said, "but then there are other Buddhists who think in more obscure terms, such as the Middle Way is simply Buddha himself, or any teaching that was given by him."

"It sounds like Buddhism has some of the same problems as Christianity, like no written document about the teachings until centuries after they were given."

"Yes, and in addition to this, there are also numerous different sects and many interpretations of Buddha's doctrine. Somewhere in the core of this malaise is a missing core principle that was taught by Buddha."

"Maybe Wayne will have some ideas," she said.

"Maybe. I'm having breakfast with him tomorrow. I'll run some things by him."

Wayne ambled in to the restaurant about thirty minutes late. He isn't the most punctual guy in the world, but I have found that a good friendship is well worth overlooking a few imperfections that we all seem to have.

"What delayed you this time?" I asked.

"Dan," he said.

"What about Dan?" I said, realizing that Dan is one of Wayne's employees.

"I was just ready to leave and he called needing help. His car broke down and he was stuck without money."

"Didn't something similar happen to him a couple weeks ago?"

"You mean when he didn't have enough money to take his baby to the doctor?"

"No. You didn't tell me about that one. I mean the one where your chain saw was stolen on the job and you had to take him a new one."

"That wasn't Dan that was Ron."

"Wayne, you're the only guy I know whose greatest fault is that you help people too much. Your guys seem to have some new crisis almost daily. Sometimes, I think they get together and take turns lining up to take advantage of you."

"You may be right," he said, looking sideways disgruntled.

"And you'd probably be rich if you didn't spend all your profits on them in addition to their salaries."

"You're probably right again," he sighed, glancing at the menu.

"But you're not going to change your ways are you?" I asked, knowingly.

"Probably not," he said. "You know, I haven't had chicken fried steak for a while. I think that's what I'll order."

The change of subject was Wayne's method of telling me he didn't want to dwell on his problems with his guys any more. I sensed he was happy to talk about almost anything as long as it did not involve his employees.

We both ordered, and as I nurtured a cup of coffee, I asked him, "Do you know anything about Buddha or Buddhism?"

"I've read a little," he said. Then he looked at me suspiciously. "Something tells me you are off on another vision quest of some kind."

"You might say that," I said. "I have been studying and thinking of the Middle Way as taught by Buddha. Do you know anything about it?"

"I'm certainly no expert, but have read a little on it. Let's see. Buddha not only taught the Middle Way, but the Four Noble Truths and the Eightfold Path. Don't ask me what they are. I do remember 'right speech' and 'right action' as two of the principles."

I could always depend on Wayne to have some knowledge of almost any subject. He is very well read for a guy with a yard care business and an outdoors look about him.

"What I am interested in is the Middle Way. What do you know about that?"

"What's there to know?" he asked. "Buddha went from extreme riches to extreme poverty, and as he was starving under the bodhi tree he came to this great realization that it was not that smart to starve to death. So he ate a little rice. Personally, I think I'm a lot smarter than Buddha. I don't need to starve half to death to realize that eating chicken fried steak and eggs this morning is good for the soul."

I chuckled. "I guess you have a point. It doesn't seem too bright to starve yourself to death in search for enlightenment."

"I heard he was down to two grains of rice a day before he got this big revelation that it was OK to eat. I think I got him beat. I'd get the same realization if I was down to two Big Macs a day."

"Very funny," I said. "But the revelation was more than to just eat. It was that both extremes are wrong and there is a Middle Way, a third choice between the two extremes."

"But how bright do you have to be to realize that you don't want to be an extremist?" he said.

"That's kind of what I was thinking. Many millions of people think that Buddha got a great revelation, yet even the man on the street already thinks that moderation is better than extremism."

"Well, look at it this way," said Wayne. "He lived in a time that the Hindu teachers were starving themselves and living naked in the woods, thinking they were finding enlightenment. I guess it wouldn't take such a big revelation to rise above the crowd with that bunch."

"Maybe not," I smiled, looking over my shoulder, hoping there were no Buddhists nearby overhearing us. "On the other hand, maybe Buddha made such a big impression on history because he did get a great revelation. Maybe there's more to the Middle Way than meets the eye."

"Well, he taught a lot of other things besides the Middle Way," said Wayne. "Perhaps it was the whole package he presented that caused him to make an impact in history."

"I'm sure that's part of it, yet he seemed to stress that the Middle Way was somehow a core teaching. Why would he put so much weight on a doctrine that is plain common sense everyone already knows?"

"Like I said, maybe the people back there were not too bright," said Wayne. "Perhaps it's something like the early Europeans believing the earth was flat."

"Maybe so, I said, "but the rest of his teachings were quite well thought out and original. This makes me think there has to be more to the Middle Way than meets the eye."

"You might be right, but if you are, I want to ask you something," said Wayne.

"What's that?"

"There's been many millions of Buddhists come and go over thousands of years. Have you heard of any of them asking this question?"

"Actually, I have been reading a lot about the subject and nobody does seem to ask this question."

"Why do you suppose that is?" he asked.

"Maybe they don't have the same source of inspiration I do," I smiled.

Wayne gave me a puzzled look, pondered a moment, and changed the subject.

CHAPTER FOUR
The Encounter

"So how did your conversation with Wayne go?" quizzed Elizabeth.

"All right I guess. I don't have any additional answers, but have formulated more questions."

"Why am I not surprised?" she smiled. Then her countenance changed and brightened, and she spoke with a sparkle in her voice, "Guess what I've decided?"

Something about her tone and radiance told me to get prepared for something significant. "I have no idea," I said a bit nervously.

"Now that I'm feeling better I want to go back to work, and guess what I want to do?"

"What's that?" I said, getting even more nervous.

"I want to work with you!"

"Really?" I said incredulously, seeing big plusses as well as some minuses as I thought about it.

"My mind is made up."

"OK," I said. "That is good, I think."

"You think? You think?" she said, her voice rising.

"I know! I know!" I corrected.

"You'd better know if you know what's good for you. You do want to work with me, don't you?"

"Yes, I think it would be great, but we'd have to find the right thing to do. You've never been in sales before, let alone real estate. Do you think you could handle it?"

"But who says we have to work in real estate? Isn't the market depressed right now?"

"Yes," I said, "but if interest rates go down the market will pick up soon."

"But they may not go down. I say let's do something else instead."

"Like what?"

"You have a wide experience in many areas of business. We could do most anything," she said.

"Any ideas?"

"You are writing a book, so maybe we could do something in printing. That way if we don't find a publisher, you could print the book yourself."

"That's actually not a bad idea," I said.

"Of course it's not a bad idea. Now you're listening to the real thinker," she smiled, obviously pleased with herself

"I can see that," I said, humoring her. "Let's think on this a while and we'll make a decision. I'll tell you this though."

"What's that?"

"If I quit real estate, I can guarantee you that the interest rates will go down and stay down for some time to come."

"Then look at it this way," said Elizabeth, "You'll be doing our country a great favor by quitting. And there's one more advantage."

"Which is…?"

"This real estate business is running you ragged. You often work all hours of the day and evening. Maybe with a different, less demanding business you can have more time to write your book."

"That would be nice," I agreed.

As we thought abut this idea we both became more positive about it, so I quit real estate and we worked toward opening up a small shop. But instead of just doing printing, we decided to make it more full service and also do advertising specialties as well as signs. The idea was that when a business owner came to us we could help him with his needs in a variety of areas, like one-stop shopping.

About six weeks passed and we were approaching opening day. I was musing over things and looked up, noticing Elizabeth looking intently in my direction. "What?" I asked.

"We're about to open our business and you look depressed. What's the matter? You should be excited."

"I am happy about opening the business and working with you," I said, "but I'm wondering why John has not contacted me. I know he was going to give us a little time to relax together, but it seems that a visit is long overdue."

"So do you think you have done your homework on the Second Key?"

"Yes. I've done more reading and thinking on this assignment than I ever have before. I'm more than ready to exchange thoughts with him. But now there's something else that bothers me even more."

"And what is that?" she asked.

"I've lost contact with him." I said solemnly.

"What do you mean, 'lost contact'?"

"As you know, he's taught us about the Oneness Principle and I have been practicing it and doing a pretty good job of tuning into him and the spiritual internet that he told us about. But then a couple of days ago it seemed as if a dark barrier was thrown up and it's almost like John, Christ and even God are not there–like there's nothing up the pipeline for me."

"What do you think is going on?"

"I am not sure," I said. "I have been worried that something may have happened to John, or perhaps I am doing something wrong and have been cut off from the Higher Lives."

"I think John can take care of himself, and I can't imagine anything you have done wrong since you saw him last."

"But something is wrong," I said, "and for the life of me I can't figure out what it is. I just hit a brick wall every time I try to tune in through the Oneness Principle. It's very distressing."

"Perhaps saying the Song will cheer you up a bit," she said hopefully.

"Perhaps," I said. We then said it together and I felt a little better, but still couldn't shake the disturbing feeling.

Over the next few days the feeling seemed to get worse no matter what I did. Then one day when my wife was out shopping I found myself home alone in deep reflection.

I got up and paced the floor and finally stopped, looked upward and exclaimed, "Where are you, John? Why can't I feel you? Why do I feel cut off? Is anybody out there???"

I continued pacing the floor with a sense that a dark cloud was thickening and my words and thoughts were going nowhere, heard by no one.

I let out a shout: "Is anyone listening??? Does anyone care???" I then fell to the floor on my knees. As I was kneeling there, the thought occurred to me that perhaps I should pray and ask God to remove the cloud. Then I began to formulate all I wanted to ask for. I not only wanted the cloud removed, but I wanted communication with John and the Spirit through the Oneness Principle re-established.

I cried out from the center of my being: "O God, remove this cloud of darkness and replace it with light and let me commune with your servants." I looked upward, and as I did, something told me to utter the phrase *open the heavens.*"

I paused a moment thinking that perhaps requesting the opening of the heavens would clear away the clouds that held me downcast. I focused myself in the soul and cried out: "Open the heav..."

I was unable to finish the sentence. Right in the middle of uttering the word "heavens" I was struck down by an invisible force, the likes of which I had never felt before. I had encountered negative forces before, but this was something from the dark side with power beyond that which I had ever previously imagined.

I fell to the floor, unable to finish the sentence and was in pain greater than anything I had ever felt. I was in an explosion when I was young and know what great physical pain is, but this was a new kind of pain that attacked my very spirit and life force. It was far greater than any physical pain I had ever imagined. It was a pain that no one could understand unless he had experienced it. The pain was in a higher part of me that had never known pain before this instant.

I lay motionless on the floor, feeling that something, someone, some group was trying to destroy me - body, mind and spirit; great fear fell upon me, a fear that would make the facing of a firing squad a walk in the park. A firing squad could only destroy the body, but this force, this presence wanted to destroy every part of what I was. I felt that if it was successful I would no longer exist.

As I lay there almost frozen, the only thought in my mind

was deliverance from this powerful enemy, an enemy so overwhelming that only God could set me free.

Using all the energy I could gather within myself, I raised myself up on my elbows in an attempt to call out to my Creator. As I raised myself up I felt a Presence awaiting me. It was a Being so high and holy that the vibration was beyond anything I had ever before imagined. I had felt light and dark before, but these two beings were so powerful, one on the light and one on the dark side, that my astonishment was great indeed.

This God Presence I felt beckoning me was even more powerful than the dark force which was attempting to destroy me. It was as if this Divine Presence would merely have to wave his hand and the dark presence would be gone.

After raising myself up I started to call upon God for deliverance, but at this moment of great tension, before I could release my cry, the dark presence spoke with great force inside my mind:

"Who do you think you are?"

Before I could speak, it continued: "Do you think you are like Moses and dare to see him who is invisible? Do you think you are a prophet? You are nothing compared to the great men of the past."

"No-thing," it repeated.

And then by some power it possessed, it passed before my eyes every mistake I had ever made, every weakness I had ever possessed, and every fear I had ever imagined.

All this happened in the instant that I began to call upon this Divine Presence for deliverance, but in the midst of my cry I began to fear that this dark presence was right. Who did I think I was? I was no Moses, no prophet, no messiah. I was just a regular guy and not much above average in most categories. As I viewed my weaknesses and the mistakes of my life that were being forced on my vision, I felt very unworthy and small. I felt like I should bow out of any mission and turn it over to souls much more able and holy than I.

In the midst of this thought, the Divine Presence invited me to finish my prayer and the intensity of its presence began to grow. But as the intensity grew, a new fear arose in my mind. The presence was more powerful than the dark force, more powerful than anything I had ever imagined. It felt as if even one twinge of unworthiness would cause me to evaporate body and soul.

Before this moment I had no fear of being in the presence of any Divine Being, but coming half way into the Presence brought an awareness of power beyond anything I had ever before imagined, even though I had heard many times before that God is all-powerful. Experiencing Divinity and reading about it are two very different things.

Unfortunately, the delay caused by the dark presence gave me time to think and analyze. If not for this short delay I would have fallen into the arms of the God Presence and been delivered from evil, but a delay and short analysis caused me to reflect on my weakness and conclude that I may not abide the power and glory that was before me.

Because of the overwhelming power, I feared the Divine Presence more than I feared the dark enemy seeking to destroy me. I fell again to the floor in the greatest quandary and the greatest moment of indecision of my life. Then the Divine Presence withdrew and I was left alone, so very alone, to struggle with the Great Destroyer.

I lay on the floor for about ten minutes in the greatest pain I had ever imagined, expecting to die or perhaps worse. My heart was beating over two hundred times a minute and the stress was increasing. The spiritual agony was affecting the physical and I didn't know how much longer I could hold on before the organs of my body would collapse.

There had to be something I could do, but how do you fight that which you cannot see?

CHAPTER FIVE
Fighting the Invisible

I raised myself up again. All I could think of was to plead to God to release me from this mighty force, but the Presence seemed to be distant, and nothing responded to my words.

Perhaps I could laugh it away, I thought. That seemed to work before. I attempted to laugh at the negative presence, but as I did so I realized that it sounded more like a plea or a cry than a real laugh. I was in such distress that placing myself in a true laughing mode was out of the question.

"The Song," I thought. "One of the main purposes of the Song is protection from all destructive forces. This has to work."

I dragged myself to the couch, laid down on it, and using all my strength, I began: "We thank you Father..." The pain seemed to intensify when I said the word *Father*. I had a very difficult time even saying it, and repeated the word several times until I shouted it out.

"Father!!!" I exclaimed. I finally got the word out but my attention was taken from the meaning of the Song, so I began again.

"We thank you Father that you have revealed..." This time it was like something did not want me saying the word *revealed*. I went through the same process until I found myself shouting it out.

Again, I began, "We thank you Father that you have revealed to us your protective universal light..." The same difficulty manifested, not on the word *light*, but the phrase *universal light*.

I began yet again and this time the difficult part was with the phrase *Holy Spirit*.

I continued this process until finishing the first stanza, having similar difficulty with the words *permeates* and *we will.* I continued over and over for close to an hour until I was finally able to complete the Song with reasonable focus.

This seemed to help a little, but I was far from being released from this horrific enemy. I was strong enough, however, to pace the floor, thinking about what to do next. As I was pacing, Elizabeth came in the door.

"The traffic out there is getting as bad as Los Angeles…" she complained. Then she looked at me and said, "You look upset or something. Are you OK?"

"No. I'm not OK," I said and then related the story to her.

She held my hand and asked, "How are you feeling now?"

"After saying the Song it was like a wave of the negative force rolled back, but it's still extremely painful. Feel my pulse and tell me how fast it is."

"Wow!" she exclaimed as she held my wrist. "It is at least double your normal rate."

"And it's slowed down a lot from what it was," *Thank God*, I silently added.

She gave me a hug. "My poor baby," she sympathized.

"When you gave me a hug just then, did you feel anything? Could you sense this presence which is trying to overpower me?"

She looked thoughtful a moment and said: "No. No, I'm sorry. I don't feel anything unusual."

"Don't be sorry," I said. "It just feels so intense that it would seem that anyone could pick up the vibration from one hundred feet away. I'm glad that is not the case."

"I just wish I could understand," she said.

"Remember when you dreamed about that entity who deceived you into looking into his eyes because you thought it was John?"

"Yes, what a horrible feeling it was, like the life was being sucked out of me."

"This is probably something like that, but different. It's not like they want any life force from me but seek only to destroy."

"Obviously, someone wants you out of the way. Maybe this mission John talks about is more important than we know."

"Maybe," I said. "But if they destroyed me, you'd think the Brotherhood would get someone else. Why would the Dark Brothers come against me with such force? I couldn't see the entities, but only feel them. It seemed as if there were millions of them combining their strength."

"That's because you're the most important man in the universe…at least my universe." She leaned over and kissed me lovingly for at least thirty seconds.

Her essence felt so good I almost felt normal for that moment. "Your universe is good enough," I said, smiling.

"Perhaps we ought to take you to a doctor tomorrow to check you out. Maybe he can give you something to take your mind off this attack."

"No. I have a bad feeling about doing such a thing. I don't think a doctor can help and he may wind up thinking I need to go to the funny farm."

"But you don't have to tell him your story, and maybe a sedative would help."

"I think I have to face this with full consciousness," I said firmly. "Something inside tells me this is important."

"OK for now," she said. "But let's get you to bed early tonight. Maybe some rest will help. You'll need your strength when we open our business in a couple of days."

I went to bed early, but couldn't sleep. The wave of negative energy seemed to be getting stronger again. I got up and paced the floor until about 4 AM and finally fell to sleep on the couch and had the strangest dream. I dreamed I was playing chess with this great and dark entity. He made a move and then waited for me to move. As I looked his direction I suddenly felt like I was dissolving body, mind and spirit into nothingness. The feeling was horrible beyond description and I found myself waking up screaming.

Elizabeth came rushing downstairs, "What is it? Are you OK?"

"I'm the least OK I've ever been," I said.

"Have you had any sleep at all?" she asked.

"Maybe a half hour," I said "I'm almost afraid to sleep."

"I won't let you be afraid," she said. "Come to bed with me and let me hold you until you drift off to sleep. It's my turn to protect you."

I looked into her reassuring eyes and felt somehow there was a power coming from her that would help and hobbled up to bed with her. When she took me in her arms and held me tight, the pain and discomfort did subside enough to allow me to sleep.

"Perhaps love is the greatest weapon against evil," I thought as I fell asleep.

For the next few days the negative energy seemed to come at me in waves and I continued to have that dream about playing chess with a dark lord. The stress and intense pain wore on my physical body and I was concerned about having the strength to open the business, but probably not as concerned as my wife.

"Perhaps we should put off opening the business for a while," she said

"I would like to," I said, "but everything is in place, we've run ads and we can't afford much delay. We need to open tomorrow as planned."

OK," she said, "but if you do not feel well, you can go home and I'll manage things."

"It wouldn't make much difference. I've only been getting an hour or two of sleep a night, and if I'm going to be uncomfortable I might as well be useful in the process."

The next day we opened the shop and a few customers wandered in. I was feeling more distress than ever so I sat at my desk while Elizabeth took care of them. Finally, I decided I needed to take a turn and forced myself to my feet to take care of the next person through the door.

As I proceeded to wait on him the negative energy seemed to intensify and I had difficulty talking coherently.

"Are you OK?" the man asked. "you don't look so good."

I started sweating and my heart fluttered away again faster than I wanted to think about, and the room started to spin. I passed out and fell to the floor. In the time I was out I was not entirely unconscious; it seemed like I was falling down a bottomless pit suffering the torments of the damned. I thought of the hell that the angel showed to Elizabeth and him telling her that the inhabitants had a need to endure their situation. Did I have a need for what I was going through? I couldn't imagine such a thing. "I do not need, want or desire this in any way!" I thought angrily to myself.

After this thought I woke up to an unfamiliar face in a uniform. Elizabeth had called an ambulance and several attendants were working to revive me. One lifted me up by the shoulder and said, "Come along sir and we'll see that you get a thorough check up."

"That won't be necessary," I said. "I'll be OK."

"That may be," said the attendant, "but we've got to make sure. Your pulse is over two hundred beats a minute so something is going on here that you need to find out about."

"Honey," said Elizabeth "perhaps you need to get checked out. Maybe they can help."

"A doctor cannot help me," I said, my voice rising. "This is something I must handle myself."

"This is no time to be against seeing a doctor," said the attendant. "Now you really need to come with us."

"I'm staying here, thank you."

"But sir…"

"I'm not going. We'll pay for your services, but I'll take care of myself."

"If you refuse to come I'll have to point out this situation to Doctor Bernstein, your family Doctor your wife mentioned."

I walked over behind the counter and sat in a chair, fearing I may pass out again. "That's my wife's doctor. I don't have one."

"Well, you certainly need one, my friend." the attendant admonished. Then he looked toward my wife and said, "See that this man gets some help."

She nodded her head as the attendants walked out the door.

"Don't you think you're being bull-headed here?" she asked. "If this problem is bothering you as much as you say, then you need to check out every option."

"And what would a doctor do?" I said. "He'd just give me some drugs which would dull my mind so I would have less power of will to defeat this thing. Then if I told him the true story he'd probably lock me away."

"Well, what did you expect me to do with you lying on the floor like that?" she said exasperated. "You could have had a heart attack for all I knew."

"I know it probably looked that way, but if this happens again please do not call the ambulance. The problem will not be a heart attack and I'm not going to die. If I truly have a mission to complete, there is a way to defeat this negative energy."

Elizabeth began pacing back and forth, stopped and looked

my way intently. "You mean that you expect me to just sit back when you pass out and do nothing? What if you died or something? How would that make me feel?"

"I know that I'm asking a lot," I replied as calmly as I could to reassure her, "but I have a feeling in my gut that we shouldn't get doctors involved. I sense they will do more harm than good. No matter what happens, I want you to know that if you follow my instructions I will be happy with you, and place no blame upon you."

She didn't seem happy with this request, but gave a feeble acquiescence to it.

During the next month the waves of attack from the invisible force continued without letting up. Even though I came close to passing out many times, I somehow seemed to be able to will myself to maintain consciousness. If it hadn't been for my strong desire to not worry Elizabeth I do not know if I would have had the strength to function.

After one hard day's work we settled down to dinner. "You're not eating much. How are you feeling?" she asked, caressing my arm.

"About the same," I said. "There's got to be a way to overcome this. There must be something I can do."

"I know John could help if he would just show up," she said. "Have you picked up any message at all from him?"

"Nothing," I said shaking my head. "I've tried again and again but there just seems to be this dark brick wall between me and John or *any* source of light."

"So, do you think it's caused by the negative force?" she said with concern.

"It seemed to start just before the attack, but it is like the attack sealed some impenetrable door between me and the Oneness Principle of communion."

"Exactly what does this distress you are experiencing feel like? I know it is horrible, but how bad is it?"

"It's bad. I won't give you the details or it would just make you even more concerned. Suffice it to say their name is Legion, for they are many; and it's as bad as being in the hell the angel showed you, except I have absolutely no need to experience this. If you put your hand in that pot of boiling water on the stove it would not hold a candle to the spiritual pain I am forced to endure.

She took my hand and held it, looking with loving concern into my eyes. It was only when she gave some loving overture to me that the spiritual pain seemed to subside. At this moment of sharing I had an idea.

"While it may be true that I am hitting a brick wall in spiritual contact, you seem to be OK. I want you to close your eyes and meditate. See if you can pick up through the Oneness Principle what I am to do."

She agreed, said a prayer to herself, and closed her eyes in silence for several moments. Then she opened them suddenly.

"The book!" she exclaimed.

"What about the book?" I asked.

"You were given an assignment to write the book and you have ceased working on it."

"That may be true," I said. "But I haven't been able to think clearly enough since the attack to read a newspaper, let alone write a book. What do the Powers-That-Be expect of me anyway?"

"It may be difficult, but that was the message I received," she said. "You've been able to force yourself to work at the business. Writing should not be any more difficult."

"It is more difficult because I have to have a mind clear enough to think. Did you get anything else?"

"I got the feeling that if you write some on the book and make an effort to continue, no matter what, you will hear from John again. He will guide you toward some key of deliverance from this negative force."

"That's the first encouraging news I've heard since this problem occurred," I said hopefully. "I'll try to write, but under this stress I don't know if I'll make any sense."

"Right now, you're just pacing the floor all hours of the night doing nothing. Can you hurt any worse in attempting to do something?"

"You're right!" I said standing up. "I will try to write no matter how difficult or how garbled the writing may be."

And so my determination and direction was set. After I had finished some work for the business I sat down at my trusty Macintosh to continue writing.

CHAPTER SIX
Finding the Key

It had been a while since I had written anything so I reviewed the more recent writings, and then typed in some notes about items that I needed to cover. I realized that I had not yet saved them, and hit *save as*. That instant the electricity for the whole house shut down for about five seconds, and then came back on.

I found this quite irritating. Here I was, making an effort to get started again, and lost all my notes.

I turned the computer on again. It started to come up, but suddenly the message *system error* appeared on the screen.

I restarted three times and the same thing happened. At this point I felt like shaking the computer. I must have been grumbling out loud. Elizabeth got out of bed and came into the work room, "Are you all right? You woke me up."

"It's this stupid computer," I said. "It ate my notes and now it won't start. I'm about to throw it out in the trash!"

She looked sympathetically at the computer and said, "I wouldn't work either if you were angry at me. Don't you know that even machines have feelings? Their energy interacts with yours and other machines, just like people."

"Don't be silly," I said. We have had this conversation before. She has always maintained that her car breaks down less than mine, not because of maintenance, but because she is *nice* to it.

"It's not silly," she smiled. "Remember when you brought your computer home and it wouldn't work right? I told you it had to spend a few days adapting to your energy as well as my computer. You laughed, but a few days later your computer worked fine."

"That's because I worked out the bugs," I insisted.

"Go ahead and think that. Here, let me start your computer."

She gave the computer a couple of gentle strokes with her hand, whispered something under her breath and turned it on. I sat there waiting for the system error to come on again, but this time the screen came up as it was supposed to. I was kind of looking forward to telling her "I told you so," but this mild disappointment was overridden by the fact that the computer seemed to be working again.

"See. I told you so," she said. She looked up at me with her smiling eyes. "You're not convinced are you?"

"It's not logical," I said shaking my head.

"You're one to talk. Just how logical has your life been since you met John?"

"You've got a point there. Let me type a couple of sentences to make sure everything is working." I opened Microsoft Word and started to type. As I did the lights started to flicker. I quit typing and the lights were steady again.

"It looks like the whole house is upset at me," I quipped. "Why don't you have a little talk with the house and see if you can make it happy again?"

I said this jokingly, but she responded with a serious note. "I'll have a talk with it on my way up to bed. Wait one minute and then I'm sure you can type without interruption."

"You think so?" I challenged.

"Wait and see," she said confidently.

She went upstairs to bed, whispering something under her breath. I waited one minute and began typing again. I worked for three additional hours with no additional problems and this time, got everything safely saved and backed up.

I turned off the computer and started to leave for bed, but then looked back at the machine and wondered. I walked back to the computer and patted it gently and said softly, "nice machine… well done."

I felt kind of silly, but what the heck.

The next morning as we were drinking coffee Elizabeth asked, "So how did the writing go?"

"It was difficult, but I forced myself to sit there and do it," I said.

"Are you going to work on it again this evening?"

"I'll see what I can do."

"Joe, I had another impression when I woke up this morning. I'm not sure, but I think it could have come from John."

I swallowed my coffee hard and said, "What'd you get?"

"That your working on the book, no matter *what* your distress, is your first step toward deliverance."

"Did you receive anything about a second step?"

"Kind of. It wasn't words, just an impression. It seemed that there is another key you must find, not just the second key, and that working on the book is a step toward finding that key. When you find this new key John will come to you again."

"That's encouraging," I said, "but it's not a lot to go on. Did you get anything else?"

"I think so," she said. "It was about the Song."

"What about the Song?"

"You must say it correctly. In fact you must sing it, not just say it."

"Sing it..." I mused. "John told us that it is not sung like a regular song with musical notes, but when thought and feeling follow the words, then the soul sings the Song."

Elizabeth looked at me somberly. "I would imagine that in your present state it is difficult to sing the Song from the soul."

"It is indeed. Nothing I have thought or spoken has penetrated the wall of blackness surrounding me. I'm sure that includes the Song," I replied downcast.

"Maybe we ought to say it now and really try to focus," Elizabeth said gently.

We faced each other, held hands and began the Song.

"We thank you Father that you have revealed to us your protective universal light...."

This time I put extra attention on visualizing the idea that the light of God was universal, that it was everywhere, even in the blackness that surrounded me. It was there waiting to manifest, but because of illusion it just seemed to be distant.

"...that within this light is complete protection from all destructive forces."

This time I saw that when we step into the natural consciousness within the light there is complete protection. Not protection because the singer is special or in a special place, but because the light is universally available to all who have eyes to see. As the dark cannot exist after the rays of the sun dispel the night, even so nothing can harm the one who moves his consciousness into the light that always IS.

"…that the Holy Spirit of Your Presence permeates us in this light, and wherever we will the light to descend."

I saw that when we step into the light in our consciousness, a door opens, allowing the descent of the Holy Spirit to alight like a dove of peace.

We went through the rest of the Song and I put all my focus on "singing" the Song "correctly."

After we finished we sat in silence a moment. Then Elizabeth asked, "What did you feel?"

"I feel my focus was an improvement, but not perfect. This attack I am suffering is too great to ignore completely, but I do feel better. I feel like I can go to work without feeling like I will pass out for the first time since the attack."

"That's great," she smiled, patting my knee. "You must note what moves you away from the dark and into the light. This will lead you to the Key and your deliverance."

I had a strange feeling, "That last line you spoke! It sounded like John. What made you word it that way?"

"I don't know," she said. "I just had an impression to say that to you."

"That was John! I know it. Say it again."

"Let me see," she stumbled. "My mind's blank. I can't remember what I said."

"Now I know it was John. Let me see… you said that I must take notice of that which moves me from the dark to the light – that this is a key."

"Yes," she said nodding. "You must note what moves you away from the dark and into the light. This will lead you to the Key and your deliverance. That was it! It seemed to come to me again."

"OK," I said. "So I do feel a little better and stronger now. What is it that has taken me closer to the light?"

"We said the Song," she said.

"But we said the song earlier. This time the effect was stronger."

"So, we put more attention on the light. Could that be it?"

"That seems too simple," I said. "I was putting attention on the light when this attack began. In fact I don't think this attack would have happened if I had ignored the light to begin with, like most people do. I'll bet if I announced to the Powers-That-Be that I was giving up my quest for light and service, this negative force would just leave me alone."

"Quite possibly," she said, "but since you're not going to give up, you must find the Key to defeat darkness while serving the light."

"You're right," I said. "And it is true that focussed attention on the light while saying the Song did help. What else has helped?"

"You said you felt a little better after doing some writing last night."

"That's right," I said grabbing a sheet of paper. At the top I wrote *focused attention*. "What would be second on the list here? Perhaps *work*."

"No, no," she said. "Not work. You've been working and it hasn't done a lot of good. When you were writing you were advancing toward your mission. You were serving."

"All right," I said. "I'll put the word *service* as second."

"Is there anything else that helped?" she asked.

"Yes," I said. "Something that particularly helped was that night you took me up to bed and I fell asleep in your arms. Each time you have shown extra love and caring, I felt better."

"Than that should be third on the list – *love*."

I wrote down *love* as number three.

"There is one more thing. This did not help you, but hindered. You feared right after the attack. You feared you were not good enough and you feared for your life and soul."

"Yes, but fear didn't bring on the attack, before it happened I had no fear whatsoever."

"But even so, fear came as you fought for your soul."

"It did," I said. "And if anyone thinks they wouldn't fear when they seem to be in the process of annihilation – body, mind and soul - then they *are* deceived. They have not been through what I have been through."

"Even so, fear *did* surface and it will hurt you more than help you."

I nodded in agreement. "I'm sure overcoming fear will help. I think since the beginning of this ordeal I have made progress. When the worst has already happened, the number of things you can fear diminishes."

"So what word can we write for the fourth category? Something that overcomes fear."

"How about courage?" I asked.

"Courage it is," she said, "now read me your list."

"Focused attention (meaning focussing intently on the light), service, love, and courage," I read.

"I am picking up that these four lead to a single key word," she said thoughtfully.

"I have a hunch you are right," I said, "but for the life of me I cannot see the key word they would lead to."

Elizabeth was silent and very still for a moment, then turned to me and said, "I think I have picked up something."

"What?"

Elizabeth closed her eyes, then opened them and looked in my eyes intently. "Live these four principles, in season and out of season, no matter what the discomfort or outward circumstances, and you *will* find the key. Find the key and you will find me again."

This statement brought joy to my heart. I knew it came from John, and I had hope anew I would meet him again soon.

"Let's say the Song again and see if we can say it correctly. The impression I received was that if we say it correctly, it will have more power."

"Yes," I said. "I think we need to apply the principle of focussed attention. Let's see what we can do."

We knelt, held hands, and said the Song together. Both of us focussed intently on the meaning reaching to the soul so it would sing with joy. In addition to concentrating on the meaning, I spent at least half my focus in tuning out the negative. I felt this was my most successful attempt to date.

After we finished we had a moment of silence and Elizabeth asked: "How do you feel?"

"Far from better, but I feel like I can manage today."

"Do you think you can manage to have a good laugh?"

"You mean try again to laugh the negative force away?"

"It worked once before, didn't it?"

"Yes, it did. But the pain has been so great I have *not* been able to bring myself to laugh convincingly."

"But if you're feeling a little stronger, this is the time to try it and use the first item on the list—focused attention."

"You're right. I *should* try while I have some strength."

I tuned into the direction of the negative force and did my best to laugh.

"I've seen you do much better than that without even trying. Now laugh again," she demanded.

I laughed again. It was more like a laugh this time, but still not a laugh from the heart.

"I've got it!" said Elizabeth. "Remember that Indiana Jones movie where the guy was coming after him with knives and instead of fighting the guy as expected, Indiana just pulled out a gun and shot him?"

"Yes, that was unexpected and funny."

"I remember you really laughed at that part. Now all you have to do is visualize this negative force as this goofball with a bunch of twirling knives coming at you while you have a gun. All you have to do is shoot him and then laugh at the situation."

"That's not a bad idea," I said, smiling.

I then attempted to visualize the negative force as being the knife-wielding guy from the movie, hacking away at the air, thinking he is putting the fear of God into everyone. I pull out a gun and shoot him through the heart, and he falls dead on the spot. Then I visualized him lying at the top of a cliff. I shove his body over it and start laughing. Something finally clicked in and I was able to let out a real laugh. It felt so good, I didn't want to stop and went with the laughter as long as I could sustain it. It must have been catching, Elizabeth also started letting out some real laughter.

After a few moments we quieted down and Elizabeth asked, "How do you feel *now*?"

"Better." I said. "And you know what's interesting?"

"What?"

"For that minute or so when I was really laughing and meaning it, I felt no pain."

"It's just a matter of time before you get back to normal," she said, kissing me. "It's getting late. We've got to get to work."

And so, for the next three weeks I focussed my attention on things other than the negative force and the pain. Some may think this would be a simple thing to do, but imagine yourself sleeping in a vat of boiling oil in full consciousness and being told the pain and situation should be easy to ignore. This may be easy to say for someone who has not experienced it, but his attitude would quickly change if he were in *my* shoes. No matter how much I tried to ignore the distress, it was always there. No matter what I did, I was forced to recognize its existence and deal with it.

Despite the difficulty in focussing, I made what I considered to be a superhuman attempt to ignore the pain and focus on the job at hand. *Ignore* is perhaps the wrong word. What I did was create an attitude of mind that did not pay attention to that which was doing everything possible to get my attention. This did not make the pain go away, but it did seem to increase my tolerance for the pain so I could go on normally.

I took away my attention from the negative force and placed it on the four items: the light (the highest I knew), love (sharing love with my wife and others as much as possible), service (I forced myself to work on the book) and courage (I suppose it took courage to move ahead in the midst of such distress).

Then one evening I noticed something wonderful. I was engrossed in writing the book and after about an hour of straight typing, I sat back in my chair to reflect a moment. It suddenly occurred to me that for the past hour I was not working in a condition of ignoring the spiritual pain, but I was working without the pain, or at least most of it seemed to be gone. In fact, it seemed that the pain had been lessening over the past few weeks.

"What then is the Key behind making this happen? What is the key word that will defeat this mighty enemy which has invaded my space?" I paced the floor and went into deep reflection.

Suddenly it was as if a light were turned on in my mind. I could see the principle that could defeat even the Prince of Darkness. I saw the principle, but what was the key word? After a moment's thought I concluded that only one word would fit exactly. This was the key to my permanent deliverance. The longer

I thought about it, the more I felt the truth of it in my bones.

Finally, I shouted out, “John!!! I have the key word! You must come to me now! You promised! I’ve gone as far as I can. Now you must take me further. John, where are you? John…”

CHAPTER SEVEN
Who Do You Think You Are?

I sat back in my chair staring at the computer screen, wondering if I would ever see John again. In fact, his visits now seemed so distant I was almost wondering if I had imagined him. Then I heard the sound of cupboard doors opening and closing in the kitchen.

"Is that you Elizabeth?" I asked as I ran upstairs.

To my amazement it was John, staring in an open cupboard. "Where do you keep your tea?" he asked nonchalantly. "I haven't had a good cup for a while. Where I've been lately, they do not know what a pleasant drink is."

"Tea! You want tea?" I exclaimed. I grabbed a variety box, "We've got lots of tea. Just tell me what you want." I grabbed him to give him an enthusiastic hug.

"Hey, relax," he said smiling. "We've got to stop meeting this way."

I laughed at his unexpected humor. Perhaps the most difficult thing I have had in getting used to him was the fact that his personality is more like a modern man than the standard vision of an ancient apostle.

I let go of him and ran upstairs to the bedroom. "Elizabeth! Wake up. John is here!"

"John who?" she said rubbing her eyes.

"*The* John!" I exclaimed.

"Oh," she whispered. "I'll be right down."

I ran back downstairs. John was sifting through the six varieties of tea available. "I'll take this original Good Earth," he said.

"Three cups coming right up," I said as I started heating up the water.

Elizabeth showed up in the hallway in her bathrobe. "John," she exclaimed holding out her arms for a hug.

He yielded to her warmly and after a few seconds drew back and said, "Your energy is much better. The blockages are removed and as long as you follow the highest you know, your illness will not return."

"I guess I'd better behave myself then," she said slyly.

After the tea was ready we all sat down at the table to talk. "I have a present for you," he said, reaching in his knapsack. He pulled out a bottle of wine and handed it to me.

I looked at it. "A Merlot from Australia" I said. "What made you decide to give me this?"

"If you're going to drink wine you might as well drink the best and healthiest. A truly healthy body has at least small traces of all ninety-two natural elements. Unfortunately, in most of the soil where wine grapes are grown, the soil is depleted of 90% or more of its original trace elements. Australia and a handful of other places still have around 50% of its trace elements available. I bring you wine from Australia because this brand, and several others, still possess reasonable trace elements. You can buy some good ones locally in your stores."

"Shall I open it now?" I asked.

"No thanks. I usually only drink on light-hearted occasions. But you will definitely like this one. After you drink the bottle I want you to absorb the flavor and body of this wine. Try to sense what is in it,, that is good for you, and use this feeling to judge any wine you buy in the future. Your inner sense will tell you, of the wines available, which ones are most beneficial for your body."

"I'll do that," I said.

John sat back and looked at me intently, "I understand you've been having a little problem with our dark friends."

"Indeed," I said, somehow feeling that he knew all about what I had been going through. "This attack has been different and more intense than anything I have ever experienced. Nothing I tried gave me any relief – not prayer, not positive thinking, not affirmations – nothing."

"Nothing until you found the Key. First you applied it unconsciously, but then you began to realize the principle. Now you believe you have distilled it to a key word."

"Do you know the word I have in mind? Is it correct?" I asked with anticipation.

"Later," he said. He looked at me intently and asked, "How much distress are you currently in?"

"It's been better the past few days, but it is still *very* intense. Since you have come tonight I have been feeling a strange vibration from this force. The intelligence behind it is very restless with your presence. Is there something you can do to remove it permanently?"

"You must defeat it yourself. I know it has been difficult for you, but every negative experience has a positive side. Overcoming this will prepare you for things to come. Even so, let me neutralize this old enemy so we can talk in peace."

John got up, walked over to me, stared into my eyes, thumped me on both sides of my forehead firmly with his middle fingers and whispered, "Sleep." Suddenly, I felt normal again.

"Wow! This is great," I said. "I feel myself again." I got up and paced back and forth a few times, soaking in the joyousness of normalcy. I never realized how great normal could feel.

"Don't get too used to it," said John. "I've just temporarily neutralized their effect on you. It *will* wear off shortly after I leave."

"But couldn't you just make them go away permanently?" pleaded Elizabeth. "Why does he have to go through any more of this?"

"You recognize that I have power over these dark lives attacking your husband, and this is true, but how did I receive this power? There was a time I suffered an attack similar to what Joseph has just had, and I also had doubts about myself that sank me into its power. I had a mighty struggle, indeed, and was left alone to battle for a long period of time until I defeated the enemy. If not for the strength gained in this great struggle, I could not be here with you now, and neutralize the force attacking Joseph." he said, looking at Elizabeth.

"Then you know and understand what I have been going through?" I asked.

"I know all too well," he nodded. "All disciples must eventually learn the danger of hesitating in moving forward for the service of the Lord of Light. Many centuries ago, when I had learned that all the apostles except me were murdered, and I realized the difficulty of my lonely mission—treading the pathways of men for two thousand years—I envied those valiant eleven who went on before me. I made a plea, and prayer to God similar to what you did, and I also felt the Presence before me, calling me to move forward in accepting His will. I was about to embrace the Presence when I, too, heard words within my mind."

"What were the words?" I asked, wondering how close they were to what I heard.

"The first words in my mind were, *Who do you think you are?*"

I perked up even more. "That was exactly what came to me. What is it with that phrase?"

"It is the most powerful weapon the Dark Brotherhood has to use against Disciples upon the Threshold. They call it their *word of power which neutralizes the approaching enemy.*"

"It certainly worked on me," I said. "They had me comparing myself to Moses, and I felt pretty small for a moment."

"But a moment is all they need to neutralize you. They planted a thought of comparison in my mind that got to me like nothing else could. It went something like this. *Who do you think you are? Do you think you are better than your eleven brethren who have given their lives for the truth? Do you think you alone deserve to live and work with the Master? Or perhaps you think you're better than your Master who suffered unto death? Give up this cowardly notion of staying alive and have the guts to sacrifice yourself once and for all.*"

"I have to admit that would be a tough thought to handle under the circumstances," I pondered.

"It was very tough and plunged me into a feeling of unworthiness. I doubted my mission, and considered I may be taking the coward's way out, or at the very least, I was being selfish to be the only apostle serving with the Master in the flesh. When I began to feel unworthy the Presence withdrew, and, like you, I was left alone with overwhelming forces of pure evil, bent on my destruction."

"But you had the Master available to you back then, didn't you? Didn't you call upon him?"

"Physically, he was working in a different location on the

earth. He did hear and register my cries, just as I heard yours. What I did not realize is, the Master *had* to leave me alone, I had to learn to master the forces of evil so they would have no power over me during the long and important mission ahead."

"So I take it that you did overcome them," said Elizabeth. "How did you do it?"

"Like Joseph, I thought I was going to die, and maybe become extinct—body, mind and soul. But what hurt almost as bad was the Master did not respond to me. I thought I had failed him and the mission was aborted. I felt that the many saints who had sacrificed their lives were looking down on me with disgust. I sank into despair and this increased the pain and suffering, which, as you know, goes far beyond physical pain. I was about to give up and say uncle. I was prepared to abandon my mission as one unworthy, and live out a normal life, then die. I had a feeling that the attack would cease if I decided this. Then I began to reflect upon the words of the Master to me when I first requested to serve with him through the coming age. His response is recorded fairly accurately in the Bible. Grab your copy over there and turn to Matthew Chapter Twenty."

I retrieved the Bible, placed it on the table and opened to Matthew.

"Now read verses twenty-two and twenty-three."

"But Jesus answered and said, Ye know not what ye ask. Are ye able to drink of the cup that I shall drink of, and to be baptized with the baptism that I am baptized with? They say unto him, We are able.

"And he saith unto them, Ye shall drink indeed of my cup, and be baptized with the baptism that I am baptized with: but to sit on my right hand, and on my left, is not mine to give, but it shall be given to them for whom it is prepared of my Father."

"As I told you before, shortly after this James decided to suffer the fate of the other apostles and serve through the normal process of rebirth, but I stubbornly clung to the idea of serving directly with the Master. I didn't realize at the time that there was some selfishness in my motive. The motive of the true disciple should be service alone, and I indeed did desire to serve, but another part of me just wanted to be with my Lord.

"As I was in the deepest of despair and pain, approaching the point of death, His words came into my mind, *Are you able to drink of the cup that I shall drink of?*

"Then I thought of his own struggle in the Garden of Gethsemane where even *he* hesitated for a moment and asked the Father for permission to bow out of the consummation of his mission. '*Remove this cup*,' Jesus said."

"I never thought of it in that light," I said. "Are you saying that even the Master himself hesitated in his mission?"

"Yes," said John. "At that moment of great tension when the Master was already in great distress over other matters (I will explain later), he was attacked with this same thought, *Who do you think you are?* Imagine how such a thought would affect you if you were in the same situation of becoming a Messiah, *and* proving the truth of life over death?"

"That would be the most overwhelming *who do you think you are* of all," I said. "I would think that in such a situation one would have to think he was out of his mind for thinking such a thought."

"Yes, and almost all would-be Messiahs are half mad, so this makes the job of the real Messiah that much more difficult for him to accept. The only way for the disciple to accept his true mission is to listen to the voice of the Spirit within. The disciple must not doubt that voice no matter what. The voice within, must override the voice without, crying, *Who do you think you are?*"

"But isn't it true that there are a lot of false messiahs out there who really believe they are following the inner voice, but instead are deceived and controlled by the ego?" Elizabeth asked.

"This is true, and part of the reason that deception is so rampant among the masses. When a true or a false disciple explains the source of his message, the description sounds very similar. To the average seeker they are both coming from the same source. It is only when the seeker learns the difference between the voice of the Spirit and that of the ego, that he can discern the true messenger from the false. It is also when the disciple learns to differentiate between the voice of the false ego and the Spirit that he can know for sure his mission is true and useful. When the true voice is recognized by the servant he then faces his greatest test. He gets hit with *Who do you think you are?* And he is tempted to doubt his purpose, and fade away into the twilight. This is the temptation which was given to both Joseph and I."

"What happens to those who yield to the temptation?" I asked.

"The moment they yield to the temptation and assume that their mission was just a fanciful idea not from God, the evil force withdraws, and they have a sense of false peace. It is *not* the peace that passes all understanding, but merely a peace from being left alone, without attack. The deceived disciple temporarily feels better, thinks he has made the right decision, departs from his purpose, and lives a so-called normal life. In effect his progress is suspended for a lifetime or two."

"So, have I failed?" I asked nervously.

"No, my friend," he said clasping my shoulder. "You have doggedly continued, no matter what they have thrown at you. It was difficult on my part, beyond words, to have to leave you alone to face these demons, especially since I have gone through the same thing. I considered there was a 50/50 chance that you would be overpowered, but you roused your strength of will and persisted."

I looked in his eyes and felt like weeping. He did not shed tears, but even so, I felt an overwhelming emotion of gratitude coming from him that I cannot put in words.

After a moment of silence I asked, "So, how *did* you defeat the dark forces?"

"I realized that my situation was a partial fulfillment of the prophesy Jesus spoke, saying I would drink the same cup as he. Then I recalled when Jesus faced this overwhelming evil, he yielded to the Father's will, and went ahead with the mission. I concluded that I must do the same, yield to the higher will and pursue my mission, no matter what. The pain did not go away, and sometimes even increased, but I used a power of will I did not know I possessed. I went about the business of teaching and aiding the infant church. Some members thought I was ill and suggested I take some time off for recovery, but I insisted on working despite the great distraction."

"The word *distraction* is an understatement," I said.

He smiled. "Perhaps. You are one of the few who know what a full attack feels like, so you understand how difficult it was for me to continue to serve. But then as I did serve in distress, just as I would have without the distress, I noticed a weakening of the hold upon me. A realization of how to defeat the Dark Brothers dawned on me just as it did you. At that moment the Master came to me, just as I have come to you. He taught me many things, but most importantly, he told me the tide of the battle had shifted, and I had already gained the victory on the subtle planes. Now I just had to use the principle to seal the door where evil dwells."

"How much longer did it take?" I asked.

"It took another month or two, and it just faded away. The last moment of release came so gradually, I couldn't put my finger on it. There was just a moment of realization that came to me, the force was gone, and I was back to my normal self."

"That's encouraging," I said. "Has the attack ever come back?"

"After overcoming the dark forces of such an attack the Master told me the only danger is to slip back into self-doubt, or guilt. I had two temporary relapses after my recovery, but shortly overcame the doubt and guilt, and I have never had the problem on a personal level since. Unfortunately, this did not make their interference go away. After that, they attempted to get to me by attacking my friends and loved ones."

"Sounds like the dark ones are the original terrorists," I said.

"This is true. Now, I understand you believe you know the principle that will defeat them, and have a key word for me."

"Yes," I said. "I am sure I now see the principle, but I am not sure that the key word I have come up with is the one *you* have in mind. It *is* an unusual one."

"It is bound to be different from the word I formulated. I spoke Aramaic when I was in your situation. The important thing is, the concept is understood, and the key word fits the principle."

He paused a moment, leaned back and said, "Explain the understanding which has come to you."

I gathered my thoughts in the hope that I truly understood in a way that would satisfy John. I started to doubt, but then pushed the doubt away, and proceeded with my explanation.

CHAPTER EIGHT
Defeating the Dweller

"Since the attack I have been racking my brain thinking of the principle that could overcome this force. I tried all the obvious ones: prayer, positive thinking, affirmations and even the Song, but nothing produced any significant change. It wasn't until I just attempted to ignore the distress and worked on the highest I knew - which at this time is the book, taking care of life's needs, and attempting to say the Song with intense meaning - that I noticed a real improvement. As I experienced some improvement I kept asking what the principle behind the progress was. A number of things helped, but not one of them seemed to be the total answer. Finally, after a period of deep reflection a word came to my mind that unfolded the principle."

"And what was that word?" asked John, who I felt did not need to ask this question.

"Yes," said Elizabeth. "What is the word? You've got me curious."

"The word is attrition," I said.

"Attrition!" said Elizabeth. "What kind of key word is that?"

"Do you know what the word means?" said John.

"Well, it seems like it is a gradual wearing away of something," she said.

"And how would you explain it?" John said looking at me.

I replied, "Elizabeth hit on the standard definition which is basically the wearing away of a thing through friction. But the word can also imply disintegration through lack of attention. I remembered that we sometimes used the word in real estate in relation to neglected property. Property can fall apart through lack of attention or attrition. In hard times the real estate industry complained that we lost sales agents through attrition. When salespeople did not have enough business to keep their attention, they fell away and went to greener pastures."

"So, in other words, all you have to do is ignore the problem and it will go away," said Elizabeth.

"It's not quite that simple," smiled John. "Isn't that right, Joseph?"

"It is," I said nodding. "Right after the attack the agony was absolutely impossible to simply ignore. The intelligence behind the attack was vying for my attention and received one hundred percent of it. There was no ignoring possible. I was continually forced to acknowledge the presence."

"So how are you applying the principle of attrition without ignoring the force?" asked Elizabeth.

"Here's what I discovered," I said, leaning toward her. "I had no power over whether or not the presence was bringing pain, and there was no way I could pretend that it was not there. So I looked for the areas where I did have power. When I started working on the book again it took all my strength to take my attention away from the force and place it on the writing, but even though it was difficult, I did manage to do so. When, after a time, I realized that this seemed to lessen the hold of the force, I began analyzing what I was doing. The answer wasn't so much that I ignored the pain and the force, because I was very much aware of it. Instead, I found that, even though it was difficult, I did have power over where I placed my conscious attention. I then found that when I sustained my attention away from the negative to the normal duties I had before me, the power of the force began to diminish. This diminishing of it's power through the denial of attention is attrition. When this word came to me this evening I realized that attrition of the enemy's power through the diversion of attention was the key to its defeat."

"So you're not ignoring it, but just not giving it your attention? Tell me again what the difference is?" asked Elizabeth, looking flummoxed.

"Generally, when you ignore something, you pretend that it does not exist and give it no attention at all. With this force there was no pretending, and because it was painful I was forced to give it *some* attention; but I found I could divert attention and thus take away some of its power. Somehow it seems to feed off my attention."

"Well spoken," said John. "You have no doubt heard the maxim, *energy follows thought*. How do you think this principle applies?"

"Great point," I said, as if a light bulb had turned on in my head. "If the negative force is able to be the focus of my thought, then it's energy can follow that thought and sustain its power. By diverting my attention or thought away from the negative, and forcefully placing it upon the positive, energy will follow, for only good energy will follow good thought."

"Well said, again," said John smiling. "But you already knew the basic principle of energy following thought along with the benefits of positive thinking. How does the principle you saw go beyond the clichés accepted by the masses?"

"The general idea of positive thinking did nothing," I said. "It was only when I roused all my will and made a decision to force the direction of my attention away from the force, bringing the principle of attrition into play that things got better."

"Along this line you might find something the Master said of interest," said John. "Grab the Bible again and turn to Matthew chapter eleven, verses twelve and thirteen."

I opened the Bible and read: "*And from the days of John the Baptist until now the kingdom of heaven suffereth violence, and the violent take it by force. For all the prophets and the law prophesied until John.*"

"Do you have any idea what this means?" he asked.

"I remember reading this scripture before," I said. "I couldn't make a lot of sense of it. It seems to say that those pursuing the kingdom of heaven suffer violence, and violent people somehow take it away from the just."

"But what period of time is mentioned by Jesus?"

"It looks like it was from the time of John the Baptist to the time that Jesus spoke those words—probably about the middle of his ministry."

"And was there a lot of violence during this period?"

"Well, John the Baptist was put to death, but it seems that

Jesus and his followers were able to go about in peace."

"So this did not seem to be a time when there was violent persecution does it?"

"I guess not."

"And have you read anything in the scriptures about violent people taking the kingdom by force during the first couple of years of the Master's ministry?"

"I don't even know if the kingdom can be taken by force," I said.

"If you want to check with your Concordance you will see that *force* and *violence* are not the only options for translation here. I can see why translators rendered the verse the way they did, but they were not looking at the context of the meaning. For instance *suffereth violence* is more correctly rendered *enthusiastically pressing forward,* and the phrase *by force* was used by Jesus as society currently uses the phrase, *Carpe Diem*, or *seize the day*."

"So how would you translate it in words we can understand?" asked Elizabeth.

"I'll do better than that. I'll just tell you what the Master said from memory with my own translation into English. You have to realize that he spoke this verse and others many times with different wordings to different groups. He said this thought dozens of times during his ministry. To get a true impression of the meaning you have to reverse the order of the verses."

John paused a moment and related the words from his own recollection.

"All the prophets and wise men before John dreamed, prophesied, and taught of the kingdom of God. Many had enticing visions, and wished with all their heart that they could reach out and take the kingdom, but they could not grasp it, enjoy it themselves or present it to their people in its fullness.

"But from the days of John the Baptist until now things are different, for the Spirit of the Lord has descended, and the Kingdom of Heaven is at hand. Many sense the opportunity and are pressing forward with forceful enthusiasm. Those who successfully press forward are those who aggressively seize the opportunity – or *Carpe Diem*, as we say today."

"*Carpe Diem*," mused Elizabeth. "Now that's a translation I can understand, especially since seeing the movie *Dead Poet's*

Society."

"So Jesus was basically saying that when the opportunity for the Kingdom presents itself, we must seize the day?" I asked.

"Basically," said John.

"What does this have to do with aiding me in mastering this evil force?"

"Let me expand on this *Carpe Diem* idea as presented by Jesus," he said. "His point was that to obtain the Kingdom, or higher consciousness, we must forcefully seize the opportunity when it presents itself. Taking the kingdom by force, as the Bible says, is not a bad way to word it.

"Many in the New Age movement are making a great mistake in teaching that we must go with the flow. The trouble is that there are two major flows of energy to go with. The first is the spiritual flow and only a few are attuned to that. The second is the flow of force toward matter, or materialism. As far as the vast majority is concerned this second flow is the problem because it is by far the most powerful. Therefore, if the average seeker goes with the flow, he will flow the wrong direction, away from the Spirit.

"The seeker must *resist* the negative flow and tune into the spiritual. He can only do this with the exercise of tremendous force of will. When he first seeks the flow of Spirit, the registration will be weak, and to hold on to it to increase its strength, he must Carpe Diem or *seize hold* of the new energy with great force of decision and will. When he does, the more prominent flow of matter will pull hard on him, tempting him to let go of the budding new energy. Going with the dominant flow at this point leads to disaster, but going with the still small voice of the Spirit leads to salvation."

He paused and looked us over as if to make sure we were registering what he was saying, and added, "But if the seeker holds on to the new energy and by force of will makes it his dominant energy, then going with the flow becomes a positive thing."

"Interesting," I said. "I have heard that true spiritual teachers walk you all around a subject before they hone into the major point. Is this what you are doing?"

"You speak of a true principle," he said. "The reason for this is that a teacher of light always desires a full comprehension from the student, and if he just answers a question in a word the student will fall short in his understanding."

He paused again, and said, "I can see you are anxious to see how this fits with your problem, so let me continue.

"To move along the ladder of spiritual progression we must set ourselves on our next step, and then, by a tremendous force of will, fix our attention and focus on the objective.

"This is the principle you must apply in overcoming this attack you are suffering. Now tell me, what are the positive items of focus you have come up with?"

"I think he's talking about the list we made," said Elizabeth, looking toward the desk.

I went to my desk and retrieved my notes. "Here are four things we came up with."

"Tell them to me," said John.

I read, "Focused attention (meaning focusing intently on the light), service, love, and courage."

John looked thoughtful for a moment and added, "Courage is more of an attitude acquired through experience, but the first three are very applicable to developing the Carpe Diem principle. By causing you great distress the negative force lives off of all this attention it has diverted. The trick is to destroy it through attrition of its energy, forcing your attention through strength of will toward the light of the soul, to service to humankind, and to the love of all. As you have found, your consciousness has been seriously diverted away from these noble pursuits because of your great distress. This causes a vicious circle which continues to feed the negative."

"You're right," I said. "Before this attack I naturally thought of positive things, but afterwards it has been extremely difficult.

"Difficult, but not impossible," said John, looking at me intently. "By seizing the kingdom with violent force of will you *can* force yourself to focus on those noble pursuits and starve the dark forces, causing them to go elsewhere for nourishment. This is why sleep is such a powerful healer. During sleep your attention is taken away from the many forces tearing your body down. A good long rest can weaken these destructive forces through attrition, so when you arise, the positive energies of the body have power over the negative ones."

"Yes, of course, you are correct here," I said. "That is the idea I saw when I received the key word. I realized that I could starve the darkness with attrition. I just needed to use the power of focused will and move my attention. It's kind of like you were saying, John, I can cause my attention to sleep as far as the negative is concerned."

"So now that you see the principle, what will you do differently than before you saw it?" said John.

"Before I saw the principle I tried to dwell on the positive, but I let the pain and distress consume my attention. Now that I see the principle, I may still feel pain, yet will force myself to not put attention on it. I will force my attention away from it until the negative force is starved to death through attrition."

"You've got it," he said. "This is one of those subtle, but important truths. There is a huge difference between putting all your attention on the positive during the good times, and *keeping* it there during times of great distress. "Joseph, I want you to teach this in a future book. It will help a lot of people if they can be helped to understand. This is one of those principles that enabled Jesus to maintain his poise, control, and faith even while on the cross."

"But not many people have an overwhelming spiritual problem to deal with," said Elizabeth. "How would this apply to them?"

"Most people have all the problems and distress they can handle," said John. "Just as it can help Joseph, it can help them. Let's say that a person finds out his spouse is having an affair. He feels a tremendous sense of betrayal. To him it may seem that the distress could not be worse. If he allows the emotional pain to consume his attention, he opens the door to a downward spiral that could ruin his life. The way out is for him to force his attention on the positive things of life while working through the pain. Let me stress, again, that the pain should not be suppressed or it will resurface. If the person allows the pain while forcing his attention on the good things of life, it will not be long before the pain is completely gone. You could say his attention will be sleeping in relation to it.

"After this, his life will be as good as or better than it was before. The pain from the betrayal then dies through attrition, and no suppression is necessary because there is nothing to suppress.

Those who do not understand this principle will often carry painful experiences with them throughout the course of their entire lives."

"Interesting," I said, "but there's one thing I do not understand." I paused a moment, and added, "You said that my attention fed the negative force and I can understand this, but when it first struck I only had my attention on the positive. Why was it able to strike me down with such power when it did not have my attention? After the attack, when I was in pain, it certainly had my attention, but not before."

"There are two reasons for this," he said. "The first reason is that even though at the time of the attack you seemed to be focused on the positive, this has not always been the case. Your soul has been on a journey of many lifetimes. During many of these lifetimes you were temporarily sidetracked into harmful and destructive paths. Like all other souls, you journeyed through valleys of depression, fear, and destruction. During this journey through the negative toward the positive, you carried a residue of the negative with you from lifetime to lifetime. And during this long journey the negative energy slowly accumulated until it developed a shadow form of its own. As this shadow body takes form around the evolving pilgrim, the body becomes occupied by lower elemental lives which combine to create a lower reflection of the worst from your own consciousness."

"We've all heard of a higher self," said Elizabeth, "but this sounds like a lower self."

"Excellent observation," said John. "Yes, you have a lower and a higher self, but the lower parts of yourself are temporary; whereas, your higher natures do not pass away.

"Every entity progressing through the great wheel reaches a point where he becomes dissatisfied with the lower nature and seeks to identify with the higher. When he is in the midst of successfully making this transition, the principle of attrition begins to threaten the life of this lower self. Now I'm not speaking in symbolism here, but of a real lower life form which occupies an astral body the pilgrim has constructed over thousands of years."

"Would this entity be what is called the Dweller on the Threshold that I have read about?" I asked.

"Yes," John nodded, "this is the Dweller. It is said to be on the threshold because when the seeker approaches the threshold of Spirit identification, the principle of attrition drains life force from the Dweller. All the fears from all past lives are stimulated together to create an overwhelming fear of extinction. This negative being then feels he must stop the seeker at the threshold of Spirit or he will die and live no more. Darkness cannot exist in light. When you make the transition over the threshold of Spirit, there isn't a place for him, and he disintegrates."

"Does the Dweller go into nothingness, never to exist again?"

"Every life, great or small, good or bad, is an eternal part of the mind of God and cannot disintegrate into nothingness. Instead, it goes into the unknown for us, but known to God, to be reworked and sent forth again on a higher turn of the spiral. That which is now the Dweller, seeking to preserve its negative life at any expense, will one day be born anew where it can progress into the Light and Love of Father/Mother God."

I sat back in my chair taking this in. Then I stood up and started pacing, which I often do when I'm thinking. "So are you saying that all this grief I have had has been from a life form that I, myself, have given birth to over millennia of wrong thinking? It feels to me that there is more than the Dweller involved. Tell me the second reason you mentioned for the attack."

"You are somewhat familiar with the Dark Brothers, but many do not realize they leave most people alone—there are *not* that many people on this planet who are adepts. Most of what average people think of as the devil tempting or tormenting them is coincidence or their own imagination. As the entity advances, the Dweller slowly comes into play and becomes his personal Satan, seeking to slow his spiritual progression, and then finally making a grandstand attempt at the threshold. The attention of the Dark Brothers only takes place when the disciple becomes a real threat to their plans. When this happens they will use whatever means necessary to thwart the disciple."

John took a deep breath, stood up facing me and grabbed my arm. "This is what happened to you. They saw you as a threat because of the mission I have given you. When you were approaching the threshold they applied their own form of meditation, and energized your Dweller, seeking to give it enough strength to actually take your life. Their powerful thoughtform caused you to doubt yourself for an instant and withdraw from the Angel of the Presence, just as happened to me many years ago. They thought they had you at their mercy, but you did not yield your will and persevered. With the understanding of the Key of Attrition you have now passed to the threshold of victory."

"So it must be true what they say," I mused. "*What does not kill you makes you stronger*." We both sat down again.

"I guess you could say that," John smiled. "When the time soon comes that you starve the Dweller through attrition, then neither the Dweller, nor the Dark Brothers will have a base from which to directly attack you. After this you need never fear them again, as long as you move ahead and not backwards."

"You said they will not be able to directly attack me. What about indirect attacks?"

"Glad you're paying attention," he said. "The brother of light can rise above direct attacks on *him,* but he cannot avoid indirect attacks. For instance, I can avoid attacks on me, but I could not stop one coming to you. If they would have succeeded, they would have gotten to me through you and to Christ through me. If the Dark Brotherhood continues to see the disciple as a threat, they will seek to destroy the mission through the manipulation of family, and friends as well as enemies."

"How about Elizabeth? Do I need to worry about her?"

"You will need to closely watch her and all others who approach your aura. You will be able to sense when they are affected by the Dark Brotherhood. Because of this experience you now know their signature."

"What do you mean he will have to watch me?" asked Elizabeth, looking concerned. "I've been through a lot and have held firm. I see no reason why you should doubt me."

"But you have not yet met your Dweller," John said softly. "Until you meet and master him, there is a danger, and you must be vigilant about keeping your mind centered in the light."

"So what do we do to prevent the Dark Brothers from using others to stop the mission?

"Three things concerning those who have not chosen the dark path," said John. "First, you do everything in your power to direct the person's attention away from the negative influence to the influence of the soul. Second, pray with them if they are willing.

Finally, say the Song with them and encourage them to say it on their own if they are willing. Saying the Song will also help neutralize those agents on the earth who seek to carry out the plans of spiritual destruction.

"Right now the Song is new upon the physical plane, but when you teach it to many—where hundreds, and then thousands, and eventually millions—will combine their strength in saying it; the spiritual power will increase and the tide of the Spirit will overwhelm material and selfish power. This will be a great aid in destroying the hold of the Dark Brotherhood, paving the way for Peace on Earth, goodwill to humankind."

CHAPTER NINE
The Oneness Principle

Elizabeth made us some more tea, refilled our cups, and we continued our conversation.

"It's time to move on now to the Second Key of Knowledge, the lost Key to the Middle Way of the Buddha," John said, taking a sip. "I believe you have been doing some thinking on this."

"Yes, I have, but I don't know how much progress I have made."

"Even so, tell me your thoughts."

I paused a moment in thought and proceeded. "As you know, the Buddha was born into wealth and power which he later renounced in search of enlightenment. He then sought light in depriving himself of all that appeals to the senses and came close to starving himself to death. Then it dawned on him that neither extreme is the way to go, but a Middle Way between the two extremes is where salvation from error and sorrow lies. After he received light on this matter he went forth teaching, expanded his thinking, and gathered many students."

"And from your studies have you come up with the key word for the Middle Way?"

"I've tossed around a lot of words and there seems to be a lot of descriptive words around this principle in Buddhist writings, but none of them so far satisfy me."

"You must choose one before we proceed," he said.

"You say it's a missing key, yet it's hard to believe anything of importance is missing since so much has been written on the subject."

"Quantity of words does not wisdom make," he smiled. "Choose."

"You once told me that we must understand what is not true before we can understand what is true. So, what I am going to do is pick the most obvious word. If it is correct then I save time, but if it is not correct I learn where not to look."

John sat silently waiting for the word. I thought I'd better say something so I said, "*Moderation* is my guess."

"But you know that's not the word," he said.

"I suppose I do," I said looking downward, feeling like an awkward school kid.

"Then why did you not eliminate it yourself and move on?"

"I wasn't completely sure."

"But you were sure," he said, looking steadily at me.

"How can you say that when I really didn't feel sure?"

"That was your lower emotions that cast doubt, but there is another part of yourself that *knew* the word was incorrect. Feel that part of yourself now and then tell me that you did not know."

Suddenly it felt as if my higher nature was amplified and the lower feelings were silenced. I contemplated the word *moderation* for a second and I knew for sure, within my higher nature, that this was not the word.

"You're right," I said. "Now as I reflect upon the word it's crystal clear to me moderation isn't the key word. I feel silly for doubting."

"You see clearly now because you are using your intuitive mind and higher feelings. You are seeing through the Oneness Principle. When you use the Oneness Principle you see through the same eyes as do the Masters of Wisdom and the Christ himself. You also see through my eyes, for my Master and I are one."

"But I still do not see the key word, yet you do. Why is that?"

"Access," he said.

"What do you mean, *access*?"

"Let me first ask you this. How much information is there available on the Internet?"

"It's about like the Library of Congress," I said.

"And how much of it do you have access to this very moment?"

"I suppose that would be nothing since my computer is turned off."

"And if you turn your computer on and go online, how much access do you have?"

"I suppose I have access to whatever address I put in the browser."

"Then you do not have access to the entire Internet at one time?"

"No. I suppose not."

"But to obtain access you must point your browser in a specific direction. Is that correct?"

"I suppose," I said.

"The mind of mortal humans is like that. A seeker must decide on the principle he wishes to understand and then type in the correct address with right thinking. After a period of contemplation he will see the truth with surety on the screen of his mind. Through the Oneness Principle, you just tuned in and saw that which was *not* the Key Word. Even though you clearly saw the vision, you doubted your connection."

"I think I see where you are going with this," I said. "I have tuned into several things about the Middle Way, but just have not come up with the right address to make the principle of the Key Word appear on the screen of my mind."

"Yes," said John, "and you have just used the Oneness Principle at this moment when you saw the principle I was trying to convey to you."

"I suppose I did," expressing some surprise. "I *did* feel like I was seeing through your eyes and wasn't even aware of it until you mentioned it. It seemed so natural."

"I want you to start being aware when you are using it. You must sharpen your skills at tuning in to prepare for a life of teaching. You must learn to see through my eyes, and the eyes of those I see through. I can't always physically be with you, but by using the Oneness Principle I can be with you at all times.

"The Master tried to teach this principle to us many times when he was here, but we were slow of understanding. He often said, *I am with you always, even unto the end of the age*. (See Matt 28:20) This truth was far more literal than I realized at the time., His Presence has been with me for almost two thousand years, even if I am physically across the globe from Him. In fact He is with us at this moment, and can see through my eyes and feel my heart."

This perked Elizabeth's interest and she meekly asked, "Is he aware of me?"

John closed his eyes a small moment and said, "He is." He paused as Elizabeth's eyes showed anticipation. He then looked at her intently, gently taking her hand and said, "*Blessed are you among the daughters of men. I have heard your secret prayers given in sorrow and they shall be answered with joy. Even now your request is being fulfilled.*"

Suddenly tears streamed down her cheeks and she could not restrain herself from crying profusely. Her weeping also had a strong effect on me, and I could do nothing else but take her in my arms and hold her tight. She continued to weep so strongly that I felt her body vibrating for a minute or so.

Finally, John took our hands and guided us back to our chairs. After we sat down he said, "Elizabeth. Is there any doubt in your mind that those were the words of the Master?"

"There's no doubt. No doubt whatsoever," she said, shedding yet more tears. "The words were beautiful, but they were more than words. It was like life and love wrapped together, rolling in a wave and carrying me away. It was amazing."

"Communion with the Master never grows old," he said. "Each one is as fresh and wonderful today as it was in the beginning. But I might add, you are correct in saying that what you received is more than words, for in the Oneness Principle words are not used. All thoughts are sent and received in packages, or quantums, and then are translated into words by the mind of the receiver as needed. What I just gave you came to me as a package of pure holy thought that I then presented to you in my own words. It appears I have translated accurately here."

"I would say so. I have never seen Elizabeth quite so affected," I said. I then looked into her eyes and asked, "And what was your secret prayer that brought up so much feeling in you?"

She grabbed a tissue, wiped her eyes and said, "I know you have been going through great torture since your attack. I can only imagine what you have been going through because of the encounter I had where I felt a draining of my life force. Fortunately, that did not last long, but it was long enough for me to have some understanding. Night after night I have been going to bed and you have stayed up pacing the floor unable to sleep. When I have lain in bed I felt so helpless. I wanted to help you so much, but there was nothing I could do. This was especially difficult at night when I would lay in bed, knowing you were up and struggling in pain.

"Even though I went to bed before you, there have been many nights I have not slept either. So what I have been doing is spending a lot of time in prayer. I have been praying and praying to God that you could be released from this terrible enemy, whatever it is. There were times I almost lost faith, for my prayers seemed to have little effect. Then when John gave me the words of Christ I knew my prayers in secret had been heard, and I was overwhelmed with joy."

She then grabbed my arm with both her hands, her eyes piercing mine, and said, "This Dweller fellow is as good as gone. I know this is the turning point and you're going to be stronger than ever when this is over. I know now that my prayers are heard and my faith in you gives you strength."

"Your faith has always given me strength," I said. "Forgive me for not realizing the toll this ordeal has had on you. I can see that I have been dwelling too much on my own problems."

After a short silence John spoke again, "I have limited time so we must get back to the task at hand. Joseph, you picked the word moderation because you need to find out what is not correct before you can understand what is. Even though you could have saved time by eliminating it yourself, there was a certain wisdom in your approach. Yes, it is true that many Buddhists merely assume that all there is to the Middle Way approach is simple moderation, or avoiding the two extremes, but let me ask you this. What was the first thing Buddha did after receiving enlightenment about the Middle Way?"

"I'm not sure. I know he gathered disciples."

"Take a look in the manuscript you have there – The Gospel of Buddha."

I took the manuscript and turned to the section right after his enlightenment. Then I found something interesting. "It says here he tarried in solitude for forty-nine days without eating."

"Would you call this a moderate act after seeing a vision of the Middle Way? If you met someone today who went forty-nine days without eating, would you call him moderate?"

"No, I guess I wouldn't."

"What would most people call a person who would go forty-nine days without food today?"

"They would think he was insane and take him to the hospital and force feed him."

"The Buddha's father had not seen him for seven years and sent a request for him to visit. After Siddhartha met his father he did not stay in the palace. Where did he stay?"

"I'm not sure," I said, turning the pages looking for the answer.

"Look about there," said John, pointing his finger at the middle of a page.

I read a moment and replied, "It says he stayed in a grove outside the city."

"So would you call this a moderate approach? Siddhartha, the Buddha, had not seen his father for seven years and instead of gracing him with his presence in his residence, he stays in a grove some distance away. Suppose you had a son whom you hadn't seen for seven years, and instead of staying with you in the spare bedroom he sleeps outdoors in a park some distance away?"

"I would think the kid is an extremist rather than moderate," I said.

"Now read what he did the next morning."

I then read the following:

"On the next morning the Buddha took his bowl and set out to beg his food.

"And the news spread abroad. *Prince Siddhattha is going from house to house to receive alms in the city where he used to ride in a chariot attended by his retinue. His robe is like a red clod, and he holds in his hand an earthen bowl.*

"On hearing the strange rumor, the king went forth in great haste and when he met his son he exclaimed: Why doest thou thus disgrace me? Knowest thou not that I can easily supply thee and thy bhikkhus with food?" (From The Gospel of Buddha Published by The Open Court Publishing Company 1894)

"Again I ask is this moderation?" queried John.

I looked at Elizabeth and this time she answered. "The man was a Prince returning home. He could have had the finest dining in the land, yet went from house to house begging for food. That was anything *but* moderate."

"Let alone the fact that after enlightenment he had no possessions except for clothing taken from the garbage of others and a single bowl with which he begged for food. I could imagine what my friends would think of me if I went around town in rags with a bowl begging for food. I'd be called anything but a moderate," I said.

"On the other hand, he lived in a different time and place," said Elizabeth. "Maybe it wasn't so extreme back then."

"You're right," I said, "but it was still extreme. After all, the man was a prince, yet he still went door to door begging for food in his own kingdom."

John smiled and said, "OK, I think we have established that by most any standard, past or present, that Siddhartha, the Buddha, was no moderate, even after his enlightenment. What hint does this give you about the Middle Way?"

"That the Middle Way does not have a lot to do with moderation as many believe. Perhaps, for understanding we should look in a different direction."

"Yes," said John. "It is said that the life of the Buddha was an example of the Middle Way. What hint does this give you?"

"Well, I guess it would mean that even an extreme action such as begging for food when you have riches at your disposal can be the Middle Way," I said.

"So an extremist action can be the Middle Way?" Elizabeth asked.

"Yes," agreed John, "but extremism is not the Middle Way any more than moderation is."

"So if extremism is not the Middle Way and neither is moderation, then what is left— extreme moderation or moderate extremism?" I said, exasperated.

"It looks as if the Middle Way is a moving target," said Elizabeth.

John's eyes lit up. "The lady has just given you a major hint, more than I planned on saying."

"Moving target. Hmmm," I said. "So this is a major hint.

Very interesting. Can I guess another key word?"

"Only one per visit," he said. "Now let us move on to the foundations of Buddha's philosophy. Not only did his actions demonstrate truth of the Middle Way, but his teachings did also.

"As did many world teachers, the Buddha taught a path to salvation or liberation. The foundation of this consisted of the Four Noble Truths and the Noble Eightfold Path. We will attempt to shed some light on these items before I leave you tonight."

CHAPTER TEN
The Four Noble Truths

John seemed to be scrutinizing my face as he said, "Since you have done some studying on this perhaps you can first relate to me the Four Noble Truths."

"I'd better get my notes," I said. I grabbed my writings giving highlights of some of the things I had read. I found the notations on the Four Nobles Truths and said "After the Buddha received enlightenment he apparently received the key to human suffering and our liberation. The first Noble Truth is that we recognize the existence of sorrow or suffering."

"So, do you think that is all there is to the first truth?" John asked. "Doesn't every person on the earth already realize that suffering exists?"

"I suppose so."

"Then what was the additional light that Buddha gave us on the subject?"

I reflected a moment on some material I had recently read and said, "Some Buddhist writers say that the first Noble Truth places an emphasis on a realization of suffering and the depth of its existence. We have to realize that happiness is temporary and eventually followed by suffering. For instance, one may be happy when he marries the love of his life but will have sorrow when they part at death."

"This thought and many other comments on the Four Nobles Truths have merit," said John. "In past ages many great teachers did not write their teachings down. Then their teachings were passed down as their *disciples* understood them and not as the master understood them."

"That makes sense," said Elizabeth. "There's got to be more to the first truth than that suffering exists."

"And there is," agreed John. "Let me give you the first truth as the Buddha intended it to be taught."

He paused and closed his eyes for a moment. I wondered if he was contacting the Buddha through the Oneness Principle. Finally he said, "Suffering is linked to form in manifestation, and form is linked to time. Form is manifested in the three worlds. The first world is the physical/etheric. The second is the emotional/astral and the third is the world of mind. Form, as it manifests in these three spheres, has both a beginning and an end. When an intelligence attaches its desire to the continuation of form, then suffering is the result when the form ends. The first great truth is that when consciousness descends into the worlds of form, then suffering is a natural result and is unavoidable."

"But isn't suffering balanced off by happiness?" asked Elizabeth.

"And isn't it true that sorrow must exist before there can be such a thing as happiness?" I added.

"The Buddha recognized this;" said John, "but one thing still bothered him. When we are in the midst of our greatest happiness we are still plagued with a sorrowful thought – that the happiness is temporary and will soon end. The two of you are a good example. Presently you have a happy relationship together, but if you look to the future you have to realize that a time will come that one of you will die before the other. When your partner is gone, how happy will you be then?"

"That's a terrible thought to place in our heads," exclaimed Elizabeth. "I don't even want to think about such a thing."

"But if you do think about such a thing, it can disturb you in the midst of happiness, as it did just now." he said.

"But isn't the basic idea that we will eventually dwell in some heavenly place and never be separated again taught in most religions? Isn't this an ultimate solution to the unhappiness on the earth?" I asked.

"Not necessarily," said John. "Did you find a permanent heaven when you visited the afterlife?" he asked, looking at Elizabeth.

"I saw heavens and hells that the occupants thought were permanent, but they were not," she said.

"So what would happen if a happily married couple were to die at the same time and go into one of the heavens you saw? Would they live happily ever after never to be separated again?"

"I saw that, after a time, many occupants of the heavens became bored, and what they thought was heaven, was not heaven after all," said Elizabeth. "This was like some kind of awakening that allowed them to move on."

"And do you recall whether friends, family and spouses awakened at the same time?" he queried.

"I don't remember," she said.

"Reflect," he said in a commanding voice.

She closed her eyes and then opened them quickly. "Yes, I see it all now," she exclaimed. "Each person awakened at different times. When a loved one moved out of heaven the ones left behind were sad and were not sure of the fate of the one who advanced."

"So there is sorrow even in the heaven of the religious person who obeyed all the rules," I said.

"Correct," said John. "In the worlds where consciousness identifies with form, whether it is here or in paradise, the possibility of separation exists, the possibility of an end exists, and the possibility of sorrow exists. In addition to this, after a certain period is spent in the non-physical reality, the entity is reborn into another body and experiences another life with new features and influences. This will separate him again from past loved ones and be the cause of a sorrowful and stirring emotion within him that he is not where he belongs."

"I thought that feeling was because we are not in our true home, that we are separated from God," I said.

"In the true reality you are not separated from God, nor are you ever separated from other souls, such as your loved ones. It is illusion to think so. This illusion is caused by our attachment to the form that the reality behind the form occupies. This sorrowful feeling that the person is not where he belongs is caused more from an inner record of associations with past loved ones than a longing for God. In other words, a separation in the current life from loved ones of centuries past can still have a sorrowful effect on the entity."

"I felt that sorrowful longing for something or someone, especially when I was younger," I said. "There were times when I felt very alone."

"And you felt so alone because buried deep inside were memories of many past relationships that seemed lost to you, seemingly never to be found again."

"Seemingly," I noted.

"Following my words closely are you?" he said, reminding me of Yoda. "Yes, *seemingly*. Nothing is ever lost. All sense of loss is based on illusion, an illusion which is dispelled when Nirvana, as taught by Buddha and the Christ, is achieved."

"I do not remember Jesus teaching anything about Nirvana," said Elizabeth.

"But he did," said John. "He merely called it by another name. Do you remember him teaching about the kingdom of heaven or the kingdom of God?"

"Of course."

"That is Nirvana," he said.

"And where did he say the kingdom is?" John asked.

"He said it is within us." I said.

"And does that kingdom within you have any form?"

"I suppose it does not," I said.

"It has no form, but it uses form. The form is not the kingdom, but that which lies behind all forms and all life *is*. In the First Noble Truth the Buddha wanted to stress the great connection that suffering has to impermanent form. Suffering is much more pervasive and extensive than people realize — it is as extensive as form itself."

He took a breath and continued, "Now let us move on to the Second Noble Truth. What can you tell me about this?"

I grabbed my notes again and read, "The second truth seems to be the cause of suffering and from what I can gather, Buddhists believe the cause of suffering is our desires. Desire is never completely satisfied and is often frustrated. This prevents sustained happiness and lays the groundwork for suffering."

"Very good," he said. "Now tell me about the Third Noble Truth."

"The third has to do with the end of suffering. Because all

suffering is related to desire, the end of suffering can come through the elimination of desire."

"And what do you think of the orthodox Buddhist interpretation of these two truths?" he asked.

"Something doesn't seem quite right to me," I said. "Some of the Buddhists writings I read talk about desire as if it were a bad thing, some great cosmic mistake needing to be stamped out by whatever means necessary. This does *not* register well with me. If it were true it would imply one of the main forces God set in existence is a big mistake. and this would imply that our Creator did not know what he was doing when he made us."

"If desire were universally bad then this would be correct," he said. "I want you to read another item from the Gospel of Buddha." He took my manuscript, turned a few pages and pointed to a paragraph. "Read this statement from Buddha after he achieved enlightenment."

I read the following: "*I now desire to found the kingdom of truth upon earth, to give light to those who are enshrouded in darkness and to open the gate of deathlessness.*"

"Notice anything unusual in that statement?" John asked.

"Yes, I do. Even though the Buddhists teach that desire is to be extinguished, here is a direct quote from the teacher himself, after his enlightenment, stating his own desire."

"Here we clearly see that Buddha still had desires, even after he had obtained Nirvana in consciousness. What was it that motivated him to seek enlightenment to begin with?" John asked.

"He desired to know the truth behind suffering and how to eliminate it."

"So would you say that his very quest for Nirvana was motivated by desire?"

"I suppose."

"His powerful desire led him to enlightenment. He was not content with his own achievement; however, he desired to establish an order upon the earth to help *others* achieve nirvana. Would we even have a Buddha and his teachings without the power of desire?"

"I guess not," I said.

"Consider the heavens and the earth and all the hosts thereof. Do you not consider that their manifestation represents the desire of God? It has been said that they are created through the Will of God, but isn't that Will a higher form of desire?"

"That's an interesting thought," I said. "Could it be that when Buddha taught about eliminating desire he was talking about lower desires; but higher desires, such as building the Kingdom of God and serving others, are OK?"

"Not exactly," said John. "The truth is that all desire, whether carnal or spiritual, high or low, carries with it a seed of destruction that can trap the evolving entity and prevent his progression on the path. On the other hand, the Buddhist writings never mention that all desire also carries with it the seeds of true progression. Buddha himself used his power of desire, first to attain enlightenment, and second to enlighten others."

"So how do we avoid the seeds of destruction from our desires?" asked Elizabeth.

"The answer was given by both of the great Masters," he said. "Buddha said it quite eloquently: *Water surrounds the lotus-flower, but does not wet its petals.*

"Water is a symbol of desire. Now picture a lotus floating in desire, or water, completely surrounded; yet, at the same time that its lower parts are immersed in water, the upward surface of the floating petals are completely free from the wetness of the water. They are ever dry, taking in the rays of the sun as if the water did not exist. This symbol is the true meaning of Buddha's admonition to eliminate desire. The Christ phrased it a little differently when he told disciples living in the world that they were not to be *of the world.* The truth is the disciple does not eliminate desire, but *masters* desire. He can float like the lotus, yet dwell in his higher nature as untouched by desire as the upper surface of the lotus petals."

"So even though Buddha still had desires, he mastered them to the extent that his higher nature was always above them?" I asked.

"Correct."

"So why did he seem to teach so adamantly that desire needed to be completely eliminated?"

"This was the way his message was remembered and written down hundreds of years after his death. His teaching on desire was distorted because his core message of the Middle Way was not understood. Followers of a teaching always desire black and white extremes that are easy to register. It was easier to teach the complete elimination of desire rather than the wisdom of effectively dealing with it, as does the lotus flower."

"So how do we effectively deal with desire?" asked Elizabeth. "I know desire is a distraction for me, especially when I want Joseph to do work around the house and he procrastinates. After waiting so long I *desire* to let him have it."

"The key is to not suppress or deny the desire, but to acknowledge its existence without letting it affect your state of being. There are two key words here that will help. The first is *observer*. He who masters the world of desire must look at the world, not as a participant, but as an observer. See the world around you as a temporary setting, as a movie you are watching. Now some people watch a good movie and get so caught up in the characters they feel that they are indeed in the movie. When the lead character gets scared, the observer will forget that he is merely observing, and he will get scared too, even though there is nothing there to harm him. People going through life make this same mistake. They get so involved with physical existence they do not realize that the real part of themselves is merely observing, and are tricked into thinking they are in the true reality."

"So you're saying that we are really here as observers, but we have somehow forgotten this and think we are in a movie that is not even real?" I asked.

"Something like that," he said. "Now the second key word is *detachment*. In order to remove the effects from the unreal—the movie—and return to being the true self, the observer—the disciple—must detach his consciousness from the movie. Only by detaching his consciousness from the story being played out on the screen can he then place it back in the consciousness of the observer sitting in the theater watching the movie. When this occurs an amazing change takes place. Can you tell me what it is?"

I ventured a guess. "Most movies have a lot of terror in them. I would think that if you identified with the lead character you would feel a lot of fear. But when you remind yourself that it's only a movie and you are really safe in the theater, you may understand the fear in the story, but not be affected by it."

"Or it could be the opposite," said Elizabeth. "I've watched romantic movies with a happy ending that left me feeling warm and fuzzy, but then when the movie was over I had to return to some not-so-pleasant difficulties in my own life."

John studied us and said, "So Joseph tells us a motivation for taking the viewpoint of the observer, and Elizabeth tells us why we are tempted to over-identify with the story. The wise observer who is detached has the best of both worlds. He can enjoy the story and take the best elements as imagined experiences to be savored, yet he can be detached in his realization that it is only a movie and not be harmed by the negativity."

"So are you saying that when Joseph procrastinates in doing repairs around the house I should just tell myself I am watching a bad movie and let it go at that?" Elizabeth asked mischievously.

"Not necessarily," said John smiling. "I might add that it's amusing to see that some things in relationships have not changed since I was in Palestine two thousand years ago. You must also take into consideration that the story is not set as it is with a regular movie or book. You have the power to be a director in addition to being an observer, but with a major difference. You have power over only one character,—the lead character in the story— which is of course, you. You have no power to directly control the actions of the other characters, but you can make them react to you."

"What's interesting about this idea is that they are now working on interactive video where we will be able to change the outcome of the movies we watch," I said.

"Yes," said John. "It is interesting that evolution within society usually takes us closer to what is true in the greater reality."

He paused and added, "So taking all this into consideration, what is the Key to Nirvana, as taken from the first three Noble Truths?"

"I would say that the key is to live in the world, yet detach ourselves from the world by recognizing a greater reality of the Kingdom of God within. By centering ourselves and being the observer we can enjoy the movie of life without being negatively affected by it."

"There is one more important step to insure entrance into Nirvana or the Kingdom of God after death," he said.

"What is that?"

"You must be detached sufficiently so when the movie is over you can switch your entire consciousness away from the unreal into the real world. Those who have not achieved Nirvana take the movie of life with them and attempt to replay the emotional scenes over and over rather than adapting to the greater reality. The negative emotions in particular are those which keep the door of heaven closed to the progressing pilgrim. But to open the door Buddha gave the Fourth Noble Truths, which includes the Noble Eightfold Path. This is our next area of discussion."

CHAPTER ELEVEN
The Eightfold Path

John continued his lesson. "The Fourth Noble Truth is the path of deliverance, or salvation, as it is called in Christian terminology. This path consists of eight ideal directives for the human aspirant, all designed to point him toward Nirvana. These are commonly called the Noble Eightfold Path. What is the first one in your notes?"

I checked my notes again. "The first on my list is *right views*."

"The first thing to note," said John, "is that all the teachings of Buddha were passed down for hundreds of years before they were written down in the Pali texts, and by the time they were translated into English, there was far from universal agreement as to the best words to represent the teachings. In addition to this, Buddhists of many different languages today are far from universal agreement, even though they are not as divided as the Christian sects.

"You use a popular English translation *right view* for this first directive. Yet many modern Buddhists insist this phrase does not do justice to the original intent. They claim that the word *right* is too dualistic and this thinking has caused them to consider other words such as *holistic, wise, high* or *perfect*."

"So what is the best word to use?" I asked.

"The word comes from the Pali *samma,* which is derived from two other words. The first part *sa* signifies *one,* and *amma* means *mother* or *mother goddess*. *Amma* was one way of signifying the *divine source* in ancient times since the Divine Mother was thought to be the source of life. Of the various English translations used, *right* is as good as any, for *samma* basically means *the one source*, or *the one divine source*— as right as one can get.

"The word *view* in the first directive, *right view,* comes from the Pali *ditthi.* It has been translated most often as *view*, but also as *belief, opinion, understanding, seeing and perception.* All of these words give an added dimension to *samma ditthi*, but let us go with *view* or *belief*, both very similar in meaning. I would say that it is the ability to formulate a right belief through right seeing, or seeing without distortion to form a sound belief."

"Is that what a seer is?" I asked.

"Yes, a seer is one who can see past the fogs of illusion to that which is real. The seer tunes out that which is not the true reality. Now tell me, what do you suppose is the orthodox version of right belief?"

"From what I've read in Buddhist literature, the most important part of right view or belief is to embrace the Four Noble Truths."

"Yes, Buddha certainly did emphasize that this was a right belief and should be embraced. Do you think that is all there is to it?"

I reflected a moment and added, "It seems that some Buddhists think there can be no right belief not associated with the teachings of Buddha, or even of the lower world which is illusion."

"Yes," said John. "Many have placed too much emphasis on telling devotees what right belief *is* rather than stimulating the seeker to formulate the highest view he can discern and to test it out. All true knowing starts with a belief, but a belief must be nourished and tested so true knowledge can be extracted from it. Hand me those pages you have printed from your computer."

I picked up about fifty pages of Buddhist writings and handed them to him. He held them up and thumbed through them like he knew exactly where to go and said, "Here's a quote from Buddha concerning this principle: *Monks and scholars should accept my word, not out of respect, but upon analyzing it as a goldsmith analyzes gold, through cutting, melting, scraping and rubbing it.*"

He paused reflectively and said, "This is an accurate statement. Very close to the way he used to speak."

"You say that as if you actually heard him teach," observed Elizabeth.

Suddenly John had an atmosphere develop around him that caused an intense feeling to well up inside of me and I knew he was feeling great emotion.

"Indeed. You are very perceptive, I heard the Buddha many times when he walked the earth. I was his dedicated disciple."

"Which disciple were you?" I asked curiously.

"If you can perceive the name through the Oneness Principle, then it is yours," he said wistfully.

"I'll give it a try," I said, closing my eyes.

After a moment's concentration a flash of knowledge came to me. It was not so much a name as a knowing of the name. "This is amazing," I exclaimed. "I know who you were in that ancient life and it makes so much sense!"

"Who was he?" asked Elizabeth, leaning toward me.

"He was Ananda, the Beloved disciple of the Buddha! This man has had the privilege of being the beloved disciple of not one great master but two, both the Christ and the Buddha."

John bowed his head in reverence. "Yes, it was a privilege. Even after examining all my past lives and karma, I do not fully understand why I had such an opportunity of association. Perhaps it was to keep me humble, for these two great beings showed me how far I had yet to go."

"Maybe it was a bit like you showing me how far I have to go," I guessed.

"Perhaps," he said with a slight smile. "Now let us move ahead with the lesson. What is the second directive on the Eight-fold Path?"

"I don't know if this is the best translation, but *right thought* is what I have here," I said.

"Yes, right thought comes from *samma sankappa* and has been translated as *thought, thinking, intention, attitude, resolve, aspiration* and perhaps other words. Though *right intention* most accurately reflects what the Buddha taught."

"Right intention seems to have quite a different meaning from right thought," I noted.

"It may seem so until you examine this directive. Tell me what you have learned about it."

I picked up my notes again and read, "Right thought seems to imply centering one's thoughts on Nirvana and not allowing oneself to be distracted by carnal or lower thoughts of self."

"That's a good western way of expressing it," he said. "But to center one's thoughts on Nirvana, one must first have the intention to do so. One cannot tune out the carnal self without the intention to do so. The direction of all thought is governed by intention. This is why it is said that Nirvana, or the Kingdom of God, is composed of the pure in heart. The pure in heart are those who have right or pure intentions, intentions not distracted by the lower self."

"Many Buddhists say we are to completely eliminate desire, but wouldn't the term *right intention* or *aspiration* imply desire of some kind?" I asked.

"It would seem so," said John. "You have to understand that the human race has made significant progress since the days of Buddha, and at that time the idea of desire was very closely associated with the pleasure of the senses. Many of the common people did not differentiate between higher and lower desire. Because of this, it was easier to just teach the people to eliminate desire. Desire has its place, as I said before, but it has to be mastered so thoroughly it cannot sway the pure intentions of the disciple."

"Interesting," I mused.

"There are three basic right intentions countered by three opposing wrong intentions," John continued. "The first right intention is the intent to focus on the consciousness of Nirvana while ignoring all distractions of the lower self. The opposing intention is to attach oneself to the world of lower desires, giving It the power to sway the mind away from the Kingdom of God.

"The second right intention is that of good will and love toward all human kind. The opposing wrong intention is that of holding on to grievances and negative emotions such as jealously, envy or anger toward your fellow men.

"The third right intention is that of harmlessness, to have the purity of heart to live life without any intentional harm toward any fellow human, no matter how degraded he may be. And what do you suppose the counter, or wrong intention, would be?" he asked, looking at Elizabeth.

"I suppose it would be the intention to cause harm," Elizabeth answered. "I think there are a few bad apples who want to hurt others, but don't most people just want to live and let live?"

"It may seem that way," said John "but the vast majority of people still have a considerable distance to go before they can truly be harmless. The problem with most people is that they do not examine their more subtle intentions, which are governed by lower desires. Let me give you an example that happens way too often.

"A man has a best friend whom he cherishes, and tells himself he only wants what is best for him and would never do him harm. Later the friend falls in love with a beautiful woman. The man also finds the woman attractive, wishing he had found her first. He unconsciously seeks for opportunities to flirt with her and catch her alone. One day, the opportunity to be alone with her arrives and he begins an affair. Later, his friend finds out and is very hurt. Now the man thought he had intentions of harmlessness toward his friend, but wound up creating great harm. Why?"

"Maybe his intentions were not so pure after all," said Elizabeth.

"And his intentions were not pure because they were controlled by lower desire," said John. "To maintain pure and harmless intent, one must become a master of his feelings. If he doesn't he will be the cause of great hurt, blaming it on others, or circumstances, rather than himself."

John took a moment and sipped his tea. He sat back and said, "The Eightfold Path has three divisions. These first two directives, right view and right intention, constitute the first part of the triad and deal with the wisdom aspect. One must see correctly to have pure intentions before he can proceed to the second triad governed by virtue. These are the next three directives. Do you have them on your list?"

I looked at my notes again. "The next three are right speech, right action, and right livelihood."

"These three are in harmony with the many virtues of Christianity, Islam, Hebrew and most other religions. The first of the virtues is right speech. The translation on this one is fine. What do you suppose this entails?"

"I can answer that," said Elizabeth mischievously. "Right speech for a married man is to always agree with his wife."

"I wouldn't argue with that one," John laughed. "No. I don't think I would dare. What are your thoughts, Joseph?"

"I won't argue with that one either," I smiled in Elizabeth's direction. "But John, I suppose you want the Buddhist take on this?"

"That would be nice," he said.

"From what I gather," I said "the most important part of right speech is to speak honestly. Second, one must speak with harmlessness by avoiding harshness, slander, gossip and so on."

"You are right that the most important part of right speech is honesty, but the depth of the principle has much more to it than is realized. Why do you suppose honest speech is important?"

"I would suppose it is tied to the principle of harmlessness. Lies are very hurtful," I said.

"But sometimes the truth is also hurtful," added Elizabeth.

"But when the truth hurts, who is the cause of the distress, the person telling the truth or the person who receives it with difficulty?" asked John.

"I never really thought about it," I said. "I would think it could go either way. If a person just blurts out to an overweight person that he is fat, then the hurt caused would be the fault of the rudeness of the truth teller."

"Yes, but we are talking about speech with harmlessness. Rudely announcing that a person is fat is not a necessary part of telling the truth. The wise person will not present any hurtful truth to another unless he is requested to do so, and even then he speaks with kindness."

"So are you saying we shouldn't tell another he is fat unless he or she asks for it?" asked Elizabeth.

"Even then you can tell the truth without using a word like *fat*," said John.

"So how on earth does a man handle a question from a female such as, *do you think my thighs are too heavy?*" I asked.

"That is a tricky one," smiled John. "If you use the word *fat* you'll either wind up dead or wish you were. But seriously, here is an example of a person asking for truthfulness when truthfulness may hurt. Even so, the true follower of the path must give an honest answer. Joseph, what answer would you give to a question like that to a woman whose thighs are heavier than normal?"

"Hey, let's make a real life situation out of this," injected Elizabeth standing up in front of me. "What do you think of my thighs; are they too heavy?" she asked turning her body, looking back over her shoulder at me intently.

"John, my friend," I said turning my head. "Perhaps we need to speak in private about the direction of your lessons. I thought you wanted me to live to write some books."

John gave a chuckle. "You're on your own here. Let's see what you are made of."

"My thighs," demanded Elizabeth. "What do you think?"

I looked at her as sincerely as possible, "My dear, your thighs are perfect as far as I'm concerned. Your whole body is great. I wouldn't change a thing."

"But there are several places that need some work, aren't there? I know my tummy needs to be a little trimmer and firmer. Now tell me the truth. What do you think?" I could tell Elizabeth was enjoying this at my expense.

I looked at Elizabeth and then at John. I swear he was amused at my difficult situation. "Look!" I exclaimed. "To me you are the most beautiful woman in the world. Your tummy, your thighs, your arms, hips, the whole package is great. I have no complaints."

Elizabeth looked at John and said, "Look at the song and dance I get when I ask a simple question. I know my body is not perfect, but I can't get a straight answer out of him. Now you of all people should be completely honest. What do you think?"

For the first time since I had known him John looked a little shaken. "I didn't sign up for this job to judge female bodies," he said.

"Then tell my husband to let me know exactly what he thinks," she pleaded.

"OK, you two," said John with a gentle reprimand. "Now take a deep breath and let us continue the lesson. Elizabeth, you have to know that you asked a loaded question and if Joseph had told you that you were too fat in any way, you would have been offended."

"So, you think I'm too fat," she flatly stated.

John rubbed his hand over his face in exasperation. "No, no, no. Not at all."

"Now John," said Elizabeth "I know that most men are wimps about telling women the truth, but I did not expect it from you."

"I do not think I have been accused of being a wimp for over a thousand years," he said looking perplexed. "It's not that Joseph and I are spineless here. We have both told the truth, but just wish to tell it in the most harmless way."

"But Joseph told me my body is perfect and that's not the truth. There are a lot of things wrong with it."

"Perhaps that is true in your eyes, but not in his. Notice that he carefully worded his reply. First he said, *your thighs are perfect as far as I'm concerned. Your whole body is great. I wouldn't change a thing.* He was truthfully expressing how he saw you from the aspect of beauty being in the eye of the beholder. It is true that he withheld an analysis of your weight or fat content, but from my limited experience with females this was very wise of him. The refusal to give a full answer or to withhold information, if done with wisdom, is an ingredient in right speech." He paused, thinking a moment and stated, "Open your Bible and read Proverbs 25:2."

I grabbed the Bible quickly, glad to have John on my side, opened it and read, "*It is the glory of God to conceal a thing, but the honor of kings to search out a matter.*"

"So does God tell us everything he knows?" John asked.

"I guess not," I said. "It adds to his glory to conceal things."

"And how many things are concealed?"

"I know that many things are concealed from me. There are a lot of things I want to know that are not in any scriptures."

"Indeed," he said. "And concealment is a part of right speech. He who speaks correctly will sometimes tell the full truth, other times he will hold back some truth, but there is one thing he will always do."

"What is that?" Elizabeth asked.

"Everything he will speak will, to the best of his ability, be true."

"So Joseph was speaking the truth when he says I have a perfect body? Come on!" Elizabeth exclaimed, glaring at me.

"Believe me, if you weighed a few pounds more or less than perfection, it would make no difference with him. He accepts you perfectly just the way you are, and when you are old and much less physically perfect than you are right now, he will still see perfection in you." said John. I relaxed a little, appreciating the defense he put forth.

"That's sweet of you to say," she said demurely.

"Now tell me," he said. "If Joseph had told you that your thighs were too big, you would have been offended, wouldn't you?"

"I just wanted to know the truth," she whimpered.

"But now you must tell the truth. You would have been offended and wouldn't have been able to get the thought out of your mind for weeks. Isn't that right?""

"Perhaps it's my turn to teach you two a mystery that seems to escape all men," countered Elizabeth. "When females ask questions like I just did, we already know if we are overweight or not. We just want reassurance that we are accepted the way we are."

"So I gave you the answer you wanted after all?" I asked hopefully.

"Maybe, but you could have been a little more convincing."

"Now that we have the greatest of all mysteries cleared up, perhaps we can move on," said John clearing his throat.

"Yes, let's move on," I said. "I'm sure John does not have unlimited time with us."

Elizabeth gave me a look that told me she was concealing some thoughts of her own as John continued. "As I said, the principle behind this virtue is more important than is realized. Wrong speech is deceptive speech, and when one knowingly deceives, he casts a cloud between himself and his own soul. Right speech is speech which is true, as the consciousness of the entity understands truth. If a person will continue to speak only the truth with no conscious deception, then he sets himself on the true path of liberation and the greater consciousness of Nirvana. Sometimes the truth is very difficult to speak, but it must be spoken if deception is to be dispelled."

"I was listening to a talk show the other day," said Elizabeth, "and a caller stated that he had an affair a while back, but it had come to an end. He wanted to know whether or not to tell his wife about it. The host told him no – that it may cause the end of his marriage and the truth served no purpose now that the affair had ended. In fact he was told to lie about it if necessary."

John shook his head and said. "It is troubling that this idea of deception has gained such wide support through the media, even embraced by many who think they know the mind of God. If a person has an affair and wishes to make amends, he needs to tell his spouse, even at the risk of losing him or her. It is better to lose in marriage than to create a bottomless pit between you and your own soul. If your spouse asks if you have had an affair, the importance of stating the truth is more important still because you are placed in a position of outright lying or telling the truth. There is no other choice when such a question is asked. The point that the deceivers do not realize is this: The spouse already knows the truth on the subtle planes, and if there is a betrayal of trust, great damage is already occurring. The betrayed spouse will already feel a spiritual gap in the relationship and may not be able to consciously explain why. Continued deceit will make this gap widen until the relationship is destroyed. The only hope of saving it is truth in communication. I cannot emphasize enough the importance of consistent honest speech in opening up the spiritual path as well as the spiritual dimension of all relationships. Just because a couple stays together does not mean they have depth to their relationship."

John paused a moment to let the information sink in and asked, "Now, the second main aspect of right speech is harmlessness. In addition to telling the truth, what can you do to apply harmlessness to your communications?"

I ventured an answer, "I would say that when you are stating a difficult truth, you should word your speech so the receiver is hurt as little as possible."

Elizabeth added, "And I would say that we should avoid negative criticism, gossip, slander, anger and all hurtful words."

"Very good," said John. "Many of the steps toward harmlessness in speech are already understood by the masses and only need to be applied. Even though the path to this aspect of right speech seems easy to understand, it is very difficult to perfect and requires continuous diligence on the part of the seeker. The person must take the attitude of the observer by watching himself and then catch himself when he violates this principle. Diligent attention to the task at hand is always good advice."

John lifted up his cup and observed, "I just realized I'm out of tea. Let us take a break and get a refill. Then we will continue."

CHAPTER TWELVE
Right Action

We refreshed our cups of tea and John continued the lesson.

"To thoroughly cover the Eightfold Path would take a book or more, but what I wish to do here is to cover the basics and a core principle or two of each directive, which is often overlooked. One problem all the religious philosophies have is that those who expound the doctrines will often write volumes on the details and miss the core meaning."

"Kind of like not seeing the forest for the trees?" asked Elizabeth.

"Exactly," said John. "The next directive is Right Action. Again, this translation is fine for our purposes. What do you suppose is meant by this statement?"

I checked my notes again and replied, "Buddhism seems very close to Christianity on this one. Buddhist teachers say it means to not kill, not steal, not have promiscuous sex, and that all actions should be honorable and harmless."

"It sounds very similar to the Ten Commandments," said Elizabeth.

"Good point," said John. "Between Right Speech, Right Belief, Right Intent and Right Action, all the Ten Commandments are covered. The action related parts of the Ten Commandments are: remember the Sabbath Day, honor your father and mother, thou shalt not kill, thou shalt not commit adultery, and thou shalt not steal."

"How about not making graven images?" I asked. "Isn't that a law governing actions?"

"Partially," he said. "Right Speech, Right Belief, Right Intent and Right Action are all influential in the commandments, but the worship of graven images is more of an error of belief than it is action. A person will worship an image other than God because of his willing belief, but he usually steals, kills or commits adultery knowing that he is doing a harmful action."

"How about the Sabbath Day? Resting on the seventh day seems more of a non-action than an action," I said.

"Correct use of the Sabbath Day strongly involves the second eightfold directive of Right Intentions, but is demonstrated with Right Action. Jesus showed the world that right use of the Sabbath involved much more than rest, or non-action, for he performed some of his greatest works, or right actions, on the Sabbath."

"I guess he really irritated those Pharisees," I grinned.

"You don't know the half of it, "smiled John. "You have to realize that in those days, rules of the Sabbath were very strictly laid down to the believers, and few dared challenge them. Jesus went forth with right action on the Holy Day with such boldness that the religious leaders felt extremely insulted their authority was challenged by an upstart."

John paused a moment and chuckled. "Some of my fondest memories are the looks on the faces of those Pharisees when Jesus defied them. I would have sworn at the time that their faces turned purple."

"That would have been fun to watch," I said, smiling.

John looked at me intently, "Don't worry. You'll have plenty of opportunity in this life to be a thorn in the side to many holding on to their unjust authority. And you have a big advantage in this age. You have much greater protection from the laws of the land than did teachers in days of old. Still, you must be wise. The use of right speech and right action will be your protection as well as your sword."

"As long as I don't get crucified, I'm willing," I said, half joking.

John looked at me with great seriousness. "You must be willing to do the work no matter what the consequences will be. Think on this as we proceed and if you have any reservations you can withdraw from the mission."

There was an uncomfortable silence. Finally, I felt that John was expecting a response from me. "I'm willing to take my chances. Will I have to give my life for the work?" I asked a little on edge.

"Yes," said John.

I was silent, not quite knowing how to respond.

"Just a moment here," said Elizabeth. "This is my husband you are talking about. I think I should have a say in this."

"Relax," said John. "Giving your life for the work of spiritual service can involve physical risk, but it goes beyond that. To give your life to the work is to dedicate all your thought, your intent and your actions to the service of humankind and the Will of God. All thoughts of self must be dropped. Your old life will be dead and lost, and a new life of unselfishness must be the goal."

Elizabeth and I both felt a little more comfortable with this interpretation. "That sounds a little more reasonable," sighed Elizabeth in relief.

"Perhaps," said John. "But to truly dedicate your entire conscious life to the work is as difficult as sacrificing your physical body. The keynote to this dedication is the attitude of doing what is necessary, whether pleasant or unpleasant, to get the job done."

"You mean like Joseph did when he went to work on the book, even though he was suffering in pain?" asked Elizabeth, looking at me.

"Exactly like that," he said. "Now let's get back to the lesson at hand. Any more questions on the Sabbath?

"I don't remember the Buddhists even recognizing a Sabbath." I said.

"Actually, they have a long tradition of holy days closely resembling the Jewish Sabbath. Instead of one day out of seven, it is one out of fourteen. These holy days are at the times of the full and new moon. It is interesting that the day of the new moon was also sacred among the Jews. You can look it up later in I Chronicles 23:31. In fact, in the days of Moses, the Sabbath was governed by the phases of the moon just as it is with the Buddhists. At that time the Israelites used the lunar month: the first Sabbath was the day of the new moon, or the first day of the month; the second Sabbath was the quarter moon; the third, the full moon; and the fourth, the waning quarter moon."

"I've never heard that before," I said.

"Some Bible scholars and ancient history students are aware of this, but the connection of the phases of the moon with the Hebrew religion does not filter down to Sunday School," he said.

He continued, "The true principle behind the Sabbath is rest, and the true rest is the attainment of Nirvana, or the Kingdom of God within. When one attains this spiritual contact then the disciple *remembers* the Sabbath continuously and his consciousness is always holy. Ancient people celebrated on the Sabbath; celebration was a symbol of the joyousness of attaining higher consciousness of the Kingdom of God."

"If the churches of today celebrated on the Sabbath maybe I would go once in a while," I said. "By the way, you have never commented on going to church. Am I expected to attend somewhere?"

"Do you want to?" he asked.

"Not particularly," I said. "I don't really learn much from the meetings I have attended, nor do I feel much spiritual elevation."

"If you do not feel you are getting something out of an investment in time, then neither God nor man will condemn you for not participating," he said.

"As long as we are on the subject of churches," said Elizabeth, "I have a question. Is there any church which is a true church of God, or one that is closest to the truth?"

John smiled and said, "Many people wonder about this. No church, philosophy, or organization has all the truth, yet none of them are completely devoid of truth. No organization is correct in all that it teaches, but neither are any of them wrong in all they teach. If there are two philosophies, one will have more light than the other, and that light to which the seeker is attracted will correspond to the light which is in him."

"But which one has the most light?" persisted Elizabeth.

"It is not wise for me to tell you that, for Joseph would write it in the book. It is important that the writings appeal to people of all philosophies, and if a person feels his religion is not approved in any way his mind will close. It's like the old saying goes; you catch more flies with honey than with vinegar."

"So you will not tell us which religion has the most light, but on the other hand, I am not required to attend any of them unless I want to? I guess I can live with that."

"If you truly desire to discover the light within any philosophy, all you have to do is study it out in your mind, reflect upon it and the truth will be revealed. Through the Oneness Principle you can even see through the mind of Christ on the subject."

John took a sip of tea and continued, "Let us finish this directive by examining the core principle. Every course of action is preceded by a decision of some kind. Every basic decision is a choice between a right action and a not-so-right action. Sometimes the right action is obvious. We all realize that it is clearly wrong to steal from the innocent. Other actions are not so obvious. For instance, is it wrong to steal food from a rich man to feed your hungry child? To steal or let your child starve? That's a difficult decision that some face in different lands. When the right action is obvious, one with pure intent will take it, but when it is not so obvious, he must check with his inner being and act by the highest that he can perceive. When the person continues to act by the highest he knows, the path becomes clearer, and the point of exact truth is eventually seen. The seeker then moves on to higher, even more difficult choices of action, until he becomes *one* with the Will of God. Becoming *one* with Higher Will assures continuous right action."

"I notice an important part of right action among the Buddhists is not killing," I said, "but they take this idea much further than the Christians. Most do not believe in killing animals for food, and I believe they go so far as to not even kill spiders or other pests. Is this the right interpretation of thou shalt not kill?"

"Do you realize you have just killed a few seconds ago?" asked John.

"What are you talking about?" I said incredulously.

"You just scratched your nose and in that act you killed a number of living microorganisms. Do you therefore think you committed a wrong action?"

"I certainly hope not," I said. "It would drive me crazy to

go through life not being able to scratch an itch."

"And what do you do when you find a lone spider wandering about your house?"

Elizabeth chuckled, "He usually picks it up and throws it outside. I think he's silly."

"But what would you do, Joseph, if you found your home overwhelmed with hundreds of spiders?" he asked. "Would you still attempt to throw them all outside?"

"Well, I have a new age friend who would just ask the spiders to leave. He claims he doesn't have insect problems because of this."

John smiled as if he could teach a whole lesson in response to this statement, but continued, "But suppose you tried everything and they still would not leave, but grew in numbers. What would you do then?"

"The answer is a no-brainer," said Elizabeth. "We would call pest control."

"I don't like to kill anything, but I have to admit I would probably call an extermination service to rid us of the problem," I said.

"And would this be a right or wrong action?"

"It's hard to say," I said thoughtfully. "Maybe I would just be acting in the interest of self, but I would think it would be a right action."

"What if you were out camping with your children and a bear attacked your son and the only way to save him was to shoot the bear. Would you shoot him?"

"I would," I said firmly.

"And what if, while you were at the bank, a bank robber entered the bank and through a sequence of events wound up holding all the people in the building hostage. He is wearing a bomb and tells police that he will press the button to detonate it and kill everyone in the building if they do not meet his demands. Time passes and the demands are not met. The robber looks through the window and sees the police rushing the building. He figures that time is running out so he announces that on the count of three he will press the button and detonate the bomb. You notice a gun on the floor a short distance from you dropped by a security guard. The robber is not looking your direction and you feel the only hope to save the people is to quickly grab the gun and shoot the robber to death before he can press the button. So what do you do in this case? Do you take one life to save many?"

"I certainly would not like to be in that situation, but yes, I would kill the robber to save many lives."

"And how about that little band of German conspirators who tried to assassinate Hitler in June of 1944 in an attempt to end the slaughter of millions? Was this a right action?"

"I would say, yes," I said.

"But what if you had a vision from God that your next door neighbor was going to be a new Hitler, responsible for the death of additional millions? Would you kill him?"

"I do not think so," I said.

"And why not?"

"A person has to be judged by what he does, not what he will do. The guy next door may have evil in his heart, but he still has free will and could change."

"You have answered wisely," said John. "And what is the core principle guiding all your decisions?"

"I'm not sure."

"Let's go back to the microscopic lives you destroyed in scratching your nose. What gives you the right to do that?"

"It may sound a little egotistical," I said, "but I guess it is because I am a more evolved and significant life form. The well being of the greater life can be preserved at the expense of the lesser lives."

"Well spoken," he said. "And why do you not kill a lone spider wandering through your house?"

"I figure he's not hurting anything and there's no just cause to take its life."

"But are you just in calling the exterminator when you are invaded by hundreds of them?"

"In this case the lesser lives are causing distress to the greater and the greater is justified in eliminating that threat. It's a tougher decision than scratching my nose, but I suppose it is the same principle at play."

"Very good," said John. "Now, how about the incident of the bear attacking your son? Are you justified in shooting it to save him?"

"I would think so."

"Why?"

"I would think that human life would have priority over the animal. It would also be a natural response for me since I love my son more than the bear."

"Then you said you would shoot the bank robber, which is a human life. Why would you be justified?"

"It would be worth taking one life to save many."

"And you feel the same way about the men who plotted to kill Hitler?"

"Yes."

"But you wouldn't kill a potential Hitler."

"No."

"So what is the thread or principle that runs through all of this?" he asked.

"Starting with the last point, we should not kill based on potential crimes. Most people's visions of the future are incorrect."

"But how about the bank robber and the bear?" he asked. "It is remotely possible that they could have changed their minds at the last moment and not hurt anyone."

"But these two were in the middle of destructive action that reason dictates must be stopped." I said. "The potential Hitler next door had not yet made any move toward harming others."

Elizabeth joined in, "I would say the principle for taking action on a real Hitler and the bank robber was said by Spock in Star Trek. *The needs of the many outweigh the needs of the few.* By killing the bank robber you would save the lives of all in the building."

"That's a good statement for humans dealing with humans, but how about humans dealing with animals?" he said. "You thought that the life of one person, your son, was worth more than the life of the bear. Is this correct?"

At that instant a scripture came to my mind. "Now I've got a scripture for us to read." After a moment I found it. "Here it is in Matthew chapter ten, verse 31: *Fear ye not therefore, ye are of more value than many sparrows.* Here the Master himself says humans are worth more than many sparrows, so that would indicate a human life is worth more than an animal's, even a greater animal such as a bear."

"And is the life of a bear worth more than a tomato?" John asked.

"Yes, of course."

"And is the life of a tomato worth more than a pebble?"

"Obviously, yes."

"What is the principle?"

"The more evolved the life, the greater its value," I ventured.

"But the composition of the greater evolution is the Key. The vegetable has the mineral in it with the added life value of sentiency. The animal has the vegetable in it with the added life value of movement and focused attention. The human has the animal in him with the added life value of self consciousness. Each added value increases the power of the life of God to descend into this world and enhance experience. All we take with us to the higher worlds is the fruit of experience, so the power to enhance experience is a key to value in all the worlds of the Creator."

"So a human life is worth more than bear." I said. "One human life couldn't be worth more than all, could it?"

"A human life is worth about seven bears," he said.

"Really," I said, "and how many sparrows?"

"Over a thousand, but don't ask me how many mosquitoes."

Elizabeth laughed, "I wouldn't trade one human life for all the mosquitoes in the world."

"One more question on this subject," I said. "The Buddhists teach it is wrong action to kill animals and that we are to be vegetarians."

"Most do believe this but there is not uniformity of belief on this subject, as the Buddha himself ate some wild pig and other meat now and then. Some current Buddhists allow meat to be eaten sparingly. Buddha was basically against the wholesale slaughter of animals, feeling that the pain caused to the animal kingdom was not worth the benefit."

"Was he correct in this teaching?" I asked.

"He was correct for that time and place, but the teaching is not correct for all times and all places," he said.

"How about this time and place?"

"This time and place in the western world is much different than the world Buddha lived in. Consider the animals we eat, such as the cow, the pig and the chicken. Now consider some we do not eat, such as the wolf, the cougar and the eagle. Of these two groups, which is the most numerous today in North America?"

"There are very few of the wild animals left compared to the way it was in ancient times," said Elizabeth, "but we have many millions of pigs, cows and chickens."

"And why is this?" asked John.

"Since they are a source of food, we take care of them," she said.

"Exactly," said John. "Even though North America is now overrun with humans and most of the wild animals have been destroyed, we find that the animal population as a whole has not decreased, but increased. Suppose that everyone in North America were vegetarians and did not drink milk or eat cheese. What do you suppose the animal population would be?"

"Much less than it is now," said Elizabeth. "Perhaps some would not even exist."

"You are correct," said John. "The population of the cow, the pig and the chicken would be like the wolf, the cougar and the eagle, perhaps worse."

"That's sad to think about," said Elizabeth.

"And let us suppose that everyone in North America became vegetarians tomorrow. What would then happen to the cow, the pig and the chicken?"

"They would lose their value," said Elizabeth.

"And then would anyone take care of them?"

"Perhaps not if they no longer have commercial value."

"You are correct," said John. "If they had no commercial value they would all be slaughtered and come close to extinction. Without commercial value only pets would have a chance of having significant numbers surviving."

"But organizations such as PETA say that commercial animals are abused by the farmer."

"There is some abuse and their living conditions are far

from perfect," said John, "but have you ever considered how difficult the condition of the animals in the wild is?"

"We went on a hayride last year north of Cascade, Idaho where we watched a farmer feed the starving elk," said Elizabeth. "We discovered that, even from ancient times, these wild animals often starved to death in the winter. Because of lack of food during this severe winter the farmer fed many of the elk, and without his good heart, I do not think they would have lived through the winter. I felt sorry watching the helpless animals standing with their feet in the snow, cold and shivering, with no food through the winter. If this is how nature takes care of animals then I say, thank God for the help that comes from humans."

"You are seeing correctly here," said John. "Even though the life of commercial animals is not an optimum situation, they have many advantages over those in the wild. First, they are usually well fed and receive good medical attention for their maladies. The second advantage is that they get to 'rub shoulders' with humans. This was especially helpful in the days of the small farmer who often gave names to his cows and pigs and had true affection for them. Now that farms are larger, there is greater distance between the farmer and the animals; and this sabotages some of the benefits the animals receive from humans. All contact of a lower kingdom with a higher produces some positive stimulation, but numerous problems have been created by mass production of animals. Large commercial farms now give greater thought to profits than to their care and quality.

Instead of giving them their natural foods, some large farms have made cannibals out of the animals by feeding them animal by-products. This is very unnatural for most farm animals and can lay the foundation for disease—for the animal and the consumer.

The large farm that cuts corners in expenses toward the animal's welfare creates a situation where the employee has little care in his relationship with the animals and often sees them as commercial objects rather than living things."

"So what is the solution to this problem?" I asked. "I can see the disadvantage of the large farms, but there are so many people demanding meat that the day of the small farmer feeding the masses seems to be a thing of the past."

"The small farmer and businessperson will always find a way to service the people in ways that are ignored by the larger companies. This crates a demand that is eventually followed by them. The way to create positive change is not to curse the darkness by attacking the large farmers, but to light a candle by creating new demand."

"And how do we do that?" I asked.

"Those concerned for both their own health and the well-being of the animals must demand and purchase the meat of animals that are raised on healthy natural foods and treated humanely by farmers. Consumers must choose free range eggs and chickens over those imprisoned in small cages. They must demand beef which is raised on natural grains and grass with little or not antibiotics or hormones.

"This demand for quality meat through more diligent care is growing now and will increase until many of the larger farmers will pay attention to the need and make needed changes. This will cause the cost of meat to go up and consumption down. The effect will be that many will seek more protein from vegetable sources and nutritious animal substitutes will be developed. As demand increases for healthier mean and for animal substitutes, humanity will gradually shift toward a vegetarian diet.

The drift toward vegetarianism is sure, but animal activists need to realize that a gradual drift using positive incentive is the safer route for the animals and humans, looking at the situation from a wholeness viewpoint."

John slid back in his chair and said, "I would like to spend more time on this subject, but we must move on to the next directive. Let's take another short break and we will continue."

CHAPTER THIRTEEN
Right Livelihood

After a short break we sat back at the table. I noticed Elizabeth looking very tired. "Are you all right?"

"I'm getting very sleepy," she yawned. "Perhaps John could come back tomorrow or you could just continue without me."

"That will not be necessary," said John, reaching for his knapsack. He opened a pocket and pulled out a small cloth pouch. "Bring me three small glasses of purified water," he commanded mysteriously.

I brought three glasses of water purified by reverse osmosis and put them on the table. John opened the pouch and took a pinch of light brown herbal type material and put it in one of the glasses. He then picked up a spoon, stirred it and gave it to Elizabeth. "Drink this," he said. "You will be refreshed and not need sleep for some time."

Elizabeth looked at the glass a little suspiciously and then took a sip. "Wow!" she said. "This has a zing to it."

He then put a pinch into the other two glasses, stirred them, and handed one to me. "In place of having a glass of wine together, let us toast using a drink worthy of a Master of Wisdom." He smiled, raising his glass to toast and Elizabeth and I joined him. The glasses clinked as he said, "To the Plan."

That sounded good to me, I figured any plan John would support would be a good one. "To the Plan," I repeated, followed by Elizabeth. I took a sip and it *did* have a zing. After we finished our drinks I sat back and commented, "That's the greatest refreshment I have had since Shamballa. You know if we packaged this we could make all the money we need to publish the writings."

"You do not quite understand yet," said John. "A decision has been made that we cannot help disciples obtain money for the work except when absolutely necessary."

"That's too bad," said Elizabeth. "This stuff is worth a fortune. I have never felt so instantly refreshed. I feel like I could go on a hike or do cartwheels."

"So why can't the Brotherhood help disciples with money? It looks like it would really make things go easier," I said.

"Have you heard the story about the caterpillar breaking out of its cocoon? When it is helped too much it dies, but when it struggles it flourishes?"

"Yes, I have heard that told before," I said "I guess it also applies to a chick breaking out of its egg. The struggle strengthens it."

"Even in my own writings it is written, *And she being with child cried, travailing in birth, and pained to be delivered.* (Rev 12:2) This is symbolic of the pain and struggle that must take place to give birth to the Kingdom of God in the human kingdom, a higher correspondence to a woman giving birth to a child."

"It's too bad you guys just cannot materialize a few gold bars," I said. "I've always had to struggle just to make a reasonable living."

"Making headway in the material world is always difficult for those who seek the spiritual path," he said. "In this age a balance between the material and spiritual must be sought. This is not the time and place to be as the Buddha and only have one change of clothes and a bowl to your name. To bring to fruition the part of the Plan that is ours will require a blending of spiritual *and* material energy. Billions of dollars will eventually be spent in the transforming work."

"If you're looking for billions, you are looking at the wrong guy," I said wryly.

"I'm looking at the right guy," he smiled. "You will initiate a path that will eventually draw more wealth toward it than you can imagine."

"It would be nice if it happens soon," said Elizabeth seriously. "We have a *lot* of bills that need to be paid."

"Thinking that way concerning your business is fine," said John, "but in doing the spiritual work you must completely free yourself from thoughts of self in connection with money that results from it. You will be allowed to use money from your books to support yourself, as the writing and marketing will be a major labor for you just as your current business is. Even here you must see the funds as a means to free your time and enhance your ability to do a greater work."

"How long will it take for the writings to be successful?"

"As long as it takes," he said. Then he looked introspective for a moment and said, "Your writings will eventually be very successful, but first you must crawl as the caterpillar, then cocoon your work, and after a great struggle you shall fly free as the butterfly with great power to present the colorful and beautiful teachings in your wings."

"Sounds encouraging," I said.

Elizabeth looked at John and asked, "Do you ever use money?"

He smiled and said, "Of course. How do you think I obtained these clothes I am wearing?"

"I don't know," she said. "We just thought that you somehow materialized the things you need."

I joined in, "We've read books about masters who materialize gold, money, or whatever they need."

He smiled and replied, "Not all things you read about the Masters are accurate. A Master can materialize items only if the purpose of his mission absolutely requires it; otherwise, we have to earn money the same way you do. It would be like making counterfeit money for us to materialize wealth and inject it into the system. Why do you think I was working for the Salvation Army when you met me?"

"I thought it was a part of a plan to connect with me."

"I didn't need to work there to ring a bell to catch your ear, but I did need to work there to earn some money. At the time I was saving up to buy a new laptop."

I was astounded at this and said, "This seems silly with the powers you have. Surely there is a better way for you to make money than to work at such a low paying job."

"Any job I take has to be short term since I can be called away at any moment. It is usually important that I do not reveal my identity. I do quite a lot of yard work, pruning trees, shrubs, etc. I might have even worked for your friend Wayne for a while had he not been so close to you. The point is we attempt to practice what we preach and earn our way rather than obtaining goods by using artificial money injected in the system. By the way, the Brotherhood never works for their students, so don't offer me a job."

"I think you read my mind," I said. "I had this weird image of you and me making signs together. That would be more unbelievable than anything that's happened so far."

John smiled at the thought as Elizabeth asked, "As Joseph says, we've read books about Masters with all these amazing powers which you also seem to have. Would it be correct to call you a Master?"

"Yes and no," he said. "I have much the same knowledge and ability as most of the Masters who work under Christ, but because of my unusual request to Jesus many years ago, I have been given a unique mission that has often required me to live in the frailties of the world as mortal as you are, but in the same body for two thousand years. When this body suffers death it is healed after three days and restored to a youthful age by the Christ. I will finish my mission when the Lord comes to teach among humankind again. After this event I will be born as a mortal infant, spend a couple of lives learning some mortal lessons I missed, and then join the ranks of the Brotherhood of Masters who know not the hand of death.

"In some ways this mission I have is a detour, but in the end no progression is lost for those who join in the purpose of God. Those lines of progression I have missed will be more than compensated later on."

"Interesting," I said.

Elizabeth looked a little perplexed. "I think it is strange with all the powers you have available, you have to do menial work for necessities. It doesn't seem right."

"Perhaps, then, this would be a good time to discuss the next directive of the Eightfold Path. What is next on your list Joseph?"

I checked my notes and read, "Right Livelihood."

"And what does one have to do or not do to obtain an honest livelihood?"

I glanced at my notes again and answered, "According to Buddhist tradition, it means that one should make a living by avoiding working in the production of arms and lethal weapons, intoxicating drinks or drugs, poisons and harmful chemicals, slavery, killing animals or breeding them for killing."

"To understand how to best apply this in the western world

today, we must again look at the core principle involved. What would you say it was?"

"That one should make a living by doing things that avoid doing harm," I said.

"And how could it be expressed in a positive way?" he asked, looking at Elizabeth.

"I suppose one should make a living by doing work that benefits others," Elizabeth answered.

"Very good," he said. "Perhaps we can say that the two key words here are harmlessness and helpfulness. Making this directive practical for the western world in this age requires a different wording than it did for ancient India. Whereas in Buddha's time many sought to avoid the responsibilities of making a living to pursue spiritual work, this age demands a different approach. Even the disciple needs to do his share of supporting the society in which he lives, be self-supporting and not expect to live off donations. The poor should seek to support themselves through their labor rather than a continual handout. Remember the saying; *he who is idle should not eat the bread of the laborer?* Those who are in difficult financial circumstances, after doing their best to take care of themselves, do need help from time to time and it is a virtue to assist them, but in this age, the consciousness of the people is realizing it is a negative thing to be an enabler. To enable a person to continue to be poor, to take drugs, to continue his alcoholism, his spousal abuse and many other evils is an evil itself. This enabling principle is a truth that was not in the public consciousness in ancient times, for things seemed to be much more black and white then."

"I've thought of that," I said. "There does seem to be many more shades of gray today than there used to be."

"It's not so much that there are more shades of gray," said John, "but merely that more is seen because there is more light in the public consciousness."

"It also seems that there is more ignorance and stupidity," added Elizabeth.

"But it only seems that way because people as a whole have more light to see the contrasting darkness," he said.

"Interesting statement," I said.

John continued, "Because things seemed to be black and white back then to all but the initiates, you were either good or evil, rich or poor, an enemy or friend, worthy or unworthy. Many past teachings overlooked the good within the evil and the evil within the good. Buddha condemned those who made weapons, yet the good within the evil was obvious during World War II. It became a good thing to make weapons to defeat Hitler in order to save the world from slavery. Buddha condemned the slaughter of animals for food and this is the ideal that the world is headed toward. At present in the Western World an immediate turn in this direction would be disastrous to the animal kingdom, causing near extinction and great suffering for farm animals. It would also deny many animals the evolutionary stimulation they need from human contact."

"Some animal rights people think that human contact is detrimental for the animals," I said.

"Human contact with animals is a lower correspondent to human contact with the Brotherhood of Light. Do angels and masters corrupt humans? Of course not. Neither do humans corrupt animals when viewed from a wholeness standpoint. Humanity makes mistakes, but overall their end purpose is to assist the animals in their progression. The eternal principle is the higher kingdom will stimulate the lower and aid in their evolution. The vegetable aids the mineral by absorbing them and stimulating the creation of what scientists call organic life. The animals eat the vegetables and transmute them into their own higher consciousness. Humans do not aid the animals to advance in consciousness by eating them, but by associating with them. This prepares them for self consciousness. In addition, the Brotherhood of Light stimulates the human toward group consciousness, which is much higher than his individual consciousness. In this way the Brotherhood of Masters consume the human as spiritual food, digesting them into the group mind, yet transmuted humans keep their individual identity as cells in the greater body." He paused a moment and asked, "Any more thoughts about Right Livelihood?"

"I've been in sales a good portion of my life and I have found that many sales pitches I have been given are very deceptive. I've either had to change the sales presentation or look for other work a number of times. I would definitely say that honesty in our employment is important today," I said.

"This idea goes beyond mere sales to all facets of work and employment," said John. "The employee must put in an honest day's work. The employer should give a fair wage and be honest with the workers and stockholders about all the public information about the company. Elizabeth, you look like you have a comment."

"I would think that Right Livelihood would mean that you would work at a job that is in harmony with the law. I know there is a large underground economy of manufacturing and selling drugs and other illegal products and services."

"Normally, this is correct," said John. "In fact, Buddhism specifically teaches to avoid a business which deals with harmful drugs."

"I notice you said normally," I said. "Does this mean that it is sometimes correct to work outside the law?"

"There are exceptions to all rules. For instance, do you think it was right to work outside the law before the Civil War and save the lives of runaway slaves through the Underground Railroad?"

"I would think that would be a virtue," I said.

"And how about those in Nazi Germany who made it their life's work to break the law and save the Jews?"

"This would also be a virtue."

"It is important to remember that there is a time and season for all things," he said. "Unfortunately, this principle can also be abused, and many who think they understand it use it as an excuse to break the law."

"It seems to me that many laws are unnecessary and unjust," I said. "Even though I am a pretty law-abiding citizen, there are quite a few I am not happy with and wouldn't blame people for breaking."

"You see that many of the laws are imperfect and yet you try to abide by them," he said. This is because you inwardly sense the principle behind group law and obey them."

"What is the principle?" I asked.

"The principle behind group law is not whether the law is perfect, or even if the law is useful for the group. The determining principle was clearly stated by Thomas Jefferson when he said, *Where the law of the majority ceases to be acknowledged, there government ends; the law of the strongest takes its place, and life and property are his who can take them.* What was Jefferson saying here?" he asked. (Quote from Thomas Jefferson to Annapolis Citizens, 1809)

I reflected a moment and said, "Even though laws may be imperfect we must submit to the ones supported by the majority or else there will be a breakdown of society and the mob will rule."

"Yes," he said, "while in the group, the wise man will submit to law which is supported by the majority, with rare exceptions, for, as I said, there are exceptions to all the laws of mankind."

"Many feel that our income tax laws are unjust as well as unconstitutional. Should we pay taxes or not?" I asked.

"Are the basic tax laws, even though their constitutionality is questionable, supported by the majority of the people?" he asked.

I reflected again and replied, "Everyone grumbles that taxes are too high, but I would say that the majority support them as a necessary evil."

"So, according to the principle I stated, should you pay taxes or not?"

"Since the majority supports them, then, according to you, I must pay."

"Let me reinforce this with another quote from Jefferson, this time from his first Inaugural speech. He advocated... *Absolute acquiescence in the decision of the majority, the vital principle of republics, from which is no appeal.*"

"But what about the idea that income taxes are unconstitutional? Wouldn't that justify the tax rebels?"

"The Constitution is a great document and I personally knew several of the Founding Fathers and gave advice about the contents. But no matter how good and true any foundation document is, the people will never be able to literally follow it one hundred percent. The majority will always drift away from it. Sometimes the drift is good but usually it is not, but if the majority supports a law then it should be obeyed by all, except in rare cases, as I said. Majority support is a natural law, stronger than any founding document. When a large segment of society refuses to obey a law supported by the majority, then lawlessness and civil unrest is imminent. "

"But what about the idea of the tyranny of the majority?" I asked.

"Tyranny by the majority is almost non-existent," he said. "In almost every example you can give me of tyranny there is a very small group involved who is causing it, not the majority. In the rule of the majority lies the path of safety."

"I can see your point," I said, "but I know a few people who will have a difficult time seeing this point. I have a friend who is always quoting Jefferson to support the rights of the minority. I don't think many are aware of your references to Jefferson and majority rule. Many constitutionalists see majority rule as mob rule."

"Jefferson, as well as other Founding Fathers, were concerned with those rights which would best serve the greatest number. To illustrate that my quotes were no anomaly, I'll give you some additional ones that you can look up the reference and include them when you write this account. Get your pen and take notes."

John then seemed to stare into space as if he were looking at a television screen and gave me the following quotes from Jefferson. Here are most of them with the references added:

"Laws made by common consent must not be trampled on by individuals" —Thomas Jefferson to Garret Vanmeter, 1781 ME 4:417, Papers 5:566

"If we are faithful to our country, IF WE ACQUIESCE, WITH GOOD WILL, IN THE DECISIONS OF THE MAJORITY, AND THE NATION MOVES IN MASS IN THE SAME DIRECTION, ALTHOUGH IT MAY NOT BE THAT WHICH EVERY INDIVIDUAL THINKS BEST, we have nothing to fear from any quarter" —Thomas Jefferson to Virginia Baptists, 1808 ME 16:321

"THE FIRST PRINCIPLE OF REPUBLICANISM IS THAT THE LEX MAJORIS PARTIS (THE LAW OF THE MAJORITY) IS THE FUNDAMENTAL LAW OF EVERY SOCIETY OF INDIVIDUALS OF EQUAL RIGHTS; to consider the will of the society enounced by the majority of a single vote as sacred as if unanimous is the first of all lessons in importance, yet the last which is thoroughly learnt ." —Thomas Jefferson to Alexander von Humboldt, 1817 ME 15:127

"[Bear] always in mind that a nation ceases to be republican only when the will of the majority ceases to be the law" —Thomas Jefferson: Reply to the Citizens of Adams County, Pa, 1808 ME 12:18

"The will of the people is the only legitimate foundation of any government, and to protect its free expression should be our first object" —Thomas Jefferson to Benjamin Waring, 1801 ME 10:236

"The measures of the fair majority ought always to be

respected" —Thomas Jefferson to George Washington, 1792 ME 8:397

"I subscribe to the principle, that the will of the majority honestly expressed should give law" —Thomas Jefferson: The Anas, 1793 ME 1:332

"All being equally free, no one has a right to say what shall be law for the others. Our way is to put these questions to the vote, and to consider that as law for which the majority votes" —Thomas Jefferson: Address to the Cherokee Nation, 1809 ME 16:456

"[We acknowledge] the principle that the majority must give the law" —Thomas Jefferson to William Carmichael, 1788 ME 7:28

"This [is] a country where the will of the majority is the law, and ought to be the law" —Thomas Jefferson: Answers to de Meusnier Questions, 1786 ME 17:85

"Civil government being the sole object of forming societies, its administration must be conducted by common consent" —Thomas Jefferson: Notes on Virginia QVIII, 1782 ME 2:120

"The fundamental principle of [a common government of associated States] is that the will of the majority is to prevail" —Thomas Jefferson to William Eustis, 1809

"The voice of the majority decides. For the lex majoris partis is the law of all councils, elections, etc, where not otherwise expressly provided" —Thomas Jefferson: Parliamentary Manual, 1800 ME 2:420

"It is the multitude which possess force, and wisdom must yield to that" —Thomas Jefferson to Pierre Samuel Dupont de Nemours, 1816 ME 14:492

"The Lex majoris partis, founded in common law as well as common right, [is] the natural law of every assembly of men whose numbers are not fixed by any other law" —Thomas Jefferson: Notes on Virginia QXIII, 1782 ME 2:172

"Every man, and every body of men on earth, possesses the right of self-government. They receive it with their being from the hand of nature. Individuals exercise it by their single will; collections of men by that of their majority; for the law of the majority is the natural law of every society of men" —Thomas Jefferson: Opinion on Residence Bill, 1790 ME 3:60

John then paused a moment and asked, "Tell me this. Would Jefferson have repeated this emphasis on majority rule again and again had he not believed in it?"

"I wouldn't think so," I replied. You gave too many quotes for that emphasis to be a mere misunderstanding."

"There's more," he said. And reading the context from which they came will not alter my point. What kind of law did he say the law of the majority fulfills?"

I glanced at my notes and read his last quote, "The law of the majority is the natural law of every society of men."

"Jefferson felt strongest among the Founders about this natural law to which all humanity gravitates because he was taught the principle, but many of these ideas rubbed off on others as we anticipated."

"But what about the calamity of mob rule?" I asked. "Doesn't this illustrate the danger of the majority getting out of hand?"

"The mob idea is sometimes used as an argument against majority rule, and usually by a minority group who want to impose ideas of their own. There are several flaws in the mob analogy. Can you name one?"

"For one thing a mob does not usually vote and the victims never do," I replied.

"Correct on point one," he said. "In true majority rule, information on both sides of the issue is given out followed by a vote. There is only one side presented to a mob and no democratic vote is taken. Now for another important question. Is the will of a mob the will of a true majority?"

"I don't know. It seems to be."

"Let me ask another question then," he said with a gleam in his eye. "Three thieves get together and agree to rob a bank. They are in 100% agreement. Is this an example of government by the majority?"

"Not really."

"Why not?" he said, looking at Elizabeth.

"The community and government which they are a part of does not support robbing banks," she said. "The three thieves, in reality, are in a minority. Even though they may agree among themselves, they are a minority in the voting community."

"And have you ever heard of a mob whose destructive actions were endorsed by the majority in any government?"

I reflected a moment. "I might be able to find an example from history, but can't think of anything in recent times."

"Like I said, *Tyranny by the majority is almost non-existent.* I said *almost* because there are exceptions to every rule, but here is the way it consistently works. Any type of mob or harmful action where the majority of a group agree to some type of tyrannical action is not a part of any democratic government. The mob, the gang, the group of thieves are all subject to the will of a greater majority who would vote to stop them in a heartbeat. And if the exception should occur and a whole town supports mob behavior, then the majority of the county will normally check it. If the county is corrupt then the majority of the state would support corrective action. Finally, if the state is corrupt then the majority of the country will normally seek what is right."

He let out a sigh and continued, "The principle is this. Tyranny, crime and harmful actions begin in small pockets of society, not supported by the greater majority. But such crimes are supported by the majority within small pockets of lawless individuals bound together for selfish purposes. These small groups are far from representing the will of the whole. Why do you suppose this is so?"

"The will of the whole would never support robbing banks," I said. "It would be like committing suicide. If the majority got together and robbed banks then all the banks would fail and the whole society would collapse."

"Exactly," said John. "Rarely will an entity seek to kill itself, and this is true not only of an individual, but also a government controlled by majority will. This is why there is safety in the will of the majority."

"But how about Hitler's Germany?" asked Elizabeth. "Didn't the majority support the persecution of the Jews?"

"Did they?" asked John in return.

"I've always thought that was the case," she said. "If not, then why were they persecuted?"

"The persecution was not directed by a democracy or any kind of majority rule, but by a small minority completely at odds with the majority of the people. Many participated in atrocities, not because of their desire or will, but to save their lives and their families' lives. It is true, however, that Hitler was elected to office before the dictatorship was set up. Do you recall what percentage of the vote he received?

We both shook our heads to say no.

"There were four major candidates and Hitler received about 30% of the vote. Hindenburg received 49.6%. A majority was needed to elect a chancellor and a runoff election was held. This time Hindenburg received the majority of 53% of the vote. Hitler did not accept the majority will and through several months of intrigue and the violent activity of his zealous Nazi followers, he was able to pressure Hindenburg, an old man, to hand power over to him.

"Thus did Hitler attain power against the will of the majority. Then immediately after he gained power he began to use force, intimidation and torture to control the majority, contrary to their will." John looked at Elizabeth and asked, "If someone places a gun to your head and commands you to pinch yourself or get shot, are you following your own will by doing this?"

"Of course not," said Elizabeth. "I'm surprised you would ask such a silly question."

"It may seem silly," said John, "but there are many out there who believe that the majority under a tyrant support him, when, in reality, they only appear to take the harmful route because they have a gun to their heads.

"I have come across a number of people here in our own country who believe there is tyranny in our own government, police enforcement and even large corporations. How would you answer them?" I asked.

John reflected a moment and replied, "One man's discipline is another man's tyranny. One father will assign chores to a goodly child and he will accept and obey. He may even appreciate the fact that he is given responsibility and made to feel like an essential part of the family. But then there are other fathers not so fortunate. Another may have a rebellious son who hates any work. Every time his father makes him do chores he sees him as a tyrant. He feels separate, as if he is not a member of the family. Now both fathers are equally just, but the two children react entirely differently. Tell me; are either of the fathers tyrants?"

"You said they were both equally just. The rules laid down seemed normal and just. The tyranny seemed to be merely in the eyes of beholder, or the rebellious son," I replied.

"Just as a family has rules, so does a society," he said "If the rules of a society are accepted as just by over half of the populace, then this is a sign that the rules do not produce tyrannical conditions. Even so, some of the minority who break the rules may cry tyranny when they have to pay the price for their rebellion. The thief may cry tyranny as he is wrestled to the ground by the police, the citizen may cry tyranny when he has to pay off the dozen parking tickets he owes and the drug dealer may cry tyranny when he is thrown in prison. None of these situations are true tyrannies, for they are breaking rules supported by the majority. A true tyrant is one who does not consider majority rule but seeks to impose his own rule to fulfill his own selfish purposes."

"Are rules that are supported by the majority always just and good then?" I asked.

"The majority will often support rules which are quite a distance from the optimum. Let us say, for instance the choice of three rules is given to the people. The first rule would be the highest good. The second would do some good, but also cause some problems. The third would be a disaster. It is very unlikely the majority would choose, or willingly accept, the third rule. It is also quite possible they would reject the first, for often only a small minority see the true highest good. The majority usually pick the safe middle which will bring some stability. This is why the path of safety lies in the will of the majority."

"But I would rather have those rules in place that produce the highest good," I said. "Isn't this an argument for a minority rule of some kind?"

"It may seem so until you study the history of the tyrants of this planet. Each of them represented a minority who thought they saw the highest good and had a destiny to impose it upon humanity. Hitler was one of these. By working with and honoring the will of the majority, progress may be slow at times;

but if the will of the majority is honored, a Hitler or Stalin will rarely come to power."

"How about the minority who sees the highest good?" I asked. "Are they to just sit back and be satisfied with mediocrity?"

John sat back. "You're being thorough tonight, aren't you?" After a thoughtful pause he continued, "Of course they are not to just sit back. I said that *in the rule of the majority lies the path of safety.* Even though it is a true principle, it does not, in the least, hamper or discourage the minority who see a higher vision. On the contrary, the stability created by honoring the will of the majority brings the security that is necessary for the innovative minority to do their work.

"Let me put it this way," he continued, "the elections of rulers, as well as the passing of laws and rules of a society are either accomplished through following the will of the majority or a minority. There is no other option. Now if we could rest assured that an enlightened minority was always at the helm to exercise their will, all may be well and good, but such is rarely the case. Many who are greedy and power hungry are drawn into politics, and if these become the ruling minority, then tyranny is not far away. Can you see then that there is danger in allowing a rule by a minority?"

"I suppose that makes sense," I responded.

"And can you see that when the will of the majority is honored, this danger is bypassed?"

"It would seem to be," I said.

"If we then avoid a rule by a minority and honor the will of the majority, are we not then taking the path of safety for the whole?"

"But the United States is not a democracy, but a representative republic. Since we are not a true democracy, are we then not following the path of safety?"

"It was the highest form of government that the majority would support when it was created by the Founding Fathers. Those who pass laws are elected by a majority of whom?"

"The people."

"And they are to represent who?"

"The people."

"How many of the people?"

"All of them?"

"This answer sounds nice," said John, "but representing all views of the people is impossible. If one person believes in gun control and another doesn't, how can he vote on behalf of two opposing wills?"

"I suppose he cannot," I said.

"So how many people is a representative supposed to represent?"

"I suppose it would be the majority."

"Yes. The best governments of this age are elected by a majority to fulfill the will of the majority. This majority will is far from perfect, but it leads away from tyranny and to the path of safety for a country."

"So how is an enlightened minority supposed to make changes?" I asked.

"For your answer look to the evolution of many of the basic inventions we see around us – the telephone, the light bulb, the automobile, the airplane, the television and many other items. When the majority first heard of these ideas they thought the dreamers were crazy. Even after they were invented and demonstrated, the majority thought they were new-fangled products that only a fool would buy. But now these once-despised products are embraced by close to 100% of the population. Why is this? Is it because a minority forced their will on the majority?"

"No."

"Why then?" he demanded.

"The enlightened minority promoted, demonstrated and taught about their ideas and products."

"Exactly," said John. "And if an enlightened minority today sees that they have a higher vision of how the country should operate, what should they do?"

"I suppose they should promote, demonstrate and teach," I said, acknowledging his wisdom. Then after taking a moment to think I added, "But it's pretty tough for someone without a position of power to influence the majority."

"No one said it would be easy," he responded. "Even the rich and powerful do not think it is easy. It took tremendous effort to bring the majority to see the value of the light bulb or telephone. No change comes easy, but there is always a way to make change if the change makes sense. The majority represent the path of safety because, in the end, the majority accept that idea which makes the most sense."

"That is certainly not the case in the beginning though," I observed.

"No. It is not. But there is a principle called the Dominating Good that the majority will always embrace after it is demonstrated. It is important that you believe, as did Jefferson, that the majority will follow common sense when they are exposed to the truth."

"I'll think on that," I said. "So what should a person do when he thinks taxes are either unjust or too high? Wouldn't that be a good time for civil disobedience as taught by Thoreau?"

"As I said, the time for civil disobedience is when the majority do not support a law. For instance, in the days of the Underground Railroad the will of the majority of the country, as a whole, had shifted against slavery. This especially applied to the black population to which the slavery laws applied. In the days of Nazi Germany many were prejudiced against the Jews, but still the majority did not want extreme persecution, and especially did not want a whole race exterminated. The will of the majority is most often violated in a dictatorship. In this case, the majority may be justified in going against certain laws, but will be afraid of civil disobedience because of the dire consequences. In the case of slavery, the consciousness of the people had expanded and outgrown outdated laws."

"But until recent history slavery was pretty much accepted by the majority throughout the earth," I added. "In the days of Jesus there was slavery in the Roman Empire and the majority seemed to accept it. Would it have been wrong for a slave to rebel at that time?"

John looked thoughtful a moment and replied, "While it is true and right that slavery would be an obvious evil in today's society, it was not seen this way by the majority in ancient Rome.

It was seen as an essential ingredient for civilization to exist and prosper. The right action for the person who realized the evil of slavery at that time was to teach and educate the people while seeking a window of opportunity to move society forward. This is what Abraham Lincoln did in our age. He wisely did not rebel against the law, but sought opportunity to change the law. Thus this one man had more power to create change than all the rebels put together. Because the majority supported slavery in ancient times, the early Christian disciples taught the people to make the best of their situation until change would come."

"I don't remember reading that in the Bible," said Elizabeth.

"Turn the Bible to Ephesians chapter six and begin reading with verse five," he said.

Elizabeth picked up the Bible, found the verse and read, "*Servants, be obedient to them that are your masters according to the flesh, with fear and trembling, in singleness of your heart, as unto Christ; Not with eyeservice, as menpleasers; but as the servants of Christ, doing the will of God from the heart; With good will doing service, as to the Lord, and not to men: Knowing that whatsoever good thing any man doeth, the same shall he receive of the Lord, whether he be bond or free.*" (Eph 6:5-8)

"The word *servant* here comes from the Greek DOUBOS, which is the word for *slave*. Both Jesus, the apostles and early Christians used this word in reference to their bond to God, for they saw themselves as committed to servitude to the will of God unto time indefinite. But when the word was used in reference to an individual being a servant of another man, it was almost always referring to a slave. There were slaves and slave owners who were members of the early church, and Paul was giving them advice. What advice did he give to the slaves?"

"He told them to be obedient to their earthly masters just as they would be to Christ," said Elizabeth.

"It even says the slaves will receive a reward from God for their service to their masters," I added.

John continued, "Note in verse eight he talks about the *bond* and *free*, verifying that slavery is part of the topic. Now read verse nine."

Elizabeth read, "*And, ye masters, do the same things unto them, forbearing threatening: knowing that your Master also is in heaven; neither is there respect of persons with him.*"

"Did Paul condemn the slave masters here, who were also Christians, or even go so far as to tell them to release their slaves?"

"It does not seem so," I said. "Instead he merely tells them to treat their slaves well."

"Now turn to First Timothy chapter six, verses one and two," he said.

Elizabeth found the passage and read, "*Let as many servants as are under the yoke count their own masters worthy of all honour, that the name of God and his doctrine be not blasphemed. And they that have believing masters, let them not despise them, because they are brethren; but rather do them service, because they are faithful and beloved, partakers of the benefit. These things teach and exhort.*"

"This makes it clear that the disciples at that time did not break the laws of the land dealing with slavery," said John. "Unfortunately, there were many in the South during the Civil War who took these ancient passages literally for the modern world and used them to justify their tyranny over human souls. Even today, there are a handful of literalists who use these and other scriptures to support their views of slavery and racism."

"I can understand Paul telling a slave to make the best of a no-win situation," said Elizabeth, "but what I don't understand is Paul merely telling the Christian slave owners to treat their slaves well instead of releasing them."

John replied, "If the church leaders had counseled the Masters to release their slaves, the Roman authorities would have become alarmed that a trend was in the works. This would have destroyed the church before a foothold was established. The early disciples had to go out of their way to give the appearance of not being an enemy to the Roman Empire."

John seemed to need a change of pace. He got up from his chair and paced back and forth saying, "But let us not lose the point I am making. This whole situation, which seems unjust by our standards, existed because the will of the majority supported it. Even more amazing from a modern vantage point is that over half the slave populace did not question the law or see injustice in it. He who does not resist a law in his mind and heart puts forth no subtle energies to assist change. Because the general will of the public, including most slaves, supported the law, this put the church in a position where it was not wise to rebel against it, but to teach the highest light that the members could comprehend, while looking forward to a more opportune day of freedom."

"Did Jesus not teach against the slavery at that time?" I asked.

"Jesus taught against the worst slavery of all, the slavery of the human soul. He taught that true eternal freedom could be had no matter what the outer circumstances were and that all human servitude was a temporary inconvenience that must be endured from time to time. If you read the New Testament you will note that he used the word *servant* (which means *slave)* many times in his teachings and often spoke of good and faithful servants of God and man as being praiseworthy, but never encouraged rebellion against their masters. He realized that the consciousness of the people was not ready for such a doctrine. As it was, they were barely able to grasp a higher vision of love toward their fellow men."

John sat back down facing me and said, "Now let me ask a question. If the teachers of the world at that time acquiesced and did not rebel against slavery because the will of the majority supported it, then how should the disciples of today approach the tax laws which are supported by the majority?"

"Actually, high taxes could be seen as a form of slavery, but one with a different set of limitations than that of ancient times," I said. "But, according to your logic, I suppose modern disciples should pay taxes and not rebel unless they have the support of the majority will."

"And if the enlightened see a better system of running the government away from high taxation, what should they do?" he asked.

ording to what you said earlier, they cannot force their will upon the majority, but should *promote, demonstrate and teach* until the majority are swayed."

"This principle of majority rule can also be interpreted in relation to the principle of harmlessness. When two paths lay before the disciple, he should always seek the more harmless of the two, which is another way of saying the most beneficial. The early disciples did not rebel against slavery because great harm would have befallen them and the church, and the message of Jesus would not have even been available to the world today. In this age, many disciples see the injustice of high taxes and some rebel against the system. In many cases this has created much grief, causing them to operate entirely outside the system and majority will, reducing their real effectiveness to create change to almost zero."

"What is the modern disciple supposed to do then?" I asked, a little exasperated, "Just sit back and let the powers-that-be walk all over him? The Founding Fathers of the United States certainly did not do this."

"But their rebellion was supported by the majority will," said John. "About a third supported the rebellion to the extent they were willing to take some risk. Then there were about a third who supported the king. The other third went the way the wind blows, but enough of these supported the rebellion in their hearts that the rebels had a bare majority on their side. This made it wise for the Founding Fathers to take action. Tell me this. When the public hears of a current tax rebel getting in trouble, how many do you suppose are cheering him on in their hearts?"

"Not too many," I said.

"I'll tell you what I think," said Elizabeth. "I think that if I have to pay taxes then so should he. Because he does not pay taxes I have to pay more."

"That's what many people think," said John. "So even though you and many others grumble about high taxes, most believe them to be a necessary evil; and less than ten percent of the general populace will support a tax rebel. Because of this low support, a rebellion often creates more grief for the rebel and others than any benefit that is gained."

"So let's get back to my question. What's a disciple to do, just roll over and play along?" I asked.

John replied, "The disciple is not to roll over, but if he wishes to make positive change he must examine the will of the majority and work with it, not against it. How many people do you suppose think that taxes are too high?"

"I'd say over ninety per cent of the taxpayers."

"You are correct, yet why is it that less than ten percent will support a tax rebel?" he asked.

"I think Elizabeth was heading in the right direction when she said that many resent the rebel because he is not paying taxes, forcing the taxpayer to bear even more of the tax burden. Also, many receive benefits from taxes and thus see them as beneficial to them," I said.

"So if you want to change the tax system, which is wiser - to work with the will of the ninety per cent or the ten percent?" he asked.

"The ninety per cent, I suppose."

"And how would you go about using that will of the ninety per cent to create change?"

I reflected a moment and replied. "The trouble with the ninety percent is that they do not seem to believe that change is possible even though they grumble about the way things are. I think people need to be educated so they can see greater possibilities and then changes can be made within the system."

"You are more correct than you realize. Now let me ask you another question. How many people do you suppose were responsible for the Renaissance that spanned two hundred years of progress in Europe?"

"Many thousands, I would think," I said.

John leaned forward, speaking softly, "It was about eighty people."

"Eighty people! That sounds impossible!" I gasped.

"Yes, about eighty people, as a driving force, serving on behalf of the Brotherhood of Light worked with the positive aspects of the majority will to create change that produced a tide of enlightenment and innovation. Now, let me ask you this question. Do you think there are eighty individuals in the world in this age who are willing to dedicate themselves to a new Renaissance, not only in lower taxes, but changing many aspects of life for the better?"

"I would hope so," I said.

"I do not have to hope, for I know so," said John. "Now your job will be to find them; find the eighty and more than eighty."

CHAPTER FOURTEEN
From Pisces to Aquarius

"I can't believe that I still do not feel tired," Elizabeth marveled. "Usually when my body tells me it's time to sleep I have to sleep. I *know* you could make a million with that herbal formula or what ever it is."

John smiled. "It is not mine to make a million on. Besides, my needs are very few. An odd job now and then supplies all I need and want for myself. People think they need much more than they do in reality. When the mind is set upon the Spirit, the needs of the physical plane seem insignificant."

"I can identify with that," I said. "I have noticed when I pursue my spiritual path; my material world seems to start crashing down on me. Then I feel like being Thoreau, finding a Walden Pond, and getting away from all the headache of making a living and paying bills."

"All disciples get that urge and some go with it." He said. "In times past, this was often beneficial for the whole of the work, but we are entering another time now, and a new approach must be considered."

"What do you mean, *another time*?" asked Elizabeth.

"The ages are represented by the signs of the Zodiac; each lasting just over 2,100 years. Several of these ages are particularly indicated in the Bible. You'll note that during the time of Moses delivering the Children of Israel, the people reverted to worshipping The Golden Calf. The calf, or bull, represented the sign of Taurus, which was then waning. Moses brought in the Age of Aries whose sign is the ram, a male sheep. This was the age of animal sacrifice, where the ram was sacrificed to God on behalf of the sins of the people.

"The next great age was that of Pisces brought in by Jesus. Its symbol was that of the fish.

"The constellation Pisces is formed by a set of dim and scattered stars that trace the images of two widely separated fish joined by a knotted cord. One fish, swimming upward, faces east toward Aries, while the other fish swims westward toward Aquarius along the plane of the ecliptic. The directions of motion of the two fish form a cross, the symbol of the Christian religion—the upright line of the cross representing spirit and the horizontal line signifying matter.

"Christian tradition evolved from making the sign of the fish of Pisces to the sign of the cross. The cross was, therefore, merely a simplification of the sign of Pisces.

"Around 800 AD the Church of Rome began to distance itself from astrology and to drop the connection of the Christian church, or Jesus, with Pisces, or even the fish, and only kept the sign of the cross. Even though this sign still had a connection with Pisces, and there were short revivals of interest, few realized the connection after this time period. It is only of recent date that Christians have revived the sign of Pisces and proudly (but unknowingly) display it on their bumpers.

"Notice that almost all of the fish symbols used by Christians today face to the left, a symbol of the past they are holding on to, instead of advancing to the consciousness of Aquarius."

"Yes, I have noticed that," I said. "I've also seen some fish symbols with the word Darwin inside. The funny thing is that these always point to the right."

"Yes," said John. " The left-pointing fish signifies the current Christian religion is attempting to hold on to the past, or the age of Pisces, and the right pointing fish of Darwin signifies the scientific approach is more in line with our current journey ahead or into the future. Of course, this does not mean current religion is all wrong or current science is all correct. In general terms, science is more in alignment with the Purpose of God than religion is.

John paused a moment and asked, "If there is a keyword for the age of Pisces, what would you say it is?"

"It would have to be something to do with Christ, since he was the key figure of the age," I said.

"And when most people think of Christ, what image comes to their minds?" he asked.

"Probably the image of him dying on the cross," said Elizabeth.

"Correct," said John. "And what single word would you associate with that?"

"Sacrifice?" she said, not quite sure of herself.

"Yes, that is the word," said John. "And all during this Piscean Age sacrifice has been the keynote. Early Christians were thrown to the lions and martyred in numerous other ways. Many soldiers were sacrificed for the Crusades. Monks, saints and religious zealots sacrificed their outer lives to find an inner one. Believers did and still do, sacrifice large portions of their money to insure a good spot in heaven."

"But where does Buddha fit in as far as the ages go?" I asked. "He seems to have worked in the age of Aries, yet the sign of the Ram seemed to have little connection with him."

"Excellent question," John smiled. "What is often overlooked, even by those who accept the ages in connection with the Zodiac, is that Christ was not born at the beginning of the age of Pisces. We were over a hundred years into it at the orthodox date of his birth.

"Buddha was born a little over 400 years before the real beginning of Pisces and about 1,750 years into the age of Aries. Because he was such an advanced soul, his consciousness was directed more toward the coming age than the one passing. Therefore, the keynote of Buddha's life was also sacrifice. Notice how the word *sacrifice* runs through his life. First he sacrificed his comfortable life, his family, and his kingdom, in search for enlightenment. Next he sacrificed all that held him to the material world, and was down to living on two grains of rice a day when he received the revelation of the Middle Way.

"Even after this he chose to emphasize the need to sacrifice all desire in order to attain Nirvana, or the Kingdom of God. In some ways sacrifice ran through his life more than it did Christ's. The truth is that the age of Pisces was ushered in through the work of two great sons of God, both Christ and the Buddha. Another interesting fact is that even as Buddha looked ahead, and anchored the principle of sacrifice for the coming age, even so did Christ see further ahead still. Christ emphasized the key word for the coming Age of Aquarius thousands of years in his future."

"And what is that key word?" I asked.

"What do you think?" asked John, throwing my question back at me. "What was one of the main points of emphasis in his teachings?"

"Love," said Elizabeth.

"Love is a thread that runs through all the ages, but the revelation of the Love of Christ was the positive message of Pisces. Guess again."

"I know he stressed service," I said.

"You've studied a little astrology," said John. "Does the word *service* fit the core idea of the Aquarian Age?"

"Standard astrology associates Aquarius with science, groups, brotherhood, humanitarianism, progress, but not usually service as a keynote," I said. "It does seem like I have read something about its symbol being related to service though."

"And what is that symbol?" he asked

"Actually, there are two," I said. "The first is the water bearer and the second are two waves. I believe I have heard it said that the water bearer is a symbol of the disciple, or servant pouring forth the water of life to a thirsty world."

"Yes," said John, "and this symbol was foreshadowed in the New Testament. Joe, please read Luke chapter 22 verses 7-13."

Then came the day of unleavened bread, when the passover must be killed.

And he sent Peter and John, saying, Go and prepare us the passover, that we may eat.

And they said unto him, Where wilt thou that we prepare?

And he said unto them, Behold, when ye are entered into the city, there shall a man meet you, bearing a pitcher of water; follow him into the house where he entereth in. And ye shall say unto the goodman of the house, The Master saith unto thee, Where is the guestchamber, where I shall eat the passover with my disciples?

And he shall shew you a large upper room furnished: there make ready.

And they went, and found as he had said unto them: and they made ready the passover."

"As Jesus' mission came to an end, notice he directed the disciples to find the man bearing a pitcher of water. In other words, he was instructing them to set their sights on the coming Age of Aquarius wherein true service would be achieved and recognized. The servant bearing the waters of life takes the seeker to the goodman of the house of God, who then leads him to a furnished upper room. What do you suppose is the higher meaning of the upper room?" he asked.

"Until now I just thought it was an upper room," I said. "Could it have something to do with higher consciousness?"

"It has everything to do with higher consciousness. And what do you suppose the meaning behind it being furnished is?" he asked, looking at Elizabeth.

Elizabeth thought a moment and replied, "When your consciousness is elevated you will be given everything you need, just as Jesus was supplied with a furnished room."

"And how would this apply to the Aquarian age as a whole?"

His question brought an intuitive flash in my mind and I replied with enthusiasm, "Yes, this makes perfect sense to me now because there are so many things that seem to correspond. Service in the Aquarian Age leads to the good man or paves the way for the progress. When we see the good, our consciousness is elevated and in the elevated consciousness we achieve abundance. Part of this fulfillment is all the technology and conveniences we have today. Aquarius is an air sign and the upper room would also be a symbol of this, illustrating that in this age the mind will rise above the lower emotions."

"Very good," said John. "Also note the pitcher symbolically teaches the same principle. Water, a symbol of the emotions, is contained by the pitcher in Aquarius and poured forth under the direction of mind. And this dialog also teaches another important principle not related to the ages. What do you suppose that is?"

Both Elizabeth and I were silent. "We're not sure," I said.

"The principle is this." he replied. "To attain knowledge, the first important step is to ask the right questions. Look what has been in you all along if you had just questioned yourself."

"You're absolutely correct!" I exclaimed. "Maybe Socrates

was on to something after all." I paused thoughtfully and asked, "You're not going to tell me you taught him, now are you?"

John laughed softly. "He was before my time, but he did have connections. Now let us get back to the reason I brought up the subject of the ages to begin with. Each age brings with it a change in consciousness for humanity as well as the servants of the race. Unfortunately, those who receive scripture and holy writings in one age develop the notion that all the precepts are eternal and will never change. When a dedicated religious person is presented with change, he will resist it with all his might, as evidenced by those who resisted Jesus and crucified him. Then looking further back, you will note the Hebrews' resistance to Moses. The same thing is happening today. The keynote of the ages is changing from sacrifice to service, yet the religious ones want to keep the emphasis on sacrifice."

"You mean like when the churches display pictures and images of Jesus suffering and being crucified?" asked Elizabeth.

"Yes," said John. "In this new age, instead of making our prime focus the crucified and dying Lord of sacrifice, we need to see Christ, who is the greatest of servants, and serve with him. It is time for civilization to focus on a living Christ, not a dead one."

"That doesn't sound like a change that would be that difficult," I said.

"All change is difficult, even desirable change. For instance, when Buddha received enlightenment and started teaching fellow teachers that they did not have to starve themselves to death to achieve Nirvana, he was met with high resistance and indignation, even though his message of change was a pleasant one."

"That is an interesting point," I observed. "You would think that such a stoic bunch who starved themselves and lived naked in the wilderness would be happy to learn that such sacrifice was unnecessary. You'd think they would at least be happy to consider the message of Buddha."

"But they were not," said John. "You, especially with the work you have to do, must realize that people often value their beliefs more than any other thing. Those who are attached will not release their beliefs for money, for comfort, for health, for life, for family, for country, or even for humanity itself."

"I never thought of it in that light," I said. "But when you mentioned that many value a belief more than humanity itself, I thought of many religious people I have met who are anxiously awaiting the end of the world when they will be saved, but most of the population will be burned with fire. You know, I think many of these people are so attached to this belief that if God Himself came down and told them it wasn't going to happen, instead of being happy the world is saved, they would be upset their belief was not correct."

"Exactly right," said John. "But what you do not realize is some would be so upset they would deny God Himself rather than change their beliefs."

"So what does this have to do with the Aquarian Age?" asked Elizabeth.

"Quite a bit," said John. "The keynote of the new age is *service* and the key thought is something like this: *The seed has been sacrificed in the age passing and the time is come to serve in the harvest. Look no more to sacrifice without fruit. See the value in the harvest and lose it not, let it not slip through thy fingers to be consumed by the wild animals below. Eat of the fruit of thy labors with joy, and share the labor of the harvest with others that abundance may be had by all who will.*"

"That's good," I said with pen in hand. "I'll write that down so I can quote it exactly."

"What must be realized is this," he said. "The basic difference between the two ages is in the emphasis. During the Piscean Age the emphasis was on sacrifice. The disciple was to sacrifice all, with no thought of ever getting it back or attaining a reward – at least in this world. Christ was seen as the example of this by sacrificing his life and receiving nothing of value on the earth. Only in the heavenly spheres did he obtain recompense. This idea of sacrifice has laid the foundation for many belief systems which will be highly resistant to change. Their type of thinking was in line with the plan in the past, but not in the present and coming future."

"Does this mean that sacrifice will not be necessary in the coming age?" I asked.

"The true principle of sacrifice will always be of great value," said John. "The lessons learned in one age will carry over into the next, but the important point to realize is the emphasis will be different. When you advance from the multiplication tables to Algebra, you do not throw the knowledge of multiplication out the window, but continue to use it. What is different is your point of emphasis. You have learned multiplication and no longer need to concentrate on it; now your emphasis will be on equations.

"Humanity is in the same situation. For thousands of years we have struggled with the lessons of sacrifice; the wise have passed the tests and are ready for the next lesson. Now they are to incorporate what they have learned from sacrifice and place attention on the new lesson of service. Instead of seeing service as a sacrifice, we must see service as an agent of harvest that will bring abundance to all who join in."

"That doesn't sound like a belief that would be difficult to embrace," said Elizabeth.

"It sounds good on paper," said John "but as it works out in the real world, it becomes a challenge to belief systems of spiritual people high and low. There are many of high potential who have sought the old ways instead of the new, and thus have taken backward paths and have become lost to the work."

"Could you give us an example of how this happens?" I asked.

"To obtain the vision, it is helpful to see examples of the old light which is setting and the new light which is dawning. I will give you examples within two groups – the churches and those slanted toward the New Age and metaphysical groups. But first, we must let Elizabeth take the bathroom break she is thinking about and then we will continue."

Elizabeth looked slightly embarrassed. "How'd you know…" Then she paused, looked at John and said, "I almost forgot who you are."

CHAPTER FIFTEEN
Right Emphasis

As our lesson continued Elizabeth was still smiling about John knowing she needed to use the john. John continued, "First, let us examine the churches. Those who are struggling to maintain the old light place strong emphasis on authority. Their attitude is 'do as the leadership says or suffer dire consequences.' Unjust authority always stresses infallible leadership, the infallible scriptures or the infallible God speaking through them. The old emphasis on sacrifice is stressed, especially the sacrifice of the member's money. Money is seen as going to God with the member getting little or no benefit from it until after death. Outside of stimulating guilt pangs and some fellowship, about the only benefit the member receives lies in the nebulous great beyond. The church does very little to assist him in living in the real world today or making a success of it."

"That sounds like most all of the churches today," I said. "Is there such a thing as an enlightened church at present?"

"Even the best of them are in kindergarten compared to what will be, yet there are some churches, and groups of individuals within churches, intuitively catching the new light and promoting it. Have you heard the term *prosperity consciousness* being promoted by religious people or groups?"

"*Prosperity consciousness*, yes, I have heard that term quite a bit and read a number of books on the subject. Are you thinking of religious motivators such as Zig Ziglar, Stephen Covey and Og Mandino?"

"Yes." he said. "They are three good examples of individuals, from a standard Christian background, who are pointing many Christians toward service that yields the harvest of abundance. The standard preachers are still into poverty consciousness, but many are listening to the new direction from the few. Today, there are an increasing number of motivational speakers, personal trainers, and prosperity teachers with a standard religious background who are teaching in church groups, businesses and seminars. These are stimulating the coming light and preparing the churches to become useful in the Aquarian Age."

"Come to think of it," I said, "a few churches put *some* stress on prosperity. I know some of the more New Age ones do, and Unity seems to. I've read a number of Katherine Ann Ponder's books on prosperity and found them very interesting. She also wrote about health. How does that fit in?"

"Katherine Ponder has done an excellent job of bridging the material and spiritual," he said. "And the subject of health is an excellent point because good health is essential to full prosperity. You will notice that the more enlightened members in all churches are seeking greater light and knowledge concerning their health."

"But don't the scriptures say that we cannot serve God and mammon?" said Elizabeth. "How can we go after prosperity consciousness and serve God at the same time?"

"In past ages, especially the Piscean age of sacrifice, it was nearly impossible. Humanity itself had to learn certain lessons, and approach a degree of enlightenment, before the material and spiritual could be balanced. The key to that balance is in the scripture itself. Repeat it one more time."

"It says you can't serve God and mammon," said Elizabeth.

"The key word here is *serve*. Do you think one can have prosperity and yet not serve mammon, or the material side?" he asked.

"I never thought about that," she said. "I suppose."

"How?"

"Perhaps if you wanted abundance for something besides self; maybe to make the world a better place," she said.

"Exactly," said John. "If you seek and obtain abundance, not just for your own needs, but to enhance your ability to serve, then you can still keep your prime focus on serving God; for when you are in the service of your fellow man you are in the service of

God."

"On the other hand," I countered, "I have seen people who are into prosperity thinking that seem to be in it only for themselves. All they want is the big house and the new car with no thought whatsoever of serving others."

"This is true," said John, "but even this is not all bad; and it is a necessary step all of us go through in our progression toward unselfishness. When the seeker finds out that abundance for self alone is not the answer, he will often use abundance for some type of service."

"I seem to recall Jesus speaking of a promise of abundant life," I said.

"Yes," he smiled, "the scripture is in John 10:10: *I am come that they might have life and that they might have it more abundantly.* In the age passing, those who sought the purpose of God had a spiritual abundance, but Jesus was looking toward the future age for the complete fulfillment of this promise. He was not only referring to his first coming, but to his second as well. He came near the beginning of the Piscean age and will come again in the Aquarian age. Between the two He will teach the world of the abundant life both spiritually and materially."

"Sounds good to me," I said. "I have been way too long without material abundance. Sometimes that hinders spiritual abundance."

"A lack in any area, whether it be in money, relationships or health can always be traced to a spiritual problem," he said. "True abundance is manifestation on *all* planes of existence."

"So where's the new and old light in the metaphysical community?" I asked.

"Even though many of the New Age and independent spiritual people see themselves as much more enlightened than those in the churches, they have a similar problem. The majority of them are stuck in studying the past, and clinging to what *was* rather than dreaming of things that have never been, and seeking to manifest them. Just as many of the past values of the church are good, but a change of emphasis is necessary, even so, many past metaphysical teachings are good, but a new emphasis is needed.

He paused and continued, "Many metaphysical groups are also caught up in the sacrifice of the Piscean Age and stress retreating from the world, living a life of poverty, or not being contaminated by business interests or the quest for progress. Many of them are anti-technology and desire to live the simple life of herding sheep, farming or even tribal living as did the ancients. Others see humankind as a disease on the planet, and desire extreme reductions in population so the earth can be preserved in some pristine condition. Little do they realize this is attachment to the past as much as their Christian brothers they are critical of."

"A lot of this looking to the past comes from a desire to preserve the environment," I said. "Are they off base on this?"

"They are off base if they approach it from a religious or emotional approach, as do the old time religions with *their* ideology," he said. "Emotional domination belongs to the passing water sign of Pisces, but mental dominance belongs to the coming air sign of Aquarius.

"Could you give us an example of wrong thinking of these people?" asked Elizabeth.

"I'll give you examples of backward beliefs generated from emotions, but with this caveat. To keep the environment in good health is an essential goal as we enter the coming age, but the plan to do this must be approached wisely, with education being much preferable to force as advocated by many."

John took a breath and continued, "One emotionally-based belief is the environment must be preserved in its pristine condition.

"This attitude of mind is largely based on a religious approach ever as much as the born againer who seeks to preserve the King James Bible and refuses to read one in modern English. Some of these pristine environmentalists see untouched nature as the literal word of God, so to speak, and do not believe this infallibility can be improved upon.

"The truth is humankind can and will improve upon nature. As the highest consciousness in nature, it is the destiny of the race of humanity to be the saviors of the animal and the vegetable kingdoms… even the earth itself."

"That's quite a statement," I said. "Many would argue that man has been the destroyer of nature."

"Yes, it seems that way so far," John said, "but there is an important concept that humanity must understand. Humans are the guiding intelligence of the physical earth, just as your consciousness guides your body. The reason humans have been careless with the environment so far is they are like children in their development. Think back to when you were a child. How much care did you take of your body?"

"Not that great," I said. "I would have eaten candy for every meal if I could."

"In other words, your immaturity caused you to be destructive to the environment of your body."

"I guess you could say that," I said.

"But did this destructive attitude last forever?"

"No."

"What made it change?" he asked.

"As it was, I did eat a lot of sugar, processed white bread and only a few things that were healthy. In my late teens I became concerned because I just never felt very good. Then one day I read a book about the benefits of healthy eating and it changed my life. I immediately cut out the refined sugars and ate whole wheat bread instead of white, and my health sharply improved. After that, I read other books and incorporated other beneficial foods. Because of this, I have been pretty healthy throughout my life."

"Humanity is much like you," said John. "In its current youthful consciousness, it wants what tastes good and not necessarily what *is* good. Because of this attitude it has been doing more harm than good for the environment. But the good news is that the human race is growing up. It is like you, just before you read the book. Humanity feels something is wrong, but do not agree on what to do. People are starting to read books and make changes just as you did. When they awaken they will put away the harmful habits and adopt new ones, making the body of the earth a healthy place to live.

"But progress will not play out as many environmentalists hope. The destiny of humanity is not to preserve a pristine environment, but to improve it and enhance it. For billions of years before the appearance of humans, the environment was on its own and had cycles of destruction so great that it makes anything man has done look like child's play. Land, atmosphere and the oceans have been entirely destroyed and reborn in their time. The intelligence of the earth itself cooperated with the great Elohiym lives in the creation of human beings, with the vision that humankind would eventually be not only a stabilizing force, but a force propelling the evolution of the planet itself."

"So you're saying that mankind is not a disease upon the earth as many environmentalists believe, but the cure?" I asked with interest.

John laughed softly, "Yes, we're like medicine that tastes bad at first, but in the end makes things better."

"So the way we will maker things better will not please some environmentalists?" I asked.

"Yes," he said. "Just as many religious authorities have fought spiritual advancement that has gone against their belief system, even so will many environmentalists fight against progressive souls who will seek to improve the whole environment of the Earth."

"Why in the world would environmentalists fight against improving the environment?" asked Elizabeth.

"Why do religious ministers fight against spiritual progress?" he countered. "The answer to both questions is the same. All authorities fight against progress that challenges what they stand for. Many who love the environment will embrace the progress to come, but others who seek only to conserve and establish a power base will be shaken. What will bother them is that the environment of the earth will be saved, not by leaving it alone, but by wisely using it and leaving it better than we find it.

"A current example is cutting down trees and planting others in their place. In this case no harm is done as long as the original cutting is done with wisdom. If we leave dense forests without management they will often suffer disease and great fires, which destroy millions of trees and cause untold numbers of torturous deaths for wildlife. Selective logging and management can reduce the number of fires and relieve much suffering to wildlife. This is a good thing, yet many protest such moves."

"But some environmentalists say that forest fires are necessary for healthy forests. Apparently the fires destroy some harmful elements and provide a basis for renewal" I said.

"That is true," John agreed, "There is some benefit from them, and limited use of fire may be necessary, but overall, large forest fires create more harm than good in modern society. Humans have the power and technology to step in and prevent these fires, aid in the health of the forests, and save untold suffering to the life that depends on the natural habitant. This is a current example of how the environment can be used and improved through the intelligence of humanity, yet all can benefit. In times to come, this wise use of the environment will grow. Mankind and the environment will become intertwined and interdependent as never before realized."

"How about clean water and air?" asked Elizabeth. "Those are strong environmental issues. Aren't the environmentalists correct on standing for these things?"

"They are correct in standing for these essential ingredients to a healthy environment, but unfortunately, many of them are their own worst enemies for an optimum solution to the problem."

"Why's that?" she asked.

"Not all, but many environmentalists want to solve these problems by returning to the past, some even hoping for a return to some type of tribal or primitive living. Unless there is something equivalent to an all-out nuclear war this is not going to happen. Humanity is going to continue to move forward, and the solutions to our problems are not to revert to the past, but to look to technology to make things better for everyone. The time is not far when we can have pollution-free vehicles traveling our busy roads. Technology will give us very clean manufacturing plants that will add insignificant pollution to the air and waters. Technology will also improve the overall environment while allowing humans to use it safely, and there's the rub. Many environmentalists want us to only look at Mother Nature, but not make practical use of it.

"Technology belongs to the Aquarian Age and will transform the planet and make it a much better place, not only for humanity, but for all the kingdoms in nature. Humanity will soon shed its selfish childlike desire for harmful candy and learn to eat its vegetables. Those who love the earth must seek true workable solutions through technology, or face becoming part of the problem as viewed by historians of the future."

"You just caused an interesting thought to form in my mind," I said. "It seems that all groups who claim to be an authority in a certain area have a large portion of their number who stands in the way of progress. For instance, many doctors who are supposed to be authorities on health stand in the way of taking natural herbs, foods and methods that promote health. Many ministers stand in the way of true spirituality. Lawyers stand in the way of just law by perverting it. Politicians stand in the way of good government, educational leaders stand in the way of improving teaching standards… The list could go on and on. But it does seem to be a strange thing that those who are authorities often seem to have less common sense about their own field than the average man on the street."

"This is a correct observation," said John, "and the same is true of environmentalists. A certain number of them will be seen by history as the greatest obstacles for solving the earth's environmental problems.

"Now let me get to the main point I wanted to make," he said. "The greatest true spiritual authorities on the earth are the disciples sent forth to do the work of the Brotherhood of Light. Many have been sent and born in situations conducive to their missions. Unfortunately, even many of these great souls have gotten caught in the same trap as the authorities of the world. Because their souls experienced numerous lifetimes in the age of sacrifice, they have come into incarnation with a preoccupation with this principle. For many of them it would be easier to accept a revelation from God demanding everything from them, above a gift that brings some happiness."

"I can kind of identify with that," I said. "When good things have presented themselves in my life I have had difficulty accepting them, somehow feeling inside there was something wrong about it. Sometimes I have had to think things through and force myself to go the logical direction."

"And that's why you are one of the few sent who are still usable to the Brotherhood. And even with you, we had to wait until your more mature years to trust you with this mission."

"What about those disciples who are stuck in the past? Are they not usable at all?"

"Not in their present state of mind. You will meet a few of them as you present the teachings and some will fear you are from the dark side because your emphasis will seem wrong to them. Some will reject you outright, but others will keep enough soul contact to nurture the inner feeling that you may be a bearer of light. Those who allow the seed of truth to grow will awaken to the practical service of the new age and join with you."

"What about those who cannot be touched? Are they on some type of lost path?" I asked. "For some reason I feel a sad feeling for them as we speak."

"Yes, it is a sad situation because these souls who have performed such great work in the past have now placed themselves in much danger. But take heart, because of their past good works and their present good intentions, many will find the path again in a future life. Only a couple of them are in danger of choosing the dark path. The first shall be last and the last first, except in those few cases where the first humble themselves as a little child."

"I take it then that there are others like me who have adjusted their consciousness to the new emphasis?"

"Yes," he said "but that number is less than we anticipated and we have had to adapt our plans to plow with the horses we have. Each usable disciple has a mission that does not compete with other working disciples and they are scattered in various areas of life, some are in avenues not considered spiritual by the majority. Some of them are considered enemies of mankind, by people who should know better."

"What about those who respond to the teachings? Will they be considered disciples?" I asked.

"When I speak of a disciple, I speak of one who has enough light and commitment to the light to volunteer to be born in a situation where he can dedicate his life to the work. A true disciple is willing to give his life for the work if required. But giving one's life is actually easier than changing direction, which the new age requires, and this is the current problem. A few of those who are attracted to your teachings will be accepted disciples. But most will be aspiring to discipleship. If successful, you will stimulate many to move into discipleship and enjoy communion with the Higher lives through the Oneness Principle."

"So what are the hang-ups that cause such problems for wayward disciples the Brotherhood has sent?" asked Elizabeth.

"There is a number of what you call hang-ups," he said. "For those with religious backgrounds, many of the new teachings will not seem to harmonize with their interpretation of the scriptures of the past.

"Others will cling to certain political views that will obscure their vision of the true mission.

"Some with metaphysical interest let their fear of conflict create a fog, making it difficult to see the true path. Others in this arena will see the teachings as too simple and will feel their knowledge of details makes their thought superior to the principles that will come forth. The lesson to be learned by all disciples is that one principle, presented in simplicity, is worth thousands of details and is far superior to a complex vocabulary."

"Complex vocabulary," I repeated. "Yes, I've met people who thought they know it all because they know a few fancy words, yet when you follow their thought they often know little."

"Most of those obnoxious types have never been disciples, but some disciples do get sidetracked by vocabulary and details," he said. "Perhaps the greatest trap for willing and able disciples is the sense of sacrifice they carry with them from previous missions. This sense of sacrifice not only applies to them, but it affects how they view followers and co-workers. Because they are having difficulty in balancing God and mammon in their own lives, they seek to solve the problem by expecting followers to support them in their financial needs, giving them the freedom to dedicate their entire attention to the spiritual plan. In the Piscean Age this direction worked well for them, but in the Aquarian age it does not, and a new approach is needed."

"And what is that new approach?" I asked.

"The approach should be on the basis of what I call *instant karma*, by which I mean that cause and effect will work out faster in the Aquarian Age than the Piscean. If the disciple serves, he or she can, in most cases, expect a recompense for that work within his lifetime and not have to wait for some afterlife experience. But what creates difficulty is when a follower or helper gives aid; he will also expect recompense, or what we call a sharing in the harvest. This shifting of energy has created an interesting situation. Have you noticed that the orthodox churches and organizations are still able to raise significant money from sacrificed donations, but those seeking real change seem starved for money?"

"I have noticed that and have been puzzled by it," I said, nodding.

"The reason for this is Piscean Age organizations are using Piscean sacrifice methods that still work for them, but their power is waning; the time will soon come when church members will wake up and demand a real value from their donations. Here's the important point: The reason many true spiritual workers are unable to raise money is they are caught in the Piscean Age method of sacrifice of their members to raise funds, and this just does not work anymore."

"If it works for the churches then why would it not work for more advanced spiritual workers?" quizzed Elizabeth.

"Because the more advanced spiritual workers draw students who are also more advanced and independent thinkers; they feel an inward revulsion to giving where their hard earned money may go down some spiritual sinkhole."

"What are the Spiritual workers to do to raise money then?" I asked.

John's face turned serious. "This is an extremely important point. The spiritual worker must not use the Piscean method of expecting to be supported by the good-hearted sacrifice of members. Some will of course, give to good causes expecting nothing in return, but the Aquarian leader will not depend on this good will. If money is expected from members, it should be money given because they have received some equivalent value from the teacher. Aquarian teachers will also set up classes and programs where they can charge membership and raise needed funds. I suppose you could call this the health spa principle. The member pays a fee and enjoys the privileges of membership. On the other hand, until the new energies are more established, avant-garde teachers will have difficulty in raising funds by any other method than an orthodox occupation."

"So how will they be able to teach if they have to maintain a full time job to support themselves?" asked Elizabeth.

"They will have to do it in their spare time," said John. "This will be difficult, but it will be much more effective than starving for funds while expecting sacrifice from followers which never seems to come."

"I have a feeling that the job thing will have to be my line of approach, at least until the book sales take off. And you say you can't tell me how long that will be?" I asked.

"It will take as long as it takes. Do not set a date for your success; you are likely to get discouraged because breaking new ground is always very difficult with more pitfalls than foreseen, and many have fallen before you. You must be prepared to persevere to the end of your life if necessary with no visible signs of success. We expect you to have success, but this is the attitude of mind you must have. It is called the endurance principle. To activate this principle one must be prepared for success to be further in the distance than expected – sometimes much further. Even so, if a person makes a decision and focuses on it until the consummation, he will succeed."

"I'm still puzzled by the fact that the Brotherhood does not seem to know all that will happen in the future," said Elizabeth frowning.

"The greater the lives, the greater the power to control that which happens within their sphere of decision," said John. "The future course of those who are in alignment with the will of God is actually quite predicable. On the other end of the spectrum, the animal and lower kingdoms which do not make conscious decisions are also quite predicable. Humankind, however, is in a category of its own. Individuals can make conscious decisions, but there is never any guarantee that they are in alignment with Higher Will. Because of this, the prediction of any future where the human race is concerned becomes a wild card, and is difficult even for a Master to foresee in the short run. But even unpredictable humans are subject to higher decisions and the Law of Cycles, so when considering a larger cycle of time, humanity as a whole is fairly predicable.

"The great unknown with humanity is how they will fare in the next thirty years. There is still a chance that a large portion of humanity could be wiped out with weapons of mass destruction, but this end is not expected or desired by most of the inhabitants of this planet. The chances are in our favor that we will have a bumpy ride, but eventually arrive at a point of stability that will allow the Christ, the Master of Masters, to teach again upon the earth. To this peaceful end the Brotherhood of Light is doing all in their power to fulfill.

John rose quickly and continued, "My time has come to go. I have given you all you can properly digest for one evening."

"But I thought we were going to discuss the last three directives of the Eightfold Path, the three that deal with right concentration," I said rising.

"We have been talking about them," he said.

I was puzzled and replied, "If I remember correctly, the last directive we covered was Right Livelihood."

"And what was our main point of focus after this?" he asked.

I reflected a moment and saw where he was going. "I think I see what you mean. We have been talking about the importance of a disciple obtaining a correct focus of concentration during the coming age. All this time we have been applying the principle of right concentration or attention."

"Yes," he said. "The lesson of the Eightfold Path continued even though you were unaware. Even so, we are not quite finished; we shall complete them when we meet again."

"When will that be?" I asked

"After you have defeated your Dweller," he said cryptically.

"Oh, no," I replied with alarm. "I almost forgot that I have to return to dealing with that terrible force."

"You will be able to obtain a short peaceful sleep after I leave and then you will have to contend with him again. But take heart; if you follow the principle of attrition, his power will be gone within a couple of weeks."

John paused thoughtfully, looked intently at me, and continued, "There is one more important point I must tell you. When a Dweller loses his life force through attrition he leaves behind an astral body which then disintegrates over a period of time. Usually that is the end of him for the disciple. But you face a fairly unique danger because the Dark Brothers have a great interest in stopping you. As I said, many disciples have been sidetracked from their missions; yet, if you are successful you can reach some of these and revive their purpose. As a final effort in using the Dweller to stop you, the dark ones are likely to send their combined life force through meditation into its dead astral body, raise it to life, and seek to destroy you."

"Wow!" I exclaimed, running my fingers through my hair. "As if I don't have enough to worry about, now you tell me that even after I subdue this thing it *still* will not be gone! This is like a bad movie." I looked at Elizabeth who was visibly as upset as I was.

John paused until the impact diminished and said, "You have

a particularly powerful Dweller that was nurtured not only on this earth, but also in your previous planet of incarnation where you made some serious mistakes."

"So what am I to do when this thing is revived and attacks me again?" I demanded. "I do not even know the nature of the coming attack or how I am to fight this phantom!"

"Yes, exclaimed Elizabeth. "What is he to do? This is my husband we're taking about and I do not want to lose him. Does he use attrition again or ignore the threat?"

"I can only give you limited help," said John. "If you do not defeat this on your own, it will not be truly defeated and you will have to face it again. If the Dark Brothers attack you through the resurrected body of the Dweller you cannot ignore the challenge or use the principle of attrition. When this happens you must face the Dweller and fight for your life." John turned and walked toward the door as he said, "I wish I could do more. May God be with you."

I grabbed John by the arm, "Wait! I don't think you have given me enough to go on. How can I fight something that I know so little about? How I can destroy it?"

He turned and looked into my eyes and suddenly I felt a strange oneness with this unusual man. I sensed a great sorrowful concern, something like a father may feel toward his son who he is going off to a battlefield where most will die. As I took in his thoughts I whispered, "What are my chances, fifty-fifty?"

"About that," he said, bowing his head slightly.

"Is there anything else you can tell me? Any advice at all?" I pleaded.

"Just one more thing," he said. "When the time of danger comes use Excalibur."

"Excalibur!" I exclaimed, almost laughing. "You mean the sword of King Arthur and Merlin? What do you mean by this statement?"

"I cannot say more. Just remember my words."

"But I do not have any sword, let alone the mythical sword Excalibur. I need to know more!"

"Excalibur is not mythical," he said. "I can say no more to you on this subject, but I must add this. No matter what happens, continue working on the book and on your contemplation of the

Lost Key of the Buddha. This period will test your ability to apply the directive of the Buddha toward right concentration. I must go."

John opened the door and walked out without looking back. He walked into the blackness of the night until we could see him no more. I felt a powerful sorrow fall over me and sensed that he was feeling it also. I did not ask for this battle John mentioned, but as we looked into the blackness in which he disappeared, I made a resolve to do all in my power to make him proud.

CHAPTER SIXTEEN
The Preparation

I slept in the next morning. It was the first undisturbed sleep I had experienced in some time and it was heavenly. The next day the Dweller that John had put to sleep roused itself and became very disturbing to me again. Its presence was very painful, yet there was a difference this time. Realizing I was going to overcome it in a short time made it easier to endure. It was a little like having a terrible toothache. Enduring it is not so bad when you are sitting in the dentist's chair, knowing it soon will be gone.

I concentrated on ignoring the discomfort of the Dweller using the principle of attrition; but even as I was attempting it, I found a greater awareness developing in the life and consciousness of the Dweller itself. I sensed a knowing within him that its life energy was waning and a fear of its own death and survival intensifying. Over time, the attacking force began to lose its consistency. I sensed it withdrawing to gather its forces to attack with an even greater ferocity.

There were times that the intensity was so great that it was difficult to not let it have my attention, but ironically, I seemed to have some success on putting all my attention on not giving it attention. That seems like a strange way to phrase it, but I can think of no other way to word it.

For the next couple of weeks I did my best to follow John's instructions and continued working on the book despite the great difficulty. Our business was also demanding more of our time so finding the time and focus to write took more determination than I had ever roused in myself. In addition, Elizabeth and I discussed our guesses as to the key word and I continued to read up on Buddhism.

For about three weeks the power of the Dweller seemed to decrease in proportion to my ability to place myself in a state of mind that did more than ignore him. Instead I did not recognize its existence or influence. I want to stress this point for those who have to face any negative force. Attempting to ignore it is not enough. One must place his or her mind in a state of consciousness that does not recognize its existence. This state of mind cuts off its nourishment and starves it to death. The interesting thing is, while attaining this state of mind, it *is* still possible to be aware of the Dweller, its life force, and its thoughts. While in this state of attrition one must live his life as if there were nothing bothering him. He must work, rest, and enjoy life as if there was nothing disturbing happening. There are many negative attacks and dark influences the seeker will face before he confronts the full force of the Dweller, and this principle of attrition will assist in overcoming all of them.

There is one more piece of advice I would give. Doors to negative force are often opened by guilt. To release oneself from negativity and properly apply the principle of attrition, one must free himself from guilt. If one has guilt and cannot shake it, he should openly discuss the problem with a friend or religious authority. The principle of confession in the Catholic, and other churches, has a true principle behind it. There are times that nothing will relieve guilt in the individual but confession. As the seeker treads the path he will eventually transcend guilt and never have another problem with it. He will learn right action through guidance from the positive Spirit, rather than a push from negative emotion and fear. Until this time comes, the guilt must be dealt with on a practical basis.

During the next couple of weeks I lived life as normally as possible as if no Dweller existed; then one evening, as I was working on the book, a *wonderful* realization hit me. The Dweller was gone! I had placed myself in the desired state of mind, which did not recognize its existence so well, that I failed to recognize the exact moment its life vanished. The last few days had been quite a bit easier to handle as I realized its power was decreasing; but the final moment of release was so natural, I seemed to have missed it.

The silent victory came when I was busy writing, as if nothing was bothering me, a time of attrition.

Shortly after this amazing realization I went to bed, snuggled up to my wife, and slept like a newborn babe. The next morning I awoke to the smell of coffee and made my way to the dining room. Elizabeth handed me a steaming cup and I shared the good news with her.

"That's wonderful," she said. Then she seemed a little downcast and added, "At least it *would* be wonderful if you didn't have to face the possessed Dweller that John talked about."

"I've been thinking of that too," I said. "On the other hand, John did not say *for sure* that the Dark Brotherhood was going to resurrect the Dweller. He merely said it *could* happen. Maybe nothing will happen. I feel absolutely no influence from the Dweller now. It's like he's dead and gone."

"My woman's intuition tells me otherwise," she said. "I would like to believe it's gone for good, but something tells me that your most terrible confrontation is looming on the horizon." She grabbed my hand and looked squarely in my eyes. "After all we've been through, Joe; I do not want to lose you now. I don't know if I could handle it."

"Well, you would think that if I have some important mission I would get some divine protection," I said wryly.

She squeezed my hand very tightly and said in a strong voice, "Listen to me! I feel very impressed to tell you something. I do not know if it is from John, God, me or what, but I know you must hear this."

"Hear what?" I gasped.

She spoke very firmly, "Divine help only comes after you have done everything possible in your power to help yourself. If you let down your guard and expect God, John or anyone else to do for you what you can do for yourself, you *will* be destroyed."

"That doesn't sound like something you would say out of the blue," I said, feeling quite disturbed.

"You're right," she said bowing her head. "I think it was from John."

"I was looking forward to forgetting about the Dweller for a couple of days. If I could have just a few days' peace without having to worry about some major confrontation, I would be a happy man. Do you receive any impression how long it will be before the confrontation comes?"

"No," she said. "But I think it will be fairly soon, and you have to be prepared."

"I hope it's at least a few days in the future so I can get a few more restful nights sleep and gather some strength back." I reflected a moment and added, "John said the key to defeating the next attack is to use Excalibur. Do you have any idea what he means by that?"

"Excalibur was King Arthur's sword that he drew out of the stone, placed there by Merlin the magician. No one could defeat King Arthur when he used the sword. He lost possession and the power of the sword when he was betrayed by his wife and best friend. Then at the end of his life the sword was given to the Lady of the Lake for safekeeping. That's what I know in a nutshell from the movies I have watched."

"Well," I said, "my question is how am I supposed to obtain Excalibur when I have absolutely no idea where it may be? There's no Lady of the Lake in these parts, neither is there any sword stuck in some stone waiting for me to retrieve it."

"The obvious answer is never the answer to John's riddles," said Elizabeth "I would guess the sword is not a sword as we know it and the stone will not be a stone; neither will the Lady of the Lake be a real lady in a real lake."

I reflected a moment. "Sometimes you really impress me. Yes, I think you are correct. There's always more to John's words than meets the eye, but if the sword is not a real physical sword, then what is it?"

"Probably some type of spiritual sword," she said. "Or maybe Excalibur is a symbol of something or some truth."

"O.K., let's suppose there is some spiritual sword I am supposed to retrieve. *Where* do I get it and how?"

"I wish I knew," she said, bowing her head.

"Well, whatever it is, we have to know. We have to find it and who knows what to do after we find it? If it is not physical then I'm not even sure if I would know how to use it if I did find it... And that's just part of the problem. I'm not even sure what I am to use it against. I have never seen the Dweller or its body."

Elizabeth grabbed me, kissed me, looked in my eyes and said

"I have faith in you. John said to use Excalibur so that means you can find it and can use it. Whatever that entails you will figure it out." She paused and I noticed a tear crawling down her cheek. "You've got to figure it out, damn it! You've got to."

I gave her a hug and said, "I'll figure it out someway. All I know is that I can't let you down. I just wish I knew how long before the confrontation, or if there will be one at all. Not knowing is maddening."

"Maybe Wayne will have some ideas." she said. "He called and said he was free for lunch. Maybe you ought to pick his brain."

"I guess it couldn't hurt," I said. I gave him a call and arranged the time and place.

I was drinking a cup of coffee at Raedean's Restaurant, thinking deeply about my problems, when Wayne walked in and sat down. He had such a disturbed look on his face that it made me forget about my problems. "What's the problem?" I asked.

"Ernie!" he growled. "That son of a bitch!"

"I thought he was the one employee you could trust."

"I thought so too," he said, squirming in his seat.

"So what did he do?"

"His wife was doing some books and record updating for me and they came across titles to four of my trucks. They forged my name on the titles and took the trucks."

"Can't you just call the cops?" I asked.

"It's not that easy," he said. "I have to somehow prove he forged my name. That could take a lot of time and money."

"Couldn't you just go steal the trucks back? You did that with a stolen trailer a while back didn't you?"

"Yes," he sighed. "But the guy who stole my trailer didn't have the title. Ernie told me that if I tried to steal my trucks back, he will show the cops the title and have me arrested."

"Have can you be arrested for taking your own trucks? That's insane."

"It's insane all right," he said "and I probably could win in the end, but it would cost me a bundle getting out of felony charges. And I may have to spend time in jail before it is all over."

"That's a terrible situation," I said. "Any idea what you're going to do about it?"

"Damn!" Wayne pounded on the table so hard several other

nearby customers looked our direction. "Maybe I just ought to catch him in a dark corner and rough him up a bit."

"I can understand the feeling," I said, "but that would probably make things a lot worse."

"It would sure make me feel better though," he added, calming down. "And how was your week? Better than mine I hope."

I reflected a moment and, even though I faced a terrible challenge, I was not sure that I would trade places with him. When you think of it, it seems that most people have about all the problems they can handle in life. "I've had my share of problems too," I said.

"Really? Tell me about them. It'll be nice to know I'm not suffering alone."

"I believe you've shared enough problems for one meal," I said, looking at the menu. "I think I'll order the meatloaf."

"Meatloaf is good," he said. "I think I'll have that too."

We gave our orders to the waitress and I redirected the conversation. "You're familiar with the story of King Arthur, Camelot and the sword Excalibur, aren't you?"

"Well, I've seen the movies like everyone else. I might have read a few things."

"Let us suppose that the whole story was a parable meant to teach spiritual truth of some kind, something like Jesus telling the story of the Prodigal Son. How would you interpret it?"

"That's an intriguing question," said Wayne showing some interest, seemingly forgetting his previous state of agitation. "I have often contemplated the meaning of the Genesis story as if it was a parable, but I never thought of applying that type of interpretation to something like Camelot. You're coming up with the darndest topics of conversation lately. It's strange, but I kind of like having my thoughts provoked."

"Good," I said. "Let's take the basic ingredients and interpret them. First of all, what would Camelot represent?"

Wayne reflected a moment and said, "Higher consciousness perhaps, or the Kingdom of Heaven."

"Sounds as good as any," I said. "Then how about Merlin?"

"Merlin was supposed to have concocted the whole plan," he said. "So what you would have to ask is who is the creator of the kingdom of heaven?"

"I guess that would be God, wouldn't it?" I said. "So you think King Arthur would represent Christ? He was a kind of spiritual son of Merlin, but a literal son of an earthly king."

"That makes sense," he said. "Jesus was descended from the earthly King David, but spiritually was the son of God. The story tells us that King Arthur was not aware of his kingdom and heritage until he drew the sword out of the stone. Do you think that Jesus was unaware of his full power and mission until he drew some spiritual sword out of a stone?"

"It's possible," I said. "What do you suppose the sword represented?"

Wayne reflected a moment, "I believe there is a scripture which calls the Word of God a sword."

"I think you may be right," I said. "I seem to recall something about that. I'm going to check the scriptures on it when I get home. So if Excalibur is the word of God what is the stone that held the sword?"

"It could be any number of things," he said, "but we've got to follow the reasoning through. When Arthur, as well as the sword, had no power, the sword was in the stone. Evidently the stone keeps the word of God neutralized so Christ, or Christ hidden in us, cannot use it."

"That's interesting," I said, nodding. "But *Arthur* comes from the Celtic word for *stone*. If Arthur is a Christ figure, then perhaps the stone is another symbol for Christ."

"Perhaps the sword in the stone is a symbol of the word of God in the physical, Christ who has forgotten who he is," he said.

"I think we're on to something," I said with rising interest. "We are all supposed to become Sons of God according to the Bible. If we have Christ, or the Word of God, in us as the scripture says, but are unaware of it, then we are powerless spiritually."

"But when we realize the power of God is not released through physical exertion but spiritual, then the sword is easily released and used," Wayne added.

"So what about the two prominent female figures, Guinevere and the Lady of the Lake?" I asked.

Wayne paused in thought and said, "Guinevere was beautiful and at first inspired Arthur, but wound up betraying him and neutralizing the power of Excalibur. I think she represented the illusion of carnal power and beauty," he said.

"Then perhaps the Lady of the Lake would represent the higher or spiritual side of Christ since she had custody of the sword," I added.

"Good point," said Wayne. "Two had custody of the sword, King Arthur and the Lady of the Lake. Perhaps they represent the male and female aspects of Christ."

"So to activate the power of Excalibur the male and female energies must work together. I think we're on to something." I said. "You've given me some good food for thought here, Wayne."

"It's not that hard to help when you ask the right questions," he said.

"Yes... Yes, you are correct," I said, thinking of John's earlier statement on questioning.

"So have you moved on from solving the Buddha's Middle Way?" he asked.

"No, but I have definitely eliminated something."

"What's that?"

"Moderation is not the Middle Way; it's more than that," I said.

"I would hope so," he smiled. "Like I said last time, it doesn't take some great mind to tell us it is not wise to starve ourselves to death. The other extreme of wine, women and song does have some appeal though."

I chuckled, "Yes, it's kind of funny that seekers back in Buddha's day were more attracted to the extreme of poverty rather than pleasure. If you're going to be an extremist I suppose you might as well take the enjoyable side."

"My point exactly," said Wayne. "So do you think there is any deeper meaning to the Middle Way than seems apparent, or were the people in that age so simple that even basic common sense impressed the hell out of them?"

"I think there's something deeper. A lot of Buddha's teachings were very profound, so it's hard to believe that his core teaching of the Middle Way was mere moderation of some kind."

"So have you come up with any other ideas?"

"A couple, but I thought I would see if you could come up with anything besides moderation."

Wayne leaned back in his chair in thought and said. "Perhaps we can use the same review that we did in looking at Camelot. Now, as I understand it, the choice of the Middle Way opens up when two choices appear before the seeker. He sees an extreme going left and another going right. The Middle Way is a choice between these two extremes, but, if you are correct, the correct choice is not necessarily the moderate choice. What does that leave us – a moderately extreme choice?"

"The choice could be moderate, but does not have to be," I added.

"OK," he said. "Then the Middle Way lies between these two extremes where we have one choice of all possibilities. If the Middle Way choice is the best choice then I would say the Middle Way is plain old common sense."

"I think you are very close," I said. "I feel we are headed in the right direction, but not quite there."

"Then maybe you ought to ask me some more questions. These questions you are asking bring thoughts to the surface that I have never considered."

"I'll have some more questions soon, I'm sure. You know it is almost as difficult to come up with good questions as it is good answers."

"On the other hand, dumb questions and dumb looks come easy with a lot of people I meet," he said, taking a bite of his meatloaf.

I smiled and then turned serious, leaning forward, "Wayne. I want to tell you something."

"What? Is anything wrong?"

I was going to begin by saying *If you never see me again* - in making an attempt to say goodbye just in case this pending attack got the best of me, but decided against it.

"What?" he said, breaking the silence.

"I think there is some great truth behind this Excalibur thing. I want you to think about it in days ahead, maybe for the rest of your life."

"I don't know about the rest of my life, but I will think about it. By the look on your face I thought you were going to tell me you were gay or something."

I laughed and it seemed to relieve the inner tension I felt. Then our conversation drifted toward more mundane matters. After lunch I went to the office.

When I finished work at the office and got home that evening I decided to check out references linking the Word of God to a sword. I found some interesting ones and decided to share them with Elizabeth after dinner.

"So how did your lunch with Wayne go?" she asked.

"Pretty good," I said. "We did some brainstorming and I have some new ideas to mull over."

"You need more than ideas," she said. "You need to know exactly how to use the sword. Any ideas on that?"

"To be honest with you, if the attack occurred tonight I don't think I would know what to do. I just hope we have some time here."

She kissed me on the cheek and said, "If it is true that the Dweller has died and left an astral corpse of some kind, the Dark Brothers will have to use it sooner rather than later. It might be going through some sort of spiritual decay."

"You're probably right," I said. "If the astral corpse has only a short time it can be revived, then I have to be on guard from this moment on. I did find one thing that may help concerning the symbolism of the sword. I'll read you a scripture on it." I found my Bible and read,

"And take the helmet of salvation, and the sword of the Spirit, which is the word of God." Eph 6:17

"You mentioned that the sword may be a spiritual symbol. Here it talks about the sword of the spirit being the Word of God," I said.

"So Excalibur could be the Word of God. Are you saying that John wants you to use the Word of God to defeat the Dark Brothers?"

"Maybe. Here are a couple more references I found:

"For the word of God is quick, and powerful, and sharper than any two edged sword, piercing even to the dividing asunder of soul and spirit, and of the joints and marrow, and is a discerner of the thoughts and intents of the heart." Heb 4:12

"And he (Christ) had in his right hand seven stars: and out of his mouth went a sharp two edged sword: and his countenance was as the sun shineth in his strength." Rev 1:16

"Repent; or else I will come unto thee quickly, and will fight against them with the sword of my mouth." Rev 2:16

"And the remnant were slain with the sword of him (Christ) that sat upon the horse, which sword proceeded out of his mouth: and all the fowls were filled with their flesh." Rev 19:21

"There seems to be something powerful about using the Word of God as a sword," she said. "Maybe the answer is just that simple. When you are attacked throw the Word of God at them."

"You mean throw the Bible at them?" I asked. "Something tells me that will not work. The scripture links the word and the sword as coming out of the mouth of Christ. I think the question is, how does one speak the Word of God? How is it used as a sword?"

"The Bible tells us that when Jesus was confronted by Satan he quoted scripture to him which seemed to help him conquer his adversary."

"But it also tells us that Satan quoted scripture at Jesus but to no effect. Would there be a difference between the Word of God spoken by him and the same Word of God by Jesus?"

"Maybe the answer to that is the key to your victory," she said.

"Maybe," I said. "It's worth thinking about."

That evening after Elizabeth went to bed, I did not feel like working on the book. All I could think of was Elizabeth's comment that the body of the Dweller may have to be used sooner rather than later. I found myself looking over my shoulder every few moments as I felt there was some truth to her words. Then I remembered John's advice to continue working as if all was normal no matter what seemed to be happening. I forced myself to sit down at the computer and began an attempt at some writing.

I was just getting in the mood as I was typing away when I heard footsteps behind me. I turned around and viewed just an empty doorway leading to the work room.

"Elizabeth," I exclaimed. "Is that you?" It had to be her I thought, for all the doors were locked and she could be the only one in the house besides me.

I didn't hear any answer so I figured that she must still be in bed asleep. Maybe I was imagining things. I turned toward the computer again and started reviewing my writings when I again heard footsteps. This time I was sure it was not my imagination.

Perhaps Elizabeth was up and around. I went upstairs to the bedroom and cracked open the door. She was lying in bed sleeping like an angel. I was mystified. I thought I heard something but now was not so sure. I looked through every room in the house and found nothing.

"Strange," I thought to myself as I went through the hallway back to my workroom.

There I was met with one of the greatest jolts of my life. Sitting in my chair, staring at the computer screen, was none other than Philo, Brother Philo as he liked to be called.

He turned, looked at me and said, "You call this a story? This is a piece of crap. I think this garbage needs deleted. Here, I'll erase your hard drive for you so you can get a fresh start."

CHAPTER SEVENTEEN
The Dark Lord

I was totally amazed to find Philo sitting in my chair attempting to delete my hard drive. I was so stunned that I spent a couple of seconds staring in bewilderment. I had to do something quickly to save my files. I leaped to the connecting cord and pulled it, instantly shutting down the computer and hopefully saving my files.

"Very clever," said Philo, standing up, glaring at me. "Looks like I'll have to take care of the files after I take care of you."

"How'd you get in here?" I demanded. "The doors are locked."

"You don't need doors when you have the friends that I have," he grinned with an evil gleam in his eye. He oozed a confidence that unnerved me.

"Maybe I'll throw you out the door without opening it then," I said.

"Go for it," he challenged.

I was happy to oblige, thinking I owed him some grief after the distress he caused my wife. I leaped to grab him and my hands passed right through his body, making it difficult to keep my balance as I slammed into the wall. "What the hell!" I said, gathering my composure.

"Hell is right," he said. "That's where I've come to send you."

"Are you Philo, an illusion or what?" I asked.

"Unfortunately for you I am the real Philo," he laughed.

I threw my open hand at him and it passed through again. "But this can't be your real body," I said bewildered.

"It's not my body, but it is real," he said showing a confidence that continued to put me on edge.

"Is it some kind of astral projection?"

"Guess again."

I reflected a few seconds and guessed, "Has this got something to do with my Dweller?"

"You're getting warm," he said, smiling, in a sing-song voice.

"What are you going to do, haunt me to death?" I said, passing my hand through him again.

"First, I'm going to rough you up a bit," he said. "And I'm going to enjoy every moment. If not for you, Elizabeth would belong to me."

"What are you going to rough me up with, your ugly face? You'll be lucky to tickle me with that ghost body you have," I said with more bravado than I felt.

He then pushed me with both hands, throwing my body against the wall. The force seemed much stronger than I remembered him being capable of from our last confrontation. "Stupid man," he said. "Did you think I was operating your computer with a ghost body? Thanks to your powerful dweller and the energy of my brotherhood, I can move this body from astral to physical at will."

I was dazed, but thinking clear enough to realize that he must be physical at this instant since I felt his attack. Without hesitation I swung and hit him square on the jaw. I usually avoid physical conflict if possible, but I must admit it felt good to see him fall backward to the floor in a daze. Then I realized that he may switch back to the astral at any moment so I kicked him in the head with great force. This seemed to knock him into unconsciousness.

I was then hit with a terrible realization. It would only be a matter of time before he regained consciousness. I couldn't go on knocking him into unconsciousness forever. What should I do? I thought back to the movie series called *Highlander* where Immortals were killed by cutting their heads off with a sword. Could it be that I was to cut the Dweller's head off with a physical sword? This seemed like as good of an idea as any. Since this was not Philo's real body but one created by me, then destroying the body of this dweller would not be like taking a human life.

I did not have a sword in the house, but did have a good sharp meat cleaver. I rushed into the kitchen to retrieve it and ran back to the body and kneeled over it. I hesitated a moment while I considered the gravity of the situation. By all appearances it seemed that I was about to destroy a human being, but mentally I knew it was only a manifestation of my own thoughts. Still it took all my will to force my hand, for it felt very distasteful for me to proceed. I brought the cleaver down with full force toward his neck.

The cleaver went through the body and anchored into the floor. Philo immediately came to life, shaking his head, standing erect and said, "You know what the problem is with your kind?"

I said nothing while desperately thinking of what my next move could be.

He continued, "You always hesitate when you have to get your hands dirty. You think of right and wrong instead of the job that needs to be done. Because of our superior will, our brotherhood will soon triumph over you weaklings."

The only thing I could think of was to test him so I took another swing. When my arm passed through his body again I came to the realization that my options had run out and if I didn't think of some way to fight him my end may be near.

Philo laughed with a wicked sound and shoved me with both hands again. I was surprised at the force; my body was thrown across the room hitting the bookcase. About a dozen books fell down on my head. I looked to the floor and noticed one of them was a Bible.

"Bible - Word of God - Excalibur," went through my mind. "It's worth a try." I picked up the book of scripture and threw it at Philo.

It passed right through his body, bouncing off the wall on the other side.

Philo looked at the Bible behind him and then stared at me with great curiosity. "I've had preachers throw words of damnation at me, but never had anyone try to hurt me with a Bible. What are you going to do next - throw holy water at me?" he said, walking toward me.

I was desperately thinking of something to do and the only thing I could think of was to speak some words from the scriptures to him.

I raised my right arm and said in a commanding voice, "Get behind me Satan!"

He stopped and I thought I was having an effect until he spoke, looking around, "Satan... Satan. Nope. I don't see any Satan around here anywhere."

I was desperate and was about to command him to leave using the name of Jesus Christ, but as soon as I attempted to say the name my lips became sealed so I could not speak.

Philo looked mockingly around again and said, "Nope. No Jesus around here either, and even if he were, he could not help someone as fearful as you are at this moment."

He was right. I was starting to fear that I had no power before his supernatural ability. I tried to quiet my fear, but the more I tried the more I seemed to fear that the end was near.

I did my best to act like I did not fear as I remembered one tactic that worked before. I laughed in his face.

To my horror he laughed back and taunted, "My Master told me to be prepared for your tactics, and the brotherhood have taken measures to neutralize all your efforts. The one thing we did not count on was your knocking me silly when my body was dense. You just about had me with that meat cleaver, but that opportunity will not come again."

"It looks like you truly have the advantage over me," I confessed. "Before you do whatever it is you are going to do, would you answer a question?"

"Perhaps. What is your question?" he said matter-of-factly.

"Do you still say you are the real Philo or could you be my Dweller impersonating Philo?"

Philo laughed and replied, "Your stupid Dweller is not bright enough to impersonate me. Yes, you are talking to the real me. And now you want to know how this can be when I can go in and out of the astral. As you might have guessed, this is not my body but the revived body of your Dweller molded to my shape. I am currently in deep meditation with my Brotherhood to revive and control your Dweller so we can experience the pleasure of your destruction and the end to this insidious work you are beginning. It took a lot of pleading and bargaining on my part, but the big guys finally let me take the body of the Dweller first.

"So when you're in this body do you experience feeling in it like a real body?"

"It's just like my real body when my consciousness is here," he said.

"That's good to know," I said.

"Good to know? Why?" he asked, sounding curious.

"Because when I sever the Dweller in two you will suffer agonizing pain."

I realized this was a gutsy statement to make and I had no power to back it up, but it was the only choice of words I could come up with that seemed like an offense at all. I didn't feel like dying by backing into a corner.

To my surprise Philo moved back in a jolt as I made the threat. I picked up a sense of fear from him as he spoke with some nervousness in his voice. "I am maintaining full control of this body," he said. "Any attempt to attack me will be met with your hand or any instrument you hold passing through the air. I, on the other hand, can give you a material blow at will and with much greater strength than my natural body. You will not catch me by surprise again."

The fear I sensed from him gave me renewed hope. He was afraid of something, something that could sever the Dweller in two. That had to be Excalibur, but where was it and how would I find it in the short time I had left? The only thing I could think of to do was to exploit his fear in hope it would reveal something. John said to use Excalibur. That must mean I have it even though I am unaware of it, so I said. "I have a weapon that you know not of, the sword of truth that can sever spirit and matter, body and soul. Touch me not or I will send you back to the bottomless pit from whence you came."

I seemed to have pushed a button this time. I saw real fear in his eyes and he seemed frozen with indecision for a moment. Then he exclaimed, "You have nothing, you hear me?" Then he shouted, "Nothing!"

I saw now that my only chance was to make a bluff. "Leave now or I will use that *nothing* which is something you fear."

He took a step backward and for a moment I thought I was making progress. Then he stood still as if he were listening to something or someone. His eyes appeared to gain confidence as he said, "My Master just spoke to me and affirmed that you have nothing and know nothing. I am to proceed according to plan."

I had no other choice but to try to bluff again, "Your Masters do not know what I know. If you know what is best for you, you will just leave."

He hesitated a moment as if having another two-way conversation and then quickly turned and shoved me with almost supernatural force. I was thrown across the room, hit the wall and must have drifted into unconsciousness for a few seconds. The next thing I knew he had me in a bear hung squeezing the life out of me. I felt one or two ribs break and knew I was in trouble. I had wrestled with Philo once before and was stronger than he. Somehow his possession of the body of the Dweller gave him extra strength.

Finally, just before my consciousness descended into oblivion he dropped me on the floor and said, "I am told not to kill you, but I do have permission to play with you and cause you all the pain I desire."

My ribs and lungs felt like they were exploding but I felt like maybe I had a chance again as he was definitely physical. I reached toward him and grabbed his leg and it was indeed material but before I could make any offensive move his leg seemed to dematerialize in my hand. He stepped back and laughed. "I told you I would not make the same mistake again." He then kicked me with such force that my body rolled over a couple of times.

I was barely conscious and after rousing myself I saw that he had me pinned against the wall, slapping me on the face. "Wake up big guy. You're not going to want to miss the fun!" Then he proceeded to strangle me until I lost consciousness again.

How long I was out I did not know, but when I opened my eyes I found myself in a dimly lit, but spacious cave surrounded by many candles. I immediately found I could not move, for I was tied, hand and foot, to some type of alter. As my blurry vision focused I was able to make out the image of a gloating Philo on my left. Then to my even greater horror I heard the voice of Elizabeth cry my name from my right. I turned my head and saw her in her pajamas in a wooden cage that seemed a creation straight from the middle ages.

"Elizabeth," I cried, "Are you OK?"

"I think so," she said. "Where are we and how did we get here?"

"I'm not sure," I said, "but we're going to get out of this."

"You never give up, do you?" smirked Philo, as he threw a

glass of water in my face. "I'd say that if you have some secret weapon to use against me you'd better use it now because in a moment you will have much more to deal with than a mere acolyte like myself. The Brothers I serve are much more powerful than me, and if you cannot defeat *me*, you could never defeat them."

He seemed to expect a response from me, but I said nothing.

He grabbed a candle and applied the flame to my foot. "Hey! What was that all about?" I yelled.

"It's about getting your attention," he decreed. "When I speak I expect a response, as will my master you will soon meet. Now let me make myself clear. Show me this weapon you think you have."

I somehow picked up the thought that Philo was a front man and part of his job was to make sure I was rendered harmless. "You still have some fear of me, don't you?" I said.

"You fool!" he exclaimed. "We'll see who fears." He then applied the candle to my other foot. "Now tell me why you think you have a weapon?"

I did not want to give him the satisfaction of hearing me scream so I bit my lip and endured the pain, but Elizabeth screamed at him. "If he really had a weapon don't you think he would have used it by now? He has no weapon. Now leave him alone!"

After a few more painful seconds he removed the candle and said, "She's right, isn't she? You were just spewing hot air. I can tell from your eyes you have nothing." He laughed in a revolting way for about five seconds.

After he was finished amusing himself with laughter he said, "Perhaps I will give you just one more test to see if there is anything to this."

He opened the door to Elizabeth's cage, grabbed her arm and pulled her screaming to the outside. He then ripped her pajama top off and held her before me. "I'm going to rape your wife. What do you have to say about that?"

I screamed at him and struggled helplessly to get loose as he made motions to overcome Elizabeth. He looked my direction and saw my helplessness and stopped. He then returned Elizabeth to the cage, threw her in and locked the door. He returned to me and said. "Now I know you have no weapon. If you did you certainly would have used it by now. Admit it. You are helpless and useless. You can't even help your own wife." He laughed again. It was a laugh that told me he was completely confident that he had nothing to fear from me.

"So, are you going to laugh me to death?" I asked.

His face instantly sobered up as he growled, "You will not be wisecracking for long. Let me reveal a mystery to you. Yes, I occupy the body of your Dweller, but your Dweller is very powerful and ancient and has enveloped around itself enough matter for more bodies than one. Watch carefully and learn."

Philo stepped back, held up his arms and chanted in a language I had not heard before. The vibration of the sound of the chant gave me the creeps and produced a chilling sensation. Unfortunately, that was not the worst of it, for to my amazement two other beings materialized on both sides of Philo. These two were dressed in hooded black robes and looked just like they were drawn out of a horror movie of some kind. Suddenly all three of them started chanting. As they did, Philo's dress changed from casual to the same attire the other two had. The combined sound of the three was even more disturbing, but then to my added horror four more men in the same black robes materialized. The seven gathered in a semicircle around me and again resumed the chant.

This time the negativity was almost unbearable. I turned and saw it was also affecting Elizabeth, for she was crouching in the cage with her hands over her ears. As the chant continued six additional figures appeared. The last person to materialize had a sword in his hand and his robe had a different appearance than the rest. It had a blackness that I had never seen before. The only way I can describe it is to say it was the opposite of the radiation of a bright white object like the sun. Instead of radiating light, this individual radiated dark. When I looked in his direction it was as if he was a living black hole sucking in all light and positive energy that was near him. Not only was his robe an intense black, but the area around his body was covered by a cloudy blackness.

This dark master turned toward Philo and said, "You have prepared these humans just as you said and you have rendered the sacrifice harmless?"

"Sacrifice?" I whispered to myself. I didn't like the sound of that word.

Philo answered, "Yes, my Lord. He has no power, nor does

he remember who he is or where he is from."

"Then perhaps there is hope," he replied in a whisper. In the movies a satanic figure always talks in some computerized slowed down voice. This entity's voice sounded fairly normal, but soft spoken. "If we reveal to him his true origins then perhaps he will join with us. If we sacrifice him he will be eliminated for only a short time and then we will meet him again, stronger than before. But if he joins with us, an enemy is lost forever."

"I understand," said Philo bowing.

Then, as if the group of thirteen had previously rehearsed, twelve of them gathered around in a circle enclosing me and the Dark Lord inside. The twelve then began making a low humming sound. Again, I strongly felt the vibration. It was indeed disturbing, for it seemed to lower my own. Then the Dark Lord turned and looked at me. I saw his eyes for the first time and was horrified to see he had no pupils or iris. His eyes were entirely white. Then I remembered John telling me earlier that the Dark Brothers have their eyes reversed as a symbol of their attention devoted entirely to self and selfishness.

I turned my head away from him when I remembered that his eyes have the power to drain life energy from his victims like a spiritual vampire. "No need to turn your head," he said. "I haven't decided to take your life just yet."

"If you think I'm joining you then you are not only evil, but also insane," I said.

"Don't be so sure of yourself," he said. "What you have been told is the dark side is, in reality, the true light, a light which is only seen through reversing the eyes. You see black around me, but that is not what these brethren see. Instead they see the true light, a light that the Brotherhood who John speaks of does not understand, for they have never embraced it. We, on the other hand, have tasted of the light of John's brotherhood. Most of us were once disciples of what you call the Brotherhood of Light, and have rejected it and embraced the dark light instead. We are the ones who have made the true choice, for we have seen both sides."

"Why would I want to embrace something that feels so terrible and evil to me? How could there possibly be happiness in your path?"

"Happiness. Is that what you are after? Did you not learn in your study of Buddha that happiness is a temporary state and only lasts a short time? We offer something much better than happiness."

"And what would that be?" I asked.

"We offer eternal pleasure, eternal fulfillment of self."

"If happiness is not eternal, how could pleasure be?" I asked.

"Happiness is based on circumstances, whereas pleasure, as we know it, involves a wholehearted identification with self and the eternal matter in the worlds of form."

"You mean your pleasure does not come and go, but remains consistent?"

"As a brother evolves up the Hierarchy, this becomes the case, for the lower members feed the higher with life essence. When you have a never-ending stream of this energy, you have endless pleasure."

"So is this like some kind of multi-level thing with pleasure as the commodity rather than money?"

"Multi-level?" he said, looking amused. He then paused a moment as if absorbing the thought and continued, "Yes, I suppose it is something like that. Once you establish yourself in the brotherhood, you achieve a continuous flow of pleasure. Compare this to the saints of John's brotherhood. They suffer pain and misfortune life after life, and for what? Some great heavenly bliss that takes an act of faith to accept? We need no faith, for we touch and feel and see pleasure in the now."

I reflected and said, "So a few at the top receive uninterrupted pleasure, but the majority receives a pittance to keep them motivated – like Philo over there, for instance."

Philo looked extremely agitated by my remark and moved slightly toward me. The Dark Master immediately responded, raised his right hand and commanded Philo, "Hold your place!"

Philo immediately resumed his placed in the circle and I saw great fear arise in his eyes as his master walked toward him and said in a raised voice, "You were allowed into this ceremony because you told us you knew your place. Is there a problem here?"

"No Master," he said in a humble tone of voice I had not seen in him before.

"And who gets the pleasure of taking the life of this victim?"

"The pleasure is all yours Master," Philo said bowing. "But you did promise me the woman."

Hearing this caused an indescribable disgust within me. His master then replied, "She is yours if you keep your place. Is this understood?"

"Perfectly," said Philo.

The Dark Master then returned to me and spoke while running his right hand through my hair, "That is how it works, my brother. Everyone keeps his place and the flow continues without end."

"But Philo just demonstrated that one can lose his place in a moment of weakness. What then?" I asked.

"There is always another eager to fill a lost place," he said.

"And where do these replacements come from?" I asked.

"Replacements for our brotherhood come from discouraged disciples of the White Light who are willing to look at the Dark Light."

"And what if that source should dry up because those in the light receive greater support and no longer become discouraged?"

The Dark Master looked angry and exclaimed, "That will never happen. Never!" He paused and continued, "There will always be a fresh supply of discouraged do-gooders. This will never change."

"So what will you do when human evolution reaches an end? Where will you get fresh souls to prey upon with your vampirism?"

"When humanity is exhausted for us those among us who have become masters of the dark light will escape to another planet of opportunity and there we will reign again, but with greater power."

"And how many become dark masters?"

"That number is not to be spoken," he said gravely.

"Well, if your outfit operates like a multi-level, then that number will be few, like maybe one percent or so." I then looked toward Philo. "You hear that Philo? You're going to be left behind with the 99%. You're going to get JACK SQUAT!"

Philo moved ever so slightly and I took some pleasure myself in knowing he was very tempted to move out of his place again.

"So what happens to the 99% who are left behind?" I asked, returning my gaze to the speaker.

The dark master seemed a little ruffled, "No one confirmed a percentage to you. Those who are left behind are still able to enjoy an extended period of pleasure."

"But after that period is over, all but their spiritual essence will be destroyed," I said. "Then they will have to begin their evolution all over again. They will wind up being millions, maybe billions, of years behind the average human of today in their progression."

"You speak gibberish, but I will say this. There is risk on the left and the right. The difference is this. During the period of our risk we enjoy domination and pleasure. During the period of your risk you experience pain and others dominate you. In the end we achieve eternal life in worlds of pleasure, worlds with pleasure greater than you can imagine here. And what is the promise of John's brotherhood? They seek an invisible Nirvana beyond the worlds of form that does not even exist. The Kingdom within spoken of by Jesus was wishful thinking. We can touch, feel and see our kingdom, but you only imagine yours."

"So you do not even believe in the higher worlds?" I asked.

"We believe in something, not in nothing," he said.

"I guess that explains the logic of this pathetic path you are on."

This statement seemed to greatly disturb him and he immediately unsheathed his sword and raised it in the air with what seemed to be the intent to thrust it in me. Elizabeth screamed and my mind was whirling, thinking as fast as I could. "You're acting out of your place!" I shouted.

Immediately, his body froze in place and he held a stationary position for a few seconds with the point of the sword a few inches from my heart. He dropped his sword and started laughing. Then the rest of the coven joined in as if that was the expected thing to do. After the laughter died down he looked at me and said. "There is no out of place for me, but you did remind me of the plan to bring you over to our side." He paused a moment and said, "Yes, I think you would indeed be a good addition to our brotherhood. It took some quick thinking to challenge me like you did. We can put that initiative to use."

I looked at him in disbelief. "You have got to be stark raving mad to think you could persuade me to join you. You might as well finish me off now because you will be severely disappointed."

"I don't think so," he said grinning. "There is something I know that you do not."

"What?" I challenged.

"Your history," he said with a grin that sent a chill through my being. "I know where you come from and why you are here. When I retrieve these ancient memories you will then know where you belong."

He then touched my forehead with his fingertips, creating a tingling sensation. I experienced an uncomfortable anticipation as images began to form.

CHAPTER EIGHTEEN
A Difficult Past

As images began to form in my mind I felt myself falling into a bottomless pit. I was spinning around as if I were in a descending whirlpool surrounded by many lives I had affected, a number of them in a harmful way.

I seemed to be going back in time, a time long before I came to this earth. Finally, I was able to get my bearings and I saw the planet where I dwelt millions of years ago. Exactly how long I cannot say. I just felt that it was indeed eons ago.

The planet was named Aeton and circled around a large orange sun not too far from our own, relatively speaking. They called the sun Soula. I found it interesting that this was close to our sun's name, Sol. I was really fascinated as I realized both had the sound of soul in them.

I saw that I lived upon Aeton during a turning point of its humanity. For thousands of years there had been a great struggle between the forces of light and dark, or spirit and materialism, and this was one of the planets where the dark side eventually dominated. I saw that in my past on Aeton I made an effort to pursue what was called the path of light. This was a time where civilization had evolved to something like the Old Roman Empire. This was a time of great conflict. I was falsely accused of treason by a jealous associate named Sabul and thrown in prison. While in prison I learned that my wife had been raped by Sabul who I once considered my friend. Later, she and my three children died mysteriously. I blamed Sabul for this also.

This whole situation was very disturbing to me for Sabul was always speaking of being on the side of light, but in truth he was as dark as the lowest of souls. Unfortunately the tribunals believed his word over mine.

I was all alone with no one I cared about remaining and I thought, "What is the difference between good and evil? If Sabul, who claims to be on the side of Light and Truth, can be so evil as to betray me and slay my family, then who is my real enemy? Who am I fighting against? If both sides be my enemy, then perhaps I should choose the enemy with the greatest benefits and the one who has a chance of victory."

I saw that even though one side did seem to pursue the path of light the conflict caused the demarcations between the two to become obscure. Both sides committed great atrocities.

As I sat for several years in a dark prison I dreamed of revenge against Sabul. This desire for revenge was the only thing that kept me alive. Finally, my time of opportunity came when the opposition we had called the Dark Army tore through the gates of my city. They destroyed half the inhabitants and gave chase to the rest. Sabul was one of those who escaped.

The leader of the opposing army was called Zinkor. He perceived that he may have some allies among the prisoners and had us all questioned. He had me and a number of others brought before his presence. I expressed a willingness to join with him if he would allow me to lead a band in pursuit of Sabul. I told him I knew Sabul well and could find the place that he would probably be hiding at.

Zinkor was pleased. He promised me my freedom *and* a command if I would find Sabul along with his followers and slay them. First he made me take an oath that I would be faithful to his command and obey without question. "What do I have to lose?" I thought and took the oath.

I departed, leading a division, and true to my word found Sabul's hiding place. I gave the men instructions to save Sabul for me. Finally, I found him and had him cornered. "Pathetic traitor," I spat out when he begged for his life. I had no sympathy as I hacked him to pieces. I made the fatal mistake of taking intense pleasure in his pain and destruction. I had never felt such a rush of intense enjoyment. It only made me want more so I ordered the destruction of the entire group who had been my friends. I happily participated and took great pleasure in every penetrating stroke of my sword. In the carnage that followed I almost went mad with glee as I fought without conscience.

When the battle was over and all in the camp were dead, I gained the respect and allegiance of the dark soldiers with me. They respected power, bravery and the overriding of any conscience to get the job done. Something in me changed to acquire the attributes respected by those who I once thought evil.

We returned to Zinkor and the soldiers recounted to him my commitment to the cause. "I had a feeling about you," he said "and am pleased to see you performed as I desired. If I place you in permanent command, will you obey my will in assisting in the destruction of all those whom you previously considered brethren?"

"They have betrayed me and are no longer my brethren," I said. "I will obey."

I thus participated in the fight of the dark against light. They were strange times. Those on the side of light were far from perfect and were highly corrupted by infiltration from the dark side. It did seem as if neither side had a claim to being in the right so I decided to follow a path that seemed most advantageous to me.

I went ahead with vigor in assisting in the fight against my old brotherhood. I advanced through the ranks of the new brotherhood and became a renowned leader, resulting in the defeat and subjugation of my new enemies. Time and time again I led conquests, relished in the pleasure of victory over our enemies, and took pleasure in their pain.

I was a powerful agent in turning the tide of power toward materialism in that life.

In my next several lives I incarnated into a world ruled by darkness and corruption, and instead of working to correct the situation, I sought to make the most of the circumstances for myself. I gravitated toward Mafia-type organizations for several lifetimes. I obtained wealth, comfort and experienced all the pleasures the flesh could give. In the process I committed many grievous crimes.

The next significant life for me was a political one. Humanity had evolved to a civilization like our world in the 1940's, and seemed to be stuck there because of the rule of darkness and the domination of totalitarianism. In this life I was a man of much power and influence, and again had every pleasure that money could buy. After several lifetimes of fulfilling all my desires I wanted something more, but was not sure what it was. I decided that it may be power, so power is what I sought.

I worked behind the scenes pulling strings to obtain my political objectives and to place those in power who furthered my ends. I had money, and used it to destroy my enemies and enhance those who would increase my power base. I became one of the wealthiest and powerful men on Aeton. Just about the time I thought I had the world at my feet, a turning point occurred.

One night, as I was lying in my bed thinking of what do to with all the power I was accumulating, there appeared at my bedside a mystical being of haunting countenance. He was dressed in a black robe and did not look directly at me, so I could not see his eyes.

He spoke to me about a "grand opportunity" to ascend to heights of power and pleasure previously unknown to me, and explained to me the various covenants and commitments I would have to make to his brotherhood. He told me that the brotherhood had already been working with me by sending me telepathic commands for several lifetimes. I had now progressed to the point where I would be allowed into full membership and could work with them in full consciousness. He explained a "fully conscious brother" was a much more powerful tool for both himself and the organization. He enumerated many benefits I would receive as a conscious member and outpost for them on Aeton.

The mistake he made was that he spoke in disgust of another brotherhood, which he called "the pseudo brotherhood of light." He talked about them as if they were the scum of the universe, ignorant and naive as children.

This piqued my imagination, for I had no memory of my past lives, and little was known on Aeton at this time of a Brotherhood of Light. The planet had descended so far into materialism that if such a brotherhood did exist it dared not show itself.

I told this being that I would think about his offer. He seemed impatient with this response and insisted I must answer soon, then vanished.

After he left I found myself, for the first time in that life, thinking about two brotherhoods in opposition to each other. The being who appeared to me seemed to have all the answers for pleasure and bliss in this life and the next. What more, I wondered, could another brotherhood offer?

The big question I had was where would I find a member of this other brotherhood? Then the next day, as I was reading the news, I found an article that caught my attention. It spoke of an order of rebels who claimed to represent the Brotherhood of Light. The state had arrested its leader; his group had assembled without the necessary licenses. This roused my curiosity, so I used my influence and a couple of bribes to have him brought to me.

I met him on a military complex in a secure room where we could speak in private. Soldiers pushed him into the room, and he fell face down. He lifted himself up grumbling about the abuse he had received. Then he asked who I was and what I wanted of him. I told him my name and explained that for now I just wanted to talk to him.

He looked surprised. "You are widely known in underground circles as the one who works behind the scenes as a person of great power and influence."

"Sounds like I am much better known underground than I am by the general population," I said. "What is your name?"

"Ja-han," he said.

"Well, Ja-han, just as you say I work behind the scenes, even so I have heard that there are two brotherhoods who work behind the scenes. I know a little about the brotherhood who controls our government, but I have only heard hearsay about yours. I have become curious and wish to know more about it. What do you offer except prison and bondage of your people?"

Ja-han looked at me in disbelief. "You know nothing of the brotherhood controlling you and your government. All of you are pawns being moved in the direction of the destruction of this planet. You are controlled by the Dark Brothers and know it not."

"I may know more than you think. I saw one of them the other day."

Ja-han's face turned very grave. He stated, "My dear sir. This is too serious of a matter for you to speak so lightly."

"I'm not trying to be funny," I said. "I really saw and talked to one the other day."

After an uncomfortable silence Ja-han said, "Tell me about

his eyes. What did they look like?"

"I didn't see his eyes," I said. "He never faced me directly. He was dressed in a black robe though."

"Perhaps you did meet one of them. What did he offer you?"

I then rehearsed to him the basic exchange I had with the visitor.

Ja-han's face turned pale as he said. "My dear Sir, you do not realize the peril you are in or what you would pose for the planet if you were to join the Dark Brothers. If you join them as a conscious participator in their dark works, there will be no turning back for you. You will lose your very soul, and that which you presently are, will be destroyed and reworked in the great refinery of the one Lord."

"Threats mean nothing to me," I said. "I am more interested in the benefits. Right now, it looks as if the Dark Lords control all the governments and sources of power on Aeton. I am not sure that your brotherhood has dominion over anything. What could possibly be the advantage of joining with your side? The moment I did so, I would become an enemy of the State and my life would become a living hell."

Ja-han stared at me and replied, "Suppose you build a house and bruise your thumb a couple of times with a hammer in the process. When the house is finished and you step back to enjoy the fruits of your labor, will you even be thinking of the passing pain you once had?"

"I don't suppose," I said, "but an entire life of being in hiding and possibly prison and death, is more than a bruised thumb."

"Not when you consider the entire scheme of things," he said. "We live many lifetimes before we achieve liberation, and this life may indeed be a bruised thumb in the series; but there will be others where I will have the joy of living peacefully in the mansion of my labors."

"But you talk about a future that may only exist within your imagination. What do you offer in the here and now besides pain, sacrifice and suffering?"

"The great Lord I follow offers one thing that the Dark Lords can never give you either now or in the future."

"And what is that?" I challenged.

"Peace," he said in a whisper that penetrated me more than a raised voice would have.

I was curious. "How can you offer peace when none of your people on Aeton have any tranquility whatsoever? All of you are fugitives and hunted by the State. How can one who has no peace offer peace?"

"But, my friend, I do have peace."

"You lie!" I shouted. "I happen to know that for the past couple of years you have been on the run and have known no rest. Even now you are held prisoner and face torture and death. How can you say you have peace?"

"Let me quiz you first," said Ja-han, unruffled by my accusations. "The fact that you made a great effort and went to some risk yourself to talk to me about my brotherhood tells me that you did not completely buy the sales pitch of the Dark Lord. There can only be one reason you hesitated to take him up on his offer."

"And what is that?"

"You have not completely given yourself to selfishness and pleasure. You have had all that money and power can buy and it is not enough."

"But the Dark Lord says there is *more*; more pleasure available than I have ever experienced," I countered.

"But if all the pleasure and power you have now still leaves a hole inside, what would more do? The vacuum inside would expand until it destroyed you."

"And you," I challenged. "I suppose you think you are all fulfilled inside even though you have nothing, and will soon die."

"Yes. Inside I am fulfilled," he said reverently. "The world on the outside is temporary and fleeting. Events are guideposts to direct our inner attention on the good, the beautiful and the true so we can obtain a joy which is eternal and shall not pass away."

"Well, if you expect to have a prayer in influencing me, then show me how to have this peace and joy."

Ja-han was silent a few seconds.

"I knew it!" I said. "You have nothing. You're all talk. I brought you here because I was curious about your cause. That was all. Nothing more. It is now time for you to return to your cell and await your death."

I got up to head toward the door to signal the guard. Ja-han rose and grabbed my arm and pleaded. "My dear sir, give me a few more moments. Please, not only for my sake, but for yours."

I was going to push him away until my eyes met his. Even though he was undergoing a moment of tension I sensed there was something peaceful and serene deep within him. "All right. I'll give you a moment, but do not waste my time."

"Good," said Ja-han as we sat back down at the table. He then looked me straight in the eyes again and asked, "Do you ever pray?"

"I recite a few of the state approved prayers," I said.

"But do you ever pray in your own words from your own heart?"

"I've never felt the need," I said. "I have always taken care of my own needs. I do not desire to plead to some imaginary being to help me."

"I want you to listen to me," said Ja-han sternly. "If you will do one simple thing I ask, I promise you will have a taste of this peace I talk about."

"I suppose you want me to pray," I said mockingly.

"Yes," said Ja-han. "If you will just cry out to God before going to sleep tonight and ask Him with all sincerity of heart for peace, it will come to you."

"I do not believe you," I said.

"I don't care if you believe or not. All I ask is that you will do this with sincerity of heart." He grabbed my right hand with both of his hands and said, "Will you please do this one thing for me?"

I looked in his eyes and again there was a radiation of warmth that seemed familiar, but one that I did not remember experiencing before in that life. "It's against my better judgment, but I will do it. If nothing else, I will prove you wrong and go on my way knowing you have nothing to offer."

"But if you do pray and experience the peace there is something you must do."

"And what is that?" I asked, surprised a prisoner would be telling me what I must do.

"You must use your means to get me out of here so I can teach you. I sense that you were once on the path of light in a previous life and have departed from it; now you are close to choosing the dark path. You cannot let this happen. Let me show you the true path and the great destiny that can be yours."

I pounded my fist on the table and shouted, "I already *have* a great destiny. Can't you see that I am one of the most powerful men on the planet?"

"Material power is based in illusion," he said. "Only the power of the invisible Spirit is real. This is what you must achieve to fill the hole inside you."

I grew impatient and rose up, "I've heard enough. Our interview is over."

I called the guards and as they took him away he shouted to me, "You must keep your word tonight."

I went about my business the rest of the day and as evening approached I seriously considered breaking my word to him. The state-approved prayers were bad enough and had turned me off to praying.

That evening as I retired to bed I thought of Ja-han and our conversation. I thought of the serene look in his eyes even though he faced great danger. I thought of his promise of peace.

I asked myself, "Do I have peace?"

Then I answered myself, "It may not be completely satisfying but it's about as good as it gets."

As I lay there thinking of reasons to not say the prayer requested by Ja-han, I thought I heard a whisper, "My peace awaits you."

I rose up with a start. I was not sure if I was hearing things or not. I tried to ignore it and turned over to go to sleep but I could not sleep. Finally I sat up contemplating saying my first personal prayer. It seemed to be a silly thing to do, but what could I lose?

I cried out, "Oh God, if there is a God, show me this peace spoken of by Ja-han."

I waited a few moments and nothing happen. I was almost relieved that nothing happened, for the more I thought about making changes, the less desirable it seemed.

I turned over to go to sleep and then I noticed it. Starting ever so softly in the core of my being, I felt the ignition of a gentle fire that seemed to expand until my whole being was filled with the most peaceful feeling one could imagine. It was a peace that passed all understanding.

The next day I wanted to learn more from Ja-han and decided

to get him out of prison no matter what it took. I hired a group of mercenaries and during a transport they overcame the guards, freed Ja-han, and returned him to one of his groups in hiding. I arranged to meet him there.

Ja-han was overjoyed to see me. "You felt the peace, didn't you?"

"Yes," I admitted. "And after that experience I knew I had to see you again. I feel that I must learn from you. Tell me about the Brotherhood of Light."

Ja-han rehearsed to me the differences between the two paths and then said, "Aeton is a dying planet with a dying humanity. The dark side prevails here and there is no turning it around. After several more generations this planet will explode and become an asteroid belt around our sun."

"What do you mean *there is no turning it around*? Does not good prevail over evil in your philosophy?"

"In the whole scheme of things it does," said Ja-han with a grim look. "And in happier times we could have turned the tide, but the race on this planet has made its group decision and has passed the point of no return."

"So what do we do?" I asked, "Throw up our hands, give up and wait to die?"

"There is much yet to do to prepare for our next step. We must gather out all those who have light within themselves, as you now have, and teach them."

"Next step?" I questioned. "What is the next step?"

"The next step is to leave this planet and find another home among the stars," he said pointing upwards.

"Find another?" I said in amazement, as our civilization had not yet perfected space travel. "How do you expect to travel to the stars? You are teaching me fables."

"We shall not go there in these physical bodies, but after death, those who are selected to leave this planet will be taken to a new home with fresh opportunity. Great watching Lives who guide the destinies of dozens of solar systems will assist in moving us to places of greater service. Your choice is to either assist in the time of the final harvest or to stay here and die with this world."

I made the choice to assist Ja-han and began working with all diligence. I soon got into trouble with the authorities and lost all my power and fortune. I spent the rest of my life as a fugitive, working underground to find and prepare those who could see the greater light. Our groups faced many dangers, but we were happy with our dreams of moving to better worlds where we could live happy lives amidst people like ourselves, worlds that were not ruled by brothers of the shadows.

Near the end of our lives Ja-han and I were eating together and I was sharing with him the type of world that I hoped would be our new home. He then looked at me soberly and said. "My friend, there is something I have not told you."

"What is that?" I asked a little nervously.

"We will be going our separate ways. I will be going to the solar system of Sirius and you will be going to another place in another system."

"I do not understand," I said. "I have grown to love and respect you more than I thought was possible and have never entertained the thought of us separating. Tell me this is not so."

"There is no separation in the higher worlds of consciousness," he said. "But we shall be separated as working individual units for some time."

"I will go to Sirius with you," I demanded.

"You cannot go," he said. "There is a problem."

"Problem? What problem?"

Ja-han spoke solemnly, "It is your karma – the debts you have to pay."

"But you told me a while back that my work and sacrifice in this life would pay for my earlier mistakes."

"This is correct," he said. "You have balanced off the mistakes of this life, but there are other lives."

"Other lives? Whatever it is I'll work it out so I can go with you."

"It is not that simple," he said sadly. "It is time for you to remember so you can understand."

He then used a regression technique on me and I reviewed my immediate past lives culminating with the one where I turned from light to dark and had lead the dark forces to victory.

I sat up a moment just to absorb what I had learned. I then paced back and forth on the floor, mumbling to myself in disbelief. I didn't want to believe what I had just seen, but somehow deep inside I knew it was correct. I stopped and let out a scream.

After I had finished my emotional outburst I turned to Ja-han and said, "This is more than I can bear. I'm not worthy to go to Sirius with you. I'm not even worthy to dust off the path upon which you walk. I helped turn the tide on this planet from light to dark. If not for me we may not have to be leaving. Aeton may very well have been a paradise by now. I can never undo what I have done. My fate can only be to stay here and be destroyed with the rest of the population."

Ja-han put his arm around me and gave me a brotherly hug. I couldn't believe that he had accepted me all those years when he knew my history. "You have a better destiny than staying here, my friend," he said. "I cannot say it will not be difficult, for the road ahead is hard indeed; but if you succeed the end will be glorious."

"You mean after all the harm I have done I will be given a chance of some kind to join the Brotherhood?"

"Indeed you will," he said smiling. "Because you have served well in this last half of your life you have earned the right to go to a place where you will be able to pay off your debts. That is if you so choose."

"Yes, I will choose to do so!" I said with enthusiasm. "What kind of place will I go to?"

"It is a planet circling a neighboring sun much younger than our own. The planet is Earth and at present it is home to a young and savage humanity. It will be a million years or so before the inhabitants reach a high degree of civilization where they can learn to live in peace. Before that time comes, there will be a struggle between light and dark and once again you will have the opportunity to shift the focus of the struggling souls one way or another. There will be risk, because you could always choose the dark side from whence there is no return in this cycle of creation."

"I'll take my chances," I said. "Earth." I mumbled. "Didn't you once tell me this was some type of prison planet?"

"Yes," he said. "Because of the great pain and difficulty of incarnating and living there among the primitive inhabitants who are in constant fear of wild beasts, it is a planet designated by the Watchers to send some of the greatest criminals of our sector to. The basic idea is that they are to learn a lesson there, but many of them become even worse and will choose the dark side. These criminals are wise and cunning, and will make your struggle to assist the population to chose the light all the more difficult. I must warn you that many of your lifetimes will be very difficult and will require the sacrifice of your life. But if you wish to redeem yourself, this is the path you must choose."

"I will do whatever is necessary to dwell with you again, my good friend."

"I will not be there to help you this time. You must gather the inner resources to persevere on your own."

"Will any others be joining me from Aeton?"

"Just a handful that also has large debts. Several have turned around as you have and some have not."

"I know it is too much to ask to expect you to come to earth during the savage years of evolution, but how about later on when the tide begins to turn?"

Ja-han closed his eyes in silence for a few moments and said, "When a son of man who is a Son of God manifests on Earth, I will join with you as one of his disciples. I will then work with you until the planet is dominated by the Light and Love of the Holy One."

"So it shall be," I said grabbing his hand.

"So it shall be," said Ja-han.

CHAPTER NINETEEN
Excalibur

The Dark Master removed his hand from my head. I got the impression that it had only been there a short time even though I had reviewed a time period covering many lifetimes in my mind. I shook my head and tried to focus my consciousness in the present.

"If you think that reviving those memories will change my mind, then you are indeed deceived. I feel more determined than ever to defy you," I said in a challenging voice.

"Perhaps," he said, "but you speak prematurely, for you have not yet seen the whole story. Before I show you the rest of your history I must tell you that Ja-han, or John as he is called now, has deceived you from the beginning. This insidious deception has lasted well over a million years for you, and it is time for you to be delivered from it."

"And what deception is that?"

"The deception is at the core of his philosophy: *The present and immediate future is full of pain and suffering; but go ahead, take it and endure, for the time will soon come that you will prevail... and then you can live a life of joy and peace.* The reality is much different. The dupes under John's Brotherhood have never-ending pain, suffering, and never prevail. The long looked-for day of deliverance never comes. John told you that to redeem yourself you had to be a factor in changing the shift of balance between the two forces. We have always dominated over the powers of the Earth and there is no end in sight to our power."

"You lie. Your time is short. Soon the power of light and love will prevail," I said defiantly.

The Dark Master paced back and forth muttering, "Soon. Soon. Everything for you deceived disciples is always soon. You have no idea how many times you thought your day of power was to *soon* be, and yet it has never come." Then he paused a moment and exclaimed in a loud voice, "And it never will!"

"Maybe you just don't understand the simple principle of faith," I said softly.

"Faith!" he shouted. "I'll show you what your faith has wrought." Then he touched my forehead again.

Again I found myself whirling back into my past. I quickly saw a long series of lives beginning back in primitive Earth times and proceeding to the present. I saw that time and time again in Earth's history, I had stood with the Brotherhood of Light and had suffered for it, as far as physical plane life goes. I saw that at the end of a large percentage of these lives I had endured torture and/or death.

After viewing this, the Dark Master removed his hand and spoke, "You thought that you would come to the Earth, pay off a few debts and then all would be well. On the contrary, all has not been well for you. As you have seen, even your last three lives have ended with your life being cut short through an untimely violent death by your enemies. In the past you have mistakenly thought that this suffering would end soon; even now you believe yourself to be at a turning point. There is no turning point. This cycle will just go on and on until you join us."

"I would never join you," I barked. "I would rather die a thousand more deaths!"

"Your strong will shall make you an asset when you join us," he said smiling, "but first it must be broken. So, you would be willing to suffer all over again, would you? Maybe you have just forgotten just how painful some of your tribulations have been. I will pick just a dozen for you and let you relive them. Then we shall see how eager you are to defy me."

He then made a motion with his hand to the group and they all began chanting the word "NO" over and over, saying it for several seconds each time it was uttered. This was done in a similar fashion that many groups chant the OM. The note, however, was uttered low on the scale and instead of producing a pleasant feeling, this chant was very disturbing. The thumbnail across the blackboard comes to mind when thinking about it.

The Dark Master touched my forehead again, and I was taken back to a primitive time when I was a tribal leader and captured by an enemy tribe. They proceeded to boil me alive, preparatory for some perverted sacrament. It was like I was back there really being boiled alive. The pain was excruciating and was made worse by the incessant chanting. There was something about the chant of NO that amplified my agony. I couldn't hold back. I screamed over and over. It was as if time was slowed down and my death did not seem to be coming. Then I thought of how my screaming must be upsetting Elizabeth, and I used all my resources to remain silent. When I silenced myself, I was disturbed even more when I heard her screaming at my plight.

The Dark Master spoke, "It matters not whether you scream or remain silent. The pain remains. Let us give you some variety and move you ahead in time."

This time I saw I was a teacher of a small band of seekers who were captured by a warlord. He wanted to make an example out of me, so he tied me up and poured molten lead down my throat. Again I relived this in slow motion, and the unbearable agony was made even worse by that satanic chanting.

This was repeated for twelve different lifetimes, which ended in a painful death or torture so distasteful, I do not wish to write more about it. The first two give the general idea. The last, which was the twelfth, ended with me being tortured by religious authorities during the Middle Ages, as described in my previous writings.

By the time I was through the twelfth torture, I must admit that my will was weakened; and I found myself thinking I would be willing to do most anything to find relief. Then something amazing happened.

The Dark Master spoke again, "Perhaps a little relief is in order here." He made another motion to the group. The "NO" turned to "YES" with emphasis on the EH sound. This time the sound was pleasant and the vibration soothing. He touched my forehead. Instantly I was back on Aeton with a sword in my hand cutting Sabul to pieces. All the pain was gone and replaced by the pleasure of revenge I had at that moment. I then relived other moments on Aeton where I took pleasure in the pain and destruction of others.

Now the first time I re-experienced this pleasure, it had no power to influence my thinking. But this time was different. This time, the contrast with the extreme pain made my perverted pleasure on Aeton seem intense beyond measure, and I found myself wanting to stay in that state of mind. It seemed to be a natural escape from the previous pain he had put me through, and because of escaping the pain, the pleasure seemed blissful indeed.

He then said, "Perhaps you wish to reject the world of pleasure and return to a suffering life." The group chanted "NO" again, and I was returned to extreme torture. This time the torture seemed worse than ever because of the contrasting pleasure I had just left behind. I then found myself shouting NO along with their chant.

"No, you say." The Master laughed, "Then I assume you accept our way of pleasure."

I was then moved ahead to another life on Aeton where I enjoyed intense pleasure at the expense of others. Again the shift caused an intensity of pleasure beyond the imagination. I found myself almost saying yes along with their chant.

"Do I hear a *yes*?" said the Dark Master coyly. "Say it clearly for me now. Say *YES*."

The temptation to say *YES* was unbelievable, but I gathered all my resources and forced myself to think about the situation. Even though every fiber of my being cried out to say *YES* I decided this was not a wise direction. I then used all the training I had received in taking attention off the Dweller through the Principle of Attrition, and applied it to my present situation. I attempted to take all attention away from the pain, the pleasure, and the Dark Master, and seek a course of action.

For the next few minutes I was completely unresponsive. This greatly agitated the Dark Master, and he retaliated by sending me back to a time of torture. Again, drawing on reserves of will that I never knew existed, I remained completely without response. The Dark Master became still more agitated. He slapped me on the face and hissed, "Which do you choose? Pain or pleasure?"

The chanting of NO intensified along with the pain. I had to use all my reserves to even speak. "I choose neither pain nor pleasure, but to follow the path of love and light wherever it may lead."

The Dark Master's countenance fell, and the circumference

of dark around him doubled in size and activity. He unsheathed his sword again, raised it in the air and screamed the most ungodly sound I have ever heard. After a long scream, a silence descended on the group. Finally, he spoke in a coarse whisper. "Of course, if you reject us you shall die. We shall take your life force and follow you into the next world, where we will weigh you down with the dark light so you cannot move on. You will not escape us either in this world or the next."

He paused, looked toward Elizabeth and added, "Neither shall she. After your body is severed with this sword she will be given to Philo, who will have his pleasure with her. We shall make sure that she will feel every measure of pain that you have just gone through. She will say *YES* and *NO* as we desire her to, and she will be ours in this world and the next."

He then laughed a laugh that was as disturbing as his scream.

After exhausting himself, he turned to me and said, "We will release Elizabeth and all will be well with her if you agree to join us."

I had never felt so helpless. I could not bear the thought of what they would do to her. "Perhaps," I thought, "I could tell them I would go along with them and then when Elizabeth is safe I would change my mind." This was a very tempting choice, but something within me told me it was not wise. And how was I to know she would be all right, even if I cooperated? She would probably choose to go to hell with me to remain by my side.

There was no good choice to make. I decided the best choice was one that would choose light and love over these Dark Brothers no matter what the consequences. Somehow, choosing the highest spiritual path would yield the best results in the end.

I looked toward the Dark Master and said, "Do with us what you will. We will reject you and all you stand for. I will only accept the Holy Spirit and follow its direction."

I had a feeling that the Dark Master wanted to scream again, but his frustration had passed beyond this point.

"Philo!" he shouted. "Tell our friend here what you will do to Elizabeth after we cut his heart out."

Philo gleefully related what he would do to her. His words did indeed make my heart sink.

"Now, one more time," said the Dark Master slowly. "Will

you join us? Both of you can escape all this pain and enter a world of pleasures undreamed of."

I looked at Elizabeth. "I love you my dear and would do most anything to avoid hurting you, but we cannot join these low lives."

Elizabeth merely mouthed silently "I love you," in return. There seemed to be nothing else she could say.

I looked toward the Dark Lord and shouted, "The answer is no. Do you understand? NO NO NO NO" I chanted over and over, mocking their previous chant.

This seemed to be very painful for the group to listen to, so I repeated it louder, experimenting with different tones.

"Philo," shouted the Dark Lord. "Come gag this wretched soul."

"Gladly," he said, and immediately retrieved a cloth and gagged me, making it impossible for me to make anything but a muffled sound.

The Dark Lord looked at me, shaking his head and said, "You have been a troubling fellow to deal with for some time now. Since the time you first came to this planet, which we control, you have had this blind faith that the balance of power could shift from our brotherhood to yours. You have indeed believed John's lies that you can play some part in this shift, and thus pay off your debts."

He paused a moment, as if considering whether to continue, and then said quietly, "Let me tell you a secret which should be very disturbing to you. There is a way to escape the negative effects of Karma, and our brotherhood knows the great secret. If it pleases us, we can murder, plunder, rape and pillage and suffer no ill effects. If you had continued on the path of the dark light, you would have had no need to suffer again and again as you have in hope of some final redemption. Instead, you could have come here and enjoyed all the pleasures of the flesh and the feeling world. With your intelligence you could have lived in comfort and power, life after life."

Philo broke protocol again and shouted, "All your effort for all your Earth lives has been for nothing. You will continue with your suffering and giving your life, and we shall continue in taking it. There is nothing you can do. I'm telling you, these guys are untouchable, and I shall be untouchable with them."

The Dark Lord raised his hand as if to make the motion that silence was in order. Immediately, Philo ceased talking. "Our young acolyte here has much to learn, but he is progressing nicely, and soon will be initiated into the secret that neutralizes karma. This is the secret you would soon have if not for your stubbornness and stupidity."

I tried to speak but could only make a muffled sound. Then Elizabeth shouted out my thoughts, "You're the stupid one. You'll get your just reward in the end."

"But the end is now," he grinned, turning toward her. "At least it is the end for you two. If we cannot persuade you to join us, we will absorb you and take pleasure in your essence. He then turned toward his followers and shouted, "The ceremony will begin."

After saying this he made some motions to the group which seemed to be in some type of sign language. The group drew to attention and began uttering a low hum. Again he raised his sword, but this time held it over my heart. I assumed that he was preparing to strike his final blow. As he held the sword over my chest, the group then began chanting some type of ceremonial words in a language I could not recognize. If I had to guess I would say Chaldean.

As I lay there, it dawned on me just how short my time was. I realized that as soon as they finished chanting their ceremonial words, the sword would descend on me making an end to me and any mission I may have in this life. As I surveyed the situation I realized I had only a moment or two of life left in this world. My mind flashed back to John's advice. I was to use Excalibur. But where in the world could it be? The only sword in the room was in the hands of the Dark Master, ready to plunge into my heart. "Excalibur… Excalibur. Where are you?" I thought to myself.

My thoughts continued, "Sorry to disappoint you John, my old friend." Now I understood what he meant when he called me an old friend. We have indeed known each other for longer than I had imagined. Since it seemed useless to dwell any further on finding Excalibur during the next few seconds, I decided I wanted the last bit of my life spent looking in Elizabeth's eyes in a silent attempt to share and communicate my love to her.

I looked in her direction and indeed her supportive eyes were looking at me, happy to catch eye contact. As I looked at her I felt extremely sad, yet joyful all in the same instant. I was sad about the situation we were in, but though all seemed lost, I seemed to find a space for happiness. I felt in that instant an intense joy as I reflected on the privilege I had of loving and sharing with her over the years. I felt a joy in reflecting on the words of the apostle Paul that love endures forever and will never fail.

As I looked at her I felt as if I could feel her words and thoughts. It seemed to be a moment in which nothing needed to be spoken. At least we would soon be together on the other side. I also found myself wondering where we were, and if our bodies would ever be found. What would the police report or news say about us? "Boise man and woman disappear from home after apparent struggle." Its funny how one's mind works, even in desperate moments.

I reminded myself to concentrate on Elizabeth since there were just a few seconds left. As I looked into her eyes again I felt an indescribable, but intense love that seemed to lift my consciousness into another world. Suddenly, instead of seeing the image of Elizabeth, I saw what appeared to be a beautiful woman with features like Elizabeth, but younger, ascending out of a lake with her hand stretched out toward me, motioning as if she wanted to give me something.

Was I imagining things or was this a sign to me that the Lady of the Lake, who has charge of Excalibur, was somehow near? Suddenly a flicker of hope surfaced in my mind and on this spark of hope my attention shifted again toward our deliverance. In the next couple of seconds the image of the Lady dissipated and Elizabeth was there with her hand stretched out toward me in the same gesture as the Lady of the Lake.

Suddenly, I felt as if I were in the middle of one of John's riddles. Is Elizabeth my personal Lady of the Lake? Does she have power to give me Excalibur? If so, where is the legendary sword? If it is not in her hand, where is it?

"Oh God," I prayed silently. "Answer me this one time, and if you deliver me, I will dedicate all my energy to fulfilling the mission you have for me."

It did not seem like a thunderous revelation, but as Elizabeth stretched her hand toward me, reaching toward my bound hand with fingers pointing toward her, I seemed to feel an energy circulating between my hand and hers. Then deep within my soul a wonderful thought surfaced. What if Excalibur is here right now? What if Elizabeth is my Lady of the Lake, reaching out to give it to me? What if all I have to do is to take it? Maybe I just need to see the sword.

It was difficult to remain calm enough to meditate, for I sensed the Dark Brothers were finishing their ceremony and only seconds remained. *Focus!* I silently shouted to myself. *See the sword!* For a couple seconds I tried to see it, but this did not seem to work. Then the thought occurred to me that the sword may be a product of male/female energy. Perhaps the energy flow I was feeling between our hands was the energy of Excalibur. Perhaps this energy could be molded with thought. I felt that I had time for one more chance, and this would have to be an all-or-nothing moment.

I concentrated on the energy flow, and attempted to blend my consciousness with Elizabeth and the flow between us. I tried to see the power of this thought substance molding itself into a sword. As I attempted this I sensed the flow of energy between us begin to increase. Feeling encouraged, I increased my concentration. As I did so, a tiny but visible ball of fire began to appear midway between Elizabeth and me.

"Holy gods!" exclaimed one of the Dark Brothers motioning toward the ball of light. "It's Excalibur!"

The Dark Master looked up. "Quick, we must finish the chant. Only seconds remain." They all resumed the chant with a slightly increased cadence.

Knowing I had only seconds made concentration extremely difficult but I forced my attention as never before, but with renewed faith. The exclamation from the Dark Brother did indeed confirm my suspicion that Excalibur was somehow within my grasp.

As I continued my focus on the ball of fiery light, the brightness and size increased until the dark domain was filled with light. I focused my attention at the center of the ball and felt a powerful energy, but still no Excalibur.

Even though I had only seconds left, it seemed as if an hour's worth of thoughts raced through my mind. Finally, I concluded my best bet was to mold this energy with the power of thought while concentrating on the sacred word. Since my mouth was bound and I could not speak, I let my mind reflect back to the one time I said it right when Elizabeth was healed. As I reflected, I visualized the beautiful sword I imagined Excalibur to be.

As I reflected on the Word and visualized the sword, something amazing happened. Excalibur began to manifest before my eyes within the ball of light. What surprised me, however, was that its appearance was much different than I visualized. Instead of the typical sword as seen in the King Arthur movies, I saw an instrument of transcendent beauty. The first part of the sword that came to my view was the blade. But instead of a blade of steel, it seemed to be a translucent crystal radiating a white light. Finally the whole image came to my view. The handle of the sword was beautiful. It seemed to be made of a translucent gold, bearing many mystical carvings. Separating the handle and the blade was a circular guard having the appearance of two wheels with six spokes each. One wheel was rotating clockwise and the other counterclockwise. At the end of each the twelve spokes was a jewel, a stone of rare beauty about an inch in diameter. Each stone was a different color, and as the two wheels slowly rotated, they emitted a rainbow of colors that seemed to be some type of living essence.

Finally, I knew for sure that Excalibur was real, but the problem was that it was hovering in midair some distance beyond my grasp. My first inclination was to reach for it, but I was quickly reminded that I was still bound tightly to an altar of sacrifice.

Then, to my horror, the Dark Brothers ceased their chanting and the Dark Master quickly raised his sword higher over my heart with intent to open my chest. At the same second that the sword was raised above me, I sent a thought in the direction of Excalibur.

"Join to the hand of the servant of the Most High."

At that instant I did not know where that phrase came from. It seemed as if I thought of it on my own, but, on the other hand, it also did not seem to be a phrase I would have come up with out of the blue, especially under such circumstances. I think my natural reaction would have been to merely shout for help. Instead, a noble phrase came forth from my mouth that seemed to be an activation key like "Open Sesame" of Arabic myth. I believe it was either from an ancient memory or planted there through the Oneness Principle.

In the instant that the sword of the Dark Master began to fall, all the cords that held me bound and gagged disintegrated into nothingness, and Excalibur was in my right hand. Once it was in my hand I had to make no effort to move it for it moved by itself. With lightening speed it merely placed itself on my chest, covering the point that the descending sword was to penetrate. In the next instant, the Dark Master's sword touched Excalibur and broke into a dozen pieces.

I quickly rose to my feet, wielding the wonderful instrument that felt so natural in my hand. The circle of the dark ones broke up and they each backed up against the wall. Each of them had a look of stark terror on their faces that I had not seen before in any human being. Philo seemed to pick up on the terror of his superiors and great nervousness showed in his face.

I looked at the Dark Master and said, "What was this you were telling me about eternal pleasure? I see no pleasure in your countenance now." I paused a second and added, "Instead, what do I see? Yes, I see fear. Greater fear I have never witnessed."

Excalibur then raised itself as if to strike. As it did so the Dark Master looked at me and exclaimed, "This is not over, you know. You only think you have won. When you fail to live up to the demands of your supposed masters, I will be there to crush you without mercy and my pleasure will be complete."

I sensed that Excalibur was about to move. I was expecting a major swing and that heads would roll, but instead it came down gently on the Dark Master. The instant it touched him, his body disintegrated. Next, as if it had a life of its own, it quickly pulled me toward the other dark brothers and within what seemed like two seconds, with a swiftness I had never witnessed, it touched them all except Philo. They too instantly disappeared and only Philo stood before me, backing toward a corner. I somehow felt that Excalibur had turned the decision as to what to do with him over to me for the sword moved by my power and not it's own.

"You can't kill me," he said haughtily. "It would be another big mistake."

"It wouldn't be killing you," I said. "What I see before me is not your real body but the last residual of my own Dweller which you have stolen."

"You would be killing me," he said. "If you slay this body

before I am ready to return, I will die. This would be the repeat of your ancient mistake."

"What ancient mistake?" I demanded.

"I was once with you on Aeton. We were once friends. I am Sabul, the one you killed with pleasure, which started you on the dark path. If you destroy me now you will make the same mistake all over again. You will lose Excalibur and follow the same dark path all over again. You'll either become a full fledged Dark Brother or be sent to another prison world to start over again. Surely this is not what you want."

"What would you have me do?" I asked.

"Tell Excalibur to take you and Elizabeth home, and just leave me be. I will then return to my body at the appointed time and will not bother you again. This is your chance to use Excalibur with kindness and harmlessness."

His words seemed to make sense to my concrete mind, but I searched my soul for direction. The answer I received was nerve wracking, for if Philo was correct, I could be in for some big trouble if I used Excalibur on him.

Even so, I said, "The mistake I made on Aeton was to take pleasure in your death and then to seek pleasure in the destruction and selfish use of many others. I have no reason to believe that you are telling me the truth. I perceive that I must destroy the last vestige of my Dweller that you occupy, or you could bring the whole group back to life and do me harm again. I will destroy the body you occupy, but not for pleasure. Instead, I will destroy it so Divine Purpose can be achieved.

As I brought Excalibur down on him, he shouted, "This is not over!"

The second Excalibur touched Philo the stolen body of my Dweller disappeared. In addition, the entire room, including the cage that housed Elizabeth, began to fade. Seconds later we found ourselves standing on the floor of our living room at home, facing each other.

Elizabeth looked at me and stepped forward to give me a hug. This made me a little nervous, as I still held Excalibur in my hand. I motioned for her to hold her distance and said, "Aren't you a little nervous that if you touch Excalibur you will be harmed?"

She stood still and said, "You're touching it and you are not harmed are you?"

"No. I guess not."

"Then I will not be harmed either." She grabbed my hand which held the sword.

"Silly me," I thought to myself. If she is indeed my personal Lady of the Lake then Excalibur can do her no harm. I then pulled her the rest of the way to my bosom and held her tight, with an enduring feeling of joy and gratitude.

CHAPTER TWENTY
The Entity

After we finished our heartfelt embrace I sat on the couch and Elizabeth sat on a chair facing me. I looked at the sword still in my right hand. "It's strange," I said. "It looks like it weighs twenty pounds or so, but I feel no weight whatsoever."

"And the jewels on the handle are beautiful," she said. "I notice the two guards are almost still now, but they were revolving much faster when attacking the dark brothers – and the rainbow of lights it produced was wonderful."

"I was so involved I didn't take it all in. It's too bad someone wasn't here with a camcorder. We are the only two witnesses and I do *not* think what happened to us can ever be accurately portrayed."

"But you'll write about it in a future book," she stated confidently.

"Yes. I suppose I will. I'm not sure how I will go about putting it on paper though."

"So what are you going to do with that sword? You can't just hang on to it forever."

"I don't know," I said. "It feels so good and natural to hold on to it that I never want to let it go."

"Well, you're going to have to put it down somewhere. We have to get ready for work in a couple of hours."

"Work," I whispered. "Operating our business seems millions of miles away after what just happened. It wouldn't be the end of the world if we opened a little late today."

"I suppose you're right. I guess we deserve a little break."

After saying this she then sat back in her chair, put her hands to her head, and exclaimed, "Wow!"

"Wow what?" I asked. "Are you all right?"

"I think so," she said. "I think I am having a good *wow* though."

"What do you mean a good *wow*?"

"I feel a presence," she said carefully.

"What kind of presence?" I asked with great curiosity.

She got up and started pacing around the room. Finally, she stopped and looked at me. "This Presence is the most wonderful, most loving, yet most powerful essence I have ever felt. I feel like I am on fire. Do I seem to be glowing or anything?"

"No," I said. "You look pretty normal."

She sat back down in her chair and replied, "I am receiving a communication."

"What is it?" I asked.

"This great being who is with me wants Excalibur back. It belongs to him."

I reflected and said, "If the Presence who is with you owns Excalibur, then we owe him our lives. But how do we give it to someone we cannot see?"

"He wants you to point the sword in my direction."

"I guess that couldn't hurt," I said, and pointed it at her face, which was about two feet from the tip of the blade.

Suddenly the guard containing the two sets of jewels started turning in opposing directions causing a rainbow of colors. At the same time the blade's radiating white crystal intensified in its brilliance. Again the sword assumed a mind of its own and started moving toward Elizabeth. This greatly alarmed me and I exerted all my strength to hold it back.

"Don't resist," said Elizabeth. "All will be well." Then to my astonishment, she opened her mouth. The sword then overcame my resistance, moved away from my grip and darted right toward Elizabeth's open mouth.

For a brief moment I wondered if I was the victim of another trick of the Dark Brotherhood. I then watched with weak knees as it entered her mouth and disappeared. As the tip entered her mouth, the sword seemed to get smaller and more ephemeral until it was no more to be seen. After the sword seemed to disappear, Elizabeth leaned back in her chair and let out a sigh.

"Are you OK?" I asked, while wondering to myself how many more times I would have to worry about either her life or her soul.

After a nerve wracking pause she finally spoke, "I think I'm OK." Then she felt her head, her ribs and then her waist. "I seem to be in one piece. Did I imagine things or did I just swallow Excalibur?"

"If I can believe my eyes, you just performed the greatest sword swallowing feat of all time," I said marveling. "How do you feel now?"

"Very strange," she said. "The power of this Presence is increasing." She got up and started pacing back and forth. "I feel like I am on fire."

"Is this Presence communicating anything to you?"

"I'm not sure. It's so overwhelming that it is difficult to concentrate."

"Overwhelming good or overwhelming bad?" I asked, seeking reassurance.

"Definitely good. It's hard to describe, but it fills the soul in such a way that there is no doubt which side it is on." She then paused in silence and closed her eyes. After a moment she opened them and said. "I am to touch both sides of your head and breath on you."

"Is that what this Presence wants?"

"Yes," she said with strong assurance in her voice.

"Go ahead," I said. "I'll just have to trust the powers-that-be on this one."

She then stepped forward and touched both sides of my head with her fingertips, took a long deep breath and breathed out on me. As she exhaled her breath, I felt a deep and penetrating peace begin at the core of my soul, which seemed to light into a warm and comfortable spiritual fire.

Elizabeth stepped back and said, "It's gone! The Presence is no longer in me. I believe it has been transferred into you. What do you feel?"

"Like you said, it is a strong Presence burning like a spiritual fire. It's like the feeling I had when I laughed at the Dark Brother beside my bed, and afterward a presence descended on me. It is also similar to the feeling of being in the New Jerusalem."

"Well, I guess one problem is solved. You do not have to worry about a place to store Excalibur. Apparently this Presence is the owner of it and he is now residing within you."

"To tell the truth I'm not sure what the situation is. I feel a Presence, and a wonderful Presence it is, but no information is coming through. It is just here with me."

"Maybe it is just settling in, looking through your eyes and making adjustments."

"Maybe," I said, a little puzzled.

"I think it is time to get a little rest," she said. "I do not remember when I have felt so exhausted."

That sounded good to me. We both went to bed and quickly fell to sleep.

My sleep did not last long. I was awakened about two hours later by an intensity of feeling that I had never felt before. The power of the Presence within me had magnified several times and I felt as if I were on fire even more than before. It was at this time I realized that the Presence of this Great Entity was not just hovering around me, but was within me sharing my very body and being. I did not quite know what to make of it except that the Entity seemed to be adjusting to me as I was toward it. Whatever the case was, the feelings associated with the Presence were wonderful, and I instinctively had great trust in it. I felt like it would leave if I asked it to, but I had no inclination except to welcome the visitor to stay as long as it wished.

I lay for the next half hour in a sort of blissful joy and then wandered off to sleep again.

Elizabeth and I slept in that morning and did not get to the office until around noon. During the day, the power of the Presence intensified even more – a thing that I did not deem possible. It felt wonderful, but made it somewhat difficult to keep my mind on my work.

The second day produced similar results. I felt as if I were literally on fire.

Then on the third day the intensity reached a crescendo, the likes of which I had never dreamed. I felt as if I was dwelling in the heart of the sun and all who looked upon me would be blinded. I felt a joy which could only be called *a fullness*. I call it *a fullness* because I do not think anything could be added to it.

This was the opposite of the feelings associated with the Dweller.

Instead of overwhelming pain, I felt a joyousness and exhilaration far beyond my wildest imagination. Sometimes I thought the intensity was too much, but then when I asked myself the question, "Do I want it to subside?" the answer was always no. Even though the intensity was so great it was almost painful, it wasn't painful—just exactly the maximum I could endure.

Instead of fear I felt a confident realization that there is indeed a dominating good which always prevails. Instead of wishing the Presence gone this time I opened my arms and heart to it inviting it to stay as long as desired. On this third day when the living fire was so intense I posed a question to Elizabeth.

"Look at me," I said.

"What for?" she asked.

"Just look," I said. "Look over my whole body."

"OK," she replied. "I've looked over your body. Now what?"

"Do I look any different?"

"Not really," she responded.

"Look harder. Do I seem to be glowing or anything?"

"Not that I can tell."

"Look closer at my skin then. Is there any light radiating from it?"

"Sorry," she said. "You just look like you always do. Has this got something to do with the Presence?"

"Yes," I said. "I thought the strength of the Presence was great on the night it went from you into me, but that was nothing compared to what I feel now. I feel like I am on fire, but it is a good fire. It feels like all who would look at me, because of the Presence in me, would just see a brilliant sun shining in its strength. I am almost surprised that I look normal."

"Maybe if I had the inner vision I would see the brilliance of the sun," said Elizabeth, "but all I see with these eyes is the physical you.

"In a way, that's a relief," I said. "If I walked around glowing, people would probably think I was an alien or something."

"I have an idea of what you are feeling since it was first in me," said Elizabeth, "but you say the power of the Presence increased over a three-day period. Perhaps it is merging with you beyond what I experienced."

"I think that is the case," I said. "I think we both felt the Presence to a similar degree the night it came, but it seems to have settled in and is merging beyond words to describe. I think this intensity can only be endured after a period of several days of adjustment. If this intensity had come all at one time I do not think I could have handled it. Here, hold my hand a minute."

She took my hand and held it.

"Do you feel anything unusual?" I asked.

"Actually I don't," she said, sounding a little disappointed.

"The feeling is so intense I thought you would feel something just by touching me. But again, I guess it is good that touching me feels normal." I paused a moment and asked, "Do you have any feelings about what I am supposed to do with this Presence?"

"It only rested on me for a short time," she said. "I just received one communication from it and that did not come in words, but an impression. I feel that you need to blend your mind with its mind until its thoughts become your thoughts – a little like the Oneness Principle that John speaks of."

That sounded like as good advice as any, and for the next several days I concentrated on merging and tuning into its thoughts. This Being was of such a high vibration and so far beyond me in spiritual attainment that I was not sure of the path of approach. I seemed to sense that the spiritual level where we were merging was beyond the power of regular spoken words.

The next few days seemed to be one of adaptation on my part. I'm sure this Being also had to make adjustments to share my body and consciousness, but at least I was sure he knew what he was doing. On the other hand, I was not sure about myself. This was an experience that had no precedent as far as my knowledge went. I therefore attempted to tune into his mind and as the days passed I seemed to be able to do this. When I acquired some ability to understand the mind of the Being who was with me, I realized that I was learning a higher form of communication.

In normal communication the mind formulates thoughts, translates them into words and speaks them to others. In this process much is lost, for the original thought is always corrupted to some extent because of the imperfection of spoken or written language.

This communication I was learning was much different. In this case my mind and the entity's mind became as one mind, intertwined and understanding each other in almost all things. I say "almost" because I sensed we still maintained our individuality and there were certain things in the entity's mind that were hidden from me.

For instance, I probed it for the Second Key of Knowledge that John was teaching me and found all his thoughts on the subject were closed to me. I assumed that I was to learn this key without it being given to me.

The three attributes of Light and Love and Power in this Being were strong beyond my previous vision or understanding. I felt such power from this Entity surging through my being that it felt as if I could point my finger at a mountain and it would be reduced to nothingness if he so willed it. Such power would have been frightening to feel if it were not tempered by an equally powerful love which I felt. The love was like a fire of unimaginable depth that was at one with my soul and spirit. It vivified my own life force and caused my thoughts to reach out to all humanity; seeking to alleviate their pain and seek peace on earth, good will to human kind.

The light and wisdom from this being was equally overwhelming. I have often considered myself a seeker who could match wits with the best of the ideologues, but before the light of this great mind I felt humble indeed. This Being was indeed a teacher of teachers, a master of angels and men.

The being stayed with me about forty days. During this period I learned that its purpose was not so much to teach me knowledge in the normal sense, but to intensify my vibration and acclimate me to this higher Presence in preparation for some future mission. I learned to understand the aspect of the Oneness Principle as never before, where two become one.

Perhaps the most unusual thing about this forty-day experience was the consistent exaltation of joy and pure bliss that I felt. I had my ups and downs in the normal sense during this time, several business problems, disappointments, etc., but nothing that happened, no matter how disturbing, was able to diminish or take away from the consistent exaltation I felt. This Being had an eternal fullness of joy, and there was nothing that could happen in the outward world that could interfere with it or take it away.

Many people have the mistaken idea that God is consistently sad because of all the evils and hurt in the world. The state of mind of this great Entity taught me otherwise. He realizes all the problems that people have and seeks to help them, but no problem, pain or distress that you or I may feel can touch or diminish His state of joy. This is because His mind is not focused on the temporary distress that humanity may have, but the eternal conquest over illusion which we all will attain at some future time. The Great Ones can see these future times of joy and merge them with the present distress, so all negativity is neutralized.

This consistent joy was perhaps the most amazing thing I gathered from this whole experience. Before this happened, I could not conceive of a positivism that could not be diminished or touched by the cares of the world. I had, of course, heard preachers talk about heaven, where we will have some type of eternal bliss; but I never seriously considered experiencing a positive joyousness in the here-and-now that could not be touched or diminished.

For instance, if I lost one thousand dollars I would, of course, be very upset. But the interesting thing about sharing this Presence was that it would not matter what happened; even if I had lost everything I owned, the experience of a fullness of joy would have continued.

I would have registered the consequences mentally and dealt with the problem on a practical basis, but the joyousness would not have been touched or diminished. The loss of the money would have seemed like a very small thing for the lower mind to handle.

I can only give the briefest description of my experiences with this Entity, but will add that even one hour of this oneness is worth a lifetime of struggle to attain.

During the forty days, I received many impressions, mainly concerning overall pictures and principles, but the last one I received is the one that lingers in my mind.

This was the message: "Teach those things which you receive through your teacher and the Oneness Principle. When you gather around you those who are willing to receive that which you have, then I will come dwell with you again and shall give you more."

"How many do I have to gather?" I asked.

"That is for me to decide," he said. "Gather around you all the lights who listen to the voice of the soul, and when all is ready I will come. Until that time I will be with you, for a link has been created between us. I will be aware of all that transpires until I come."

Shortly after receiving this message the entity left. The time afterwards required quite an adjustment to feel "normal," but on the positive side I was still aware of the link, and this connective energy I constantly sensed helped to make normal living and being bearable again.

During this forty-day time period, I did only the essential work to keep the business going as well as my relationship with my wife. A couple of days after the Entity left, Elizabeth and I were having breakfast.

I looked wistfully in the distance and said, "He's gone."

Elizabeth looked intently at me and said, "You mean the Entity?" (That's how we had been referring to him since he came.)

"Yes, the Entity. He gave me a message and then just left."

"When did He leave?"

"Two days ago."

"Two days! Why didn't you tell me?" she exclaimed.

"I didn't know what to say," I replied. "I also could not believe he was gone. I thought maybe he would come back."

"Maybe it's for the best," said Elizabeth. "You've been pretty spaced-out since our experience and have been getting behind on some necessary work. In the real world we have to pay the bills, you know. In addition, I have felt a little neglected. If I had not experienced the Entity myself, I'm sure I would be giving you a bad time about your lack of attention. As it is, I guess I have to give you credit for functioning in the mundane world these past few weeks."

"Thanks," I said. "Having the Visitor was indeed a great experience but it did make it difficult to see everyday problems as worthy of much attention."

"Perhaps the problems the Entity has to deal with are of such a different nature than us mere mortals that the things that concern us seem insignificant to Him."

"Quite possible," I said.

"So what was the purpose of the whole experience?"

"He told me it was to prepare me, to adjust my vibration, to focus our vision into one vision."

"But to prepare you for what?" she inquired.

"He said that it was for the Gathering of the Lights, which was to come shortly. He sent me that phrase a number of times – *The Gathering of Lights*."

"So what do we do now?" she asked.

"I am to continue to write, learn from John, increase my own soul contact, and gather around us like-minded souls who embrace the light. Then when the time is right he will come and dwell inside me, or perhaps the group, and guide us."

"Guide us where?"

"He did not reveal all the *whys and wherefores* to me, but merely told me it involved the gathering of lights and the bringing together of heaven and earth, or spirit and matter. Eventually the will of God shall be done on earth as it is in heaven."

"And where do you suppose John has been through all this?"

"I sense He is aware of all that has happened, and has been waiting for the Entity to leave before he comes again. When I asked the Entity about John he merely said, *one teacher at a time*. From this I gathered that receiving from two teachers brings two points of vision that can slow down the learning process and sometimes bring confusion."

"So now the Entity is gone, we can probably expect John most any time," she observed. "Have you done any more thinking on the Second Key?"

"Not much," I said. "The Entity directed my thoughts in other directions. I have a guess about the Key Word, but am not sure about it."

"Wayne's called about the tenth time, wanting to go to lunch. You haven't paid much attention to your friends since the Entity came." She picked up the phone and handed it to me. "Here, call him and tell him you're available."

"You're right," I said. I called him telling him I wanted to do lunch and at noon we met at Raedeans.

As we sat down at the table Wayne said, "I thought maybe aliens abducted you. During our last visit you acted a little strange, and then it seemed you fell off the face of the earth. What's going on?"

"I didn't mean to ignore you. I've been very preoccupied in addition to having more than I can accomplish with our business, but things have pretty much returned to normal."

"I was beginning to think you have been a bad boy and that Elizabeth was keeping you in a cage or something."

I laughed at the irony that a short time ago Elizabeth was trapped in a cage. "No such luck," I smiled. "There are some things going on that I can't share with you now, but I shouldn't be ignoring you now for some time."

"Now you're just getting me curious," he said. "I think there's something about this vision quest you've been on that you're not telling me. You haven't joined a cult have you?"

"Nothing like that," I said, laughing. "Speaking of this quest, I do want to pick your brain again."

"Go ahead," he said. "By the way, I hope my comments on Excalibur were helpful."

I sat back and let out a sigh. "More than you know. It was a lifesaver."

"That's good to know," he said, not understanding the irony.

"As a matter of fact, I think I at least owe you lunch for your helpful insights. Order anything you want."

"OK," said Wayne looking at the menu. "I guess I'll get the prime rib sandwich."

"Sounds good," I said. "I'll have one too." After we placed our orders I said, "You know, I'm still thinking about this Middle Way idea. We've concluded that it is not merely moderation. You mentioned that since the Middle Way involved some choice, then the correct choice would involve plain old common sense. That makes sense to me."

"You mean common sense?" Wayne smiled.

"I suppose," I chuckled. "But suppose we had to reduce the whole idea of the Middle Way to one word. Any idea of what it could be?"

"I can't think of anything much better than common sense," he said. "When you have two choices, you have to apply common sense to make the best choice."

"You have a point, but I've been thinking of a single word that may apply."

"And what word have you come up with?"

"I was thinking of *discernment*."

"And you're thinking of this word because…"

"If you're faced with two paths or a choice between two decisions, you must use your power of discernment to discover the correct one."

"There's only one problem with that," he said.

"What's that?"

"People often do not do what they know to be the best decision. For instance, I discern that I need to lose some weight, and I also discern what I need to eat and not eat, but I do not do it. I have the power to discern the Middle, or best way, but not the common sense to follow through. When Buddha discerned a choice he followed through, as did all the great masters. It would seem that the Middle Way would be more than just discerning, but acting on that discernment. I'm not exactly sure if this can be reduced to a word, but common sense has to be a part of the equation."

"Here I thought I may have had it down pat with *discernment*, but you're right. Discernment alone would not be the Middle Way. Even so, it has to be part of it. For instance, you have to discern a truth before you can use the common sense to act upon it."

"Perhaps you could say that the key would be to discern and then act on that discernment," he said. "This is basically what Buddha did. He saw a greater light and then acted upon it. Now that I see the greater light of how to lose weight, I just need to act upon it."

"At least you're not alone," I said, patting my own belly. "Looks like not many of us are following the Middle Way if this is the case."

Wayne looked at me intently and said, "Are you sure you're not taking a course in Buddhism, metaphysics or something like that?"

"What makes you say that?"

"I'm not sure, but it just seems like you are working on something assigned to you."

I paused a moment, thinking of how to best answer him. "I'm not taking any regular course, but I guess I could say I am studying some lessons I have come across."

"Whatever it is, it didn't seem like you would have come up

with all these questions just for the sake of conversation. It'll be interesting to see what you come up with next."

"Believe it or not, I'm not sure what I'm going to come up with next. By the way, how's things been going since I last saw you?"

"Actually, it has not been that bad for a change. Just the usual frustrations – nothing life or death. How about you?"

"It's been kind of life or death for me," I mused.

Wayne chuckled with what he thought was a mild attempt at humor.

CHAPTER TWENTY-ONE
Dark Motives Explained

That evening at dinner Elizabeth asked, "How's Wayne doing?"

"Not bad. We talked a little about the second key, but about all it did was to convince me that my next guess is probably not correct."

"Perhaps you just need to remember John's advice – that you must first find out what is *not* true in order to find the truth. If you have really eliminated your next guess then you may be one step closer to finding the key."

"The trouble is that if *discernment* is not the key word, I'm out of guesses. Wayne mentioned *common sense*, but that's two words so I'm pretty sure that's not it either. I'm not sure what I'm going to present to John when he comes."

"Isn't it about time John showed up again?" she asked.

"Yes, it is," I said. "In fact, he'll be here tonight. About an hour from now to be exact."

"And how do you know this? Have you been holding out on me?" she asked tersely.

"I wouldn't think of it," I countered, hoping to avert chastisement. "I seem to be more sensitive to some things since that Entity came. I just seem to know that John will be here in about an hour. I'm not sure if this is a one-time knowing or if it will continue."

"About an hour you say. I guess I'd better get some tea ready just in case you are right."

"Let's go one better than that," I said. "Write a note saying

Welcome John, come right in and tape it on the door. Then leave the door unlocked."

"That's an interesting idea," she said. "I wonder if it is possible to surprise him."

"You never know," I said, smiling.

Elizabeth wrote the note and placed it on the door, turned on the porch light and we waited with great anticipation.

Right on schedule we heard footsteps at the door and after a few seconds saw the door slowly creak open. John stepped halfway in with the note in his right hand and said wryly, "Does this note refer to me or to some other John?"

"You are the man!" I exclaimed. We both hurried toward him and gave him a hug. "For a while we thought we'd never see you again," I said.

"There's no such thing as *never*," he replied.

"So are you aware of what happened to us?" I asked as we sat down at the table.

"I'm not only aware," he said, "but the Brotherhood is fully aware. The whole event is safely recorded and stored in the Master's archives. The science you call virtual reality will simulate the recording. It will play back features that have always been available to us by using a combination of the mind *and* the elemental life forces of certain minerals."

"I could spend a day listening to a greater explanation of such things, but I pick up from you that you will take us other directions tonight," I said.

"That is correct," he said. "And I perceive that you are becoming more sensitive to my vibration. This cheers my heart."

"And I've got some tea ready to lighten your heart," said Elizabeth cheerfully.

"Actually, I'm not in the mood for tea tonight. I do not think you will be either after I show you your gift."

"Gift?" we both said with anticipation.

"Yes," he smiled. "In light of your recent victory over the dark forces I think we should have a little celebration." He then opened his knapsack and pulled out a bottle of Dom Pérignon.

I took it gingerly in my hands and looked at it. "I've heard of this champagne and have been tempted to buy a bottle, but couldn't bring myself to spend the hundred dollars or so."

"This is worth more than that," he said with a grin. "Note the year."

Elizabeth looked at the label and said, "Nineteen eighty three."

"Yes," he said. "This was an excellent year for the champagne. This bottle that I will share with you will rival the quality that Dom Pérignon himself produced. And, by the way, you have to spend quite a bit more than a hundred dollars to get *this* '83 vintage."

"Why do I get the feeling that you actually knew Dom Pérignon?" I asked.

John looked up and smiled, "Because I *did* know him. Dom Pierre Pérignon was a Benedictine Monk who not only sought the spiritual side of life, but made best of the practical. He was blind when I met him about three hundred years ago, but had acutely developed his other senses to the extent that he was known far and wide for his fine taste and smell, and the fine vintage which he bottled. I stayed with him, his brother and several other monks for a couple of days, but did not reveal my true identity. As I was saying goodbye, Pierre grabbed my hands in his and held them tight. *You're John, aren't you?* he said whispering in my ear. I was surprised he knew this and whispered back in his ear the word *yes*. He was weeping when I left him."

I felt strong emotion coming from him as we sat in silence for a moment. Finally, Elizabeth broke it, "So where did you get this bottle? From what you tell us of your money supply it is a little off limits for you."

"I didn't have to purchase it," he said. "Yesterday I was visiting with a fairly wealthy student in France. When I told him about your confrontation and victory over the Dark Brothers he went to his wine cellar, brought up this bottle, and gave it to me. He insisted that I give it to you with his appreciation."

"Give him my appreciation in return," I said. I then opened the bottle, and we began drinking while having some light-hearted conversation, gradually becoming more serious. As the conversation continued, we realized John was well versed on all the unusual events that happened to us.

I felt it was time to get a few questions answered. "So what happened to Philo? He told me that if I destroyed the Dweller's body he occupied, then he would die."

John put down his glass after taking a sip. "Very smooth beverage, is it not?"

"Indeed it is," I said, awaiting his reply.

"There's something you must always take into consideration when listening to any dialog from those on the dark side," he said, playing with his glass. "They lie a lot. They will tell the truth when it furthers their cause, but they will also deceive for the same reason."

"So Philo's unharmed then?"

"I didn't say that either," he said.

"That's encouraging," said Elizabeth. "I wouldn't feel sorry for him no matter *what* happens to him. Not what after he's put us through."

John looked at his glass saying, "Give me another half of a glass and you two can finish off the bottle."

After Elizabeth filled his glass to more than half, he added, "Philo was lying to get your sympathy when he said Excalibur would kill him, but the fear you saw in his eyes was not a lie. He was indeed afraid."

"So what *did* happen to him?" I asked.

"He snapped back into his body when he was in the midst of a deep and specialized meditation. He was in a coma for a few days and has been quite ill since then. He is just now starting to recover."

"And how about the rest of his associates?"

"Three of them were regular mortals, like Philo, and they are also recovering. The rest of them are full-fledged Dark Brothers who do not have physical bodies of their own, but either borrow bodies from others or manifest them through illusionary techniques."

"So what was their fate?" I asked.

"One of the worst torments they suffered from the ordeal was the shattering of their ceremonial sword. It was their version of Excalibur and has been very dear to their order for over 100,000 years. In their illusion, they have always believed their weapons were invincible. When they watched their precious sword crumble to the might of Excalibur each of them experienced a fear that struck them to the core. Then, after you destroyed the body of your Dweller, which they were using, their consciousness was thrown out of their astral or subtle bodies. For a period of time, they drifted aimlessly in what was for them a bottomless pit. This is a most terrifying experience to a Dark Brother for having no contact with soul, the astral-emotional self or the physical; these entities can feel no foothold for their consciousness and feel aimlessly adrift."

"So are they still experiencing this bottomless pit?" asked Elizabeth.

"No," he said. "Their groundless drift was temporary this time. They have now reestablished contact with their astral bodies, but they have all been badly shaken; they received a taste of what will happen to them when their moment of dissolution comes. When that time comes, all their lower bodies will return to their native elements and their essential nature will be drawn back into their soul to be recycled in a future creation many ages from now."

"But the Dark Master seemed to think they could escape such a fate. Was he lying or deceived?"

"There was some truth to what he said, but no matter which avenue of the dark path they take, they will not attain eternal life. Let me explain. The dark path is the path of extreme selfishness, and those who take it up must eventually reject all communication of Spirit which comes through the soul. Because the Spirit is life, this rejection shuts off the source of life, which leads to a condition of dying and eventual death of consciousness for this creation. Perhaps the words of the Master which I recorded will aid your understanding. Find your Bible and read John 15:5-6.

I opened the Bible and read:

"I am the vine, ye are the branches: He that abideth in me, and I in him, the same bringeth forth much fruit: for without me ye can do nothing. If a man abide not in me, he is cast forth as a branch, and is withered; and men gather them, and cast them into the fire, and they are burned."

"This isn't exactly as I wrote it, but it is close enough. When Jesus talked about being in us, he was talking about the Christ Principle, which was uniquely manifest through him. The Christ principle is basically soul energy, which interplays between matter and Spirit. Thus, the Christ principle is the mediator between matter and Spirit or God and man. Since Jesus was the perfect manifestation of the Christ Principle, he also became a mediator for us between humanity and God.

"Christ and this mediating principle of soul is thus the vine, and he who has soul contact, which allows the Holy Spirit to manifest, becomes a living branch. Now what happens to the entity who does not make this connection?"

"The scripture indicates it will be withered and burned up," I responded.

"Yes. If we are to have good firewood, it must first be severed from its source of life. It then dries out and no longer bears any leaves or fruit, but is good only for burning. This analogy holds true for those on the dark path. They shut off the life-giving Spirit and dry up, as far as the spiritual life is concerned. In this severed state, the fire of the Spirit eventually burns their outer shells, allowing their eternal part to eventually be recycled in the hope that soul contact can be reestablished in a future creation. Unfortunately, billions of years of spiritual progress will be lost for these souls."

"So how does the Dark Master plan to avoid this death or disintegration?"

"You were pretty close when you compared his idea to a multilevel program. Actually, the old pyramid scheme concept would be more precise, as some multi-levels with good products benefit a large percentage of a group. I explained to you earlier that the Dark Brothers are spiritual vampires. Just like the vampires in the movies need human blood to perpetuate their existence, even so do the Dark Ones need the life essence of gullible believers, pawns, and their disciples to sustain their lives. Because they have rejected the soul and have no spiritual contact, they must take the life essence from others who have enough good will to still maintain some spiritual contact. That which sustains them is the opposite of the Brotherhood of Light. Our life essence comes from the top down; for instance, my spiritual link is the Christ. He also has a link, who is the Ancient of Days, our spiritual Father. Above him are other links which connect us all through the Oneness Principle, to the life of the One God. The Dark Brotherhood, on the other hand, receives their energy from the bottom up."

He paused a moment, looked at Elizabeth and said, "I think I could take that cup of tea now."

Elizabeth made us a fresh batch. We settled back down and I

added, "This is interesting. The Brotherhood of Light receives their life from above, but the dark side does the opposite and draws their sustaining force from below."

After finishing a sip of tea, John replied, "True, but you must keep in mind that all life comes from above even though it circulates in the tiniest atom. Those in the light merely receive it directly; those outside the light receive it indirectly, as reflected light. All people on the planet, except that small handful who have completely committed themselves to the dark side, receive life through the soul, which links the whole human race together. Then, when the individual becomes a disciple, his consciousness tunes into the Holy Spirit through the soul, and his awareness and ability to receive the God energy is dramatically increased. Because the Dark Brotherhood consciously rejects all life through the soul they must seek it through its reflection. It is like attempting to receive light and heat from the moon rather than the Sun."

"So let me get this straight," I said. "The Dark Master I met receives no life from above, but takes it from the coven we encountered which included Philo? Any life energy Philo has is a shadow of the real energy and is siphoned off from those whom he deceives?"

"Correct."

"And if I understand your earlier teachings correctly, Philo and others who supply this energy get it from dedicated, but deceived supporters giving of their own power?"

"Yes," he replied. "And this is one reason that many feel weak in the presence of a dark disciple. Their essence is siphoned off and their will diminished. Disciples such as Philo are allowed to keep what they need to sustain them and then pass the surplus up their Hierarchy."

"So there are hierarchies on both sides then?"

"Yes, but the masters in the Hierarchy of Light receive from above and give the waters of life to a thirsty world. The Dark Masters scorch the earth by taking surplus waters and nourishing only themselves. Theirs is a world of lack, for they create spiritual as well as physical famine wherever they are accepted and there is never enough life force to go around. The Brotherhood of Light receives from the Never-Ending Source, and lives in a plane of everlasting abundance and fullness. They seek to lift a starving world up to their own consciousness, rather than to just use them."

"But even the good guys must get something out of their service," observed Elizabeth. "I can't imagine even God creating and serving the universe and getting nothing out of it."

"You have enunciated a true principle," John replied. "No matter how pure or altruistic a person is, there must be a personal benefit or the will-to-serve will diminish, and nothing gets done. The Dark Ones receive perceived benefit by a forced taking. Because this is where they see their reward, this is where they place their attention. The Brotherhood of Light receives benefits through giving. The benefits are not immediate, as with the Dark Ones, but because of an understanding of eternal laws, they realize that giving comes back with interest, and benefits not just themselves, but the *whole* of which they are a part. The Dark Ones receive their immediate reward through force; whereas those in the light receive never-ending benefits through the free will of all."

"But even the Dark Brotherhood can only siphon off energy when ignorance of the true light exists," I said. "What made the Dark Master think he could have eternal life?"

"Because you have asked I will explain that which has not been given out before." He paused a moment in thought and continued. "Unlike the Brotherhood of Light, who has an unlimited and eternal life supply from the Eternal Source, the Dark Brotherhood relies on reflected energy, which is limited and only available when victims are in a state of deception. When the Dark Brotherhood was founded upon the earth ages ago, it seemed that people were so easy to deceive that their vampirism could continue. The lower members and the incarnated disciples did not seem to consider that a time would come when a true age of enlightenment would come and the deception would end. They felt that no matter how much the Brotherhood of Light tried to assist humanity they could always pull humanity back into darkness and keep their scheme going forever."

"Surely, they realize the earth and life on it will end someday," I said.

"Yes, they know this, but even when this occurs in the far future, they believe they will be able to survive in the astral world in preparation for moving to another earth-like world. Now, the sad thing is that on a small number of worlds, they do actually achieve their goal, and dominate a planet from beginning to end. This happened on Aeton, and unfortunately, it was with your assistance. As you now know, you barely escaped joining with them."

"Thank God," I said. "It makes me shudder just to think about it. Remembering how much damage I have done makes it difficult to feel worthy of service."

"This is one of the reasons that past lives are generally not revealed. All who retrieve their memories have this difficulty. There are acts in my history that would make me ashamed if I put my attention on them, and my long period of lonely service is the final payment for my debts which are as egregious as your own. . One must realize that we all make mistakes on the way to true learning and focus on the task at hand. You have done much since arriving on earth to pay off your debt, and now you have a window of opportunity to finish the payment through service – if you are diligent and faithful."

"I'll be sure to keep an eye on him," said Elizabeth, smiling.

John continued, "Now, as I said, the Dark Brotherhood only succeeds in the end on a small number of worlds. Generally, light eventually dominates the dark; and when the inhabitants are able to see in the light of day, the deception of the Dark Ones is entirely rejected and they are no longer able to feed upon the masses."

"What happens then?" I asked.

"When their outside energy supply is cut off, their astral bodies begin to disintegrate, and they are forced to feed upon each other to keep their vehicles intact. The stronger then overpowers the weaker until only a handful remains with astral life force."

"So at first they are spiritual vampires and then they turn into spiritual cannibals," said Elizabeth. "Interesting."

"So where do they get the idea that they will obtain eternal life?" I asked again.

"You've heard the phrase *hope springs eternal*. The truth is that both sides, the light and the dark, have their particular hopes. On each planet where there is a struggle between light and dark, good and evil, ages will pass where evil, or materialism, will dominate. This gives them the false belief and hope that such domination will continue and they will have the final rule of the populace. Because of the Principle of Dominating Good, which rules in the universe, light almost always dominates, or disperses, the dark in the end. Out of a hundred planets like ours, approximately ninety-nine will achieve enlightenment. That leaves the inhabitants of one yet to be delivered in a future age, or the one lost sheep given in the parable by Jesus. There are also times when an entire solar system is dominated by the dark side, but this is rare."

"Let me see if I understand this," I mused. "The Dark Brothers can escape death of the lower self by dominating a planet with deception and darkness so the light of truth never manifests, but this only happens with one out of a hundred planets. That's not very good odds to base their hope on."

"There are two other factors which encourage them," he said. "The first factor has been a great mystery, and is the reason for the perpetuation of evil within the universe."

"I like mysteries," smiled Elizabeth.

"You may not like this one," he said, "but what I am about to tell you is becoming essential knowledge for disciples. You have heard it said, in many of the scriptures of the world, that, at the end of the age, evil will be conquered and only good and peace will exist. In other words, the scriptures give the impression that evil will be completely destroyed. This is not entirely correct. It is true that the light usually dominates in the end, and when it does, the astral, or emotional, bodies of the Dark Brothers begin to lose life force and disintegrate. This forces them into the *bottomless pit* mentioned in my writings. When confined to the bottomless pit indefinitely, their consciousness is taken in by their oversoul to be recycled for fresh opportunity in a future creation.

"But, as I said, when their ultimate defeat becomes obvious, and they can no longer extract life force from a deceived people, they begin feeding upon each other. When this happens, a handful at the top of their hierarchy gathers life essence from the lower and escape to one of two places. As the Dark Master told you, they escape to a developing world. This would be a planet in a primitive state. Here, they hope to use their developed cunning more successfully this time round. The Dark Master you met is one who escaped from Aeton. He attempted to bring you to the dark side back then, and this was the reason he was so successful at refreshing your memories and so familiar with them."

"What is the second place of escape?" I asked.

"A small handful of the Dark Brothers are able to develop

their minds so the mental dominates the emotional. Now, in the course of natural evolution, this leads to plain common sense and enlightenment. But in the case of a Dark Brother, who has no soul contact, it leads to cunning, extreme selfishness, and extremes of evil that have not entered into the imagination of humankind. Actually, it is the universe's way of keeping even the greatest lives on their toes. It appears that no entity in creation is able to just sit back on their laurels and rest forever. There always exists a destructive intelligence who seeks to take life energy which is not his to gather. This happens in all the worlds composed of physical, emotional or mental matter – the visible and invisible worlds of form."

"So what percentage of the Dark Brothers escapes to another world? I think I guessed about one percent when I was confronting the Dark Master. I remember he said the number was not to be revealed."

John let out a short laugh. "The leaders do not want to reveal the number because it is so low. It tickles me, though, that you unknowingly revealed it to the group when you said 99% would not make it, including Philo. If you recall, the Dark Master was somewhat shaken when you said that."

"I don't know if I was paying that much attention to the nuances of the situation," I replied wryly.

"I don't suppose so," he said reflectively. "But you were right on the mark. Many of the underlings are now thinking about the figure you threw out, and disturbingly so. When truth is spoken, it creates an energy field which will just not go away."

"Let me make sure I understand again," I said. "Most planets like ours eventually pass into the light, which exposes the deception of the Dark Brotherhood. This light ends their ability to siphon off their needed life energies and they become spiritual cannibals. The strong extract life force from the weak, until only about one percent is strong enough to survive. This one percent then moves on to either a primitive planet or a higher plane. I still do not quite see how someone at the bottom like Philo can have much hope of being the one percent."

"There are several reasons for hope," he said "The first is they have never experienced the higher joys of pure spirit, so they believe that intense-feeling pleasure is the ultimate good for self.

When they indulge themselves in the pleasures of materialism, it becomes addictive, like a drug habit. As you know, there are many drug addicts who would sell their souls for a few days of intense pleasure. The addiction to pleasure robs them of their power to plan a logical future."

"So their addiction to pleasure causes them to focus on the present moment only?" queried Elizabeth.

"It causes enough distraction that, even though it is obvious only a few will escape, they do not think the matter through, and believe the false promises presented to them. Lower disciples such as Philo know that all will not survive, but almost every Dark Brother in existence has the ego to see him as one of the strong who will triumph no matter what."

"So all the underlings like Philo think they will be so powerful when the time comes that they can preserve their life force. Interesting. It almost makes me feel sorry for the poor fool," I said.

"I don't feel sorry for him," said Elizabeth stiffly. "Not one little bit."

I smiled at Elizabeth's emotion and asked, "So what is the fate of the few who escape? Do they really obtain eternal life as the Dark Master said?"

John finished off his cup of tea and replied, "If their belief system were accurate, a few elite could obtain eternal life. But because of their pyramid-like filtering scheme, the higher you go in their hierarchy, the less are the chances for survival. As long as the physical universe exists, a few powerful Dark Masters will be able to maintain their existence. They believe that a Dark Master has a good shot at eternal life and pleasure because they think the Universe will last forever without destruction, and in this they err. Even the universe has a birth and eventual death, and when it dies, many eons hence it will take the lives of all the Dark Brothers with it."

"You mean there will come a time when there will be no more Universe?" I gasped.

"Not exactly," he said. "The essential ingredients of the universe and every living thing in it are preserved. After the universe dies it will be reborn again, but purged of the lower shells of the Dark Brothers to begin evolution again on a higher turn of the spiral."

"It doesn't seem fair that the weaker Dark Brothers perish early on, and the stronger and more destructive ones live on," I observed.

"Life is always fair in the end," John replied. "The Dark Brother who is returned to his native element on this planet will be created anew with fresh opportunity much earlier than one who has escaped to another planet or sphere. The longer his recycling is delayed, the greater the pain and distress of the destruction, and the longer the wait will be for new creation. Some of these details mean little to the lower levels of the Dark Hierarchy, to one immersed in sensuality, a few years of pleasure is as good as the promise of eternal bliss."

"That's an interesting thought," I said. "I know there are people who would sell their souls to a supposed eternity of damnation for a few years of having their desires fulfilled."

"Exactly," John said. "And this tendency continues in some form all through the Dark Hierarchy."

"So what happens to the Brotherhood of Life?" asked Elizabeth. "Are they ever destroyed?"

"It is impossible to destroy the eternal part of ourselves revealed through the soul," he said. "The worst that can happen is for an entity to shift his attention away from the soul and reject it entirely. This is what happens to the Dark Brothers. Their attention is away from the real and on the unreal. That which is destroyed is not the real part of them, but they are deceived into thinking this is the case. The eternal part of them will continue to exist and eventually put forth a new creation, but billions of years will be lost as well as the loss of all their former associations.

"All those who do not choose the dark path eventually learn their lessons and become one with the soul and Spirit. They are able to raise their consciousness above the worlds of form. Then, when the forms change, or come to an end, their life will continue because their attention is on the eternal rather than that which is transitory.

"It then matters not if the earth, the solar system, or even the universe dies as to physical form, for they are not dependant upon form and, as it is written, their rest shall be glorious."

John got up and stretched. "That's enough attention paid to the lost souls. We've got a lot to cover in a short time, so let us move on after a short break."

CHAPTER TWENTY-TWO
Conversations with John

We all stretched and got some fresh air on the back patio before resuming our conversation at the table. "I have one more question about the Dark Brothers," said Elizabeth. "If the Brotherhood of Light wins out on ninety-nine out of a hundred worlds and most people will choose good when light is thrown upon the situation, then why have they been such a problem here upon this earth?"

John leaned forward and replied, "When the people of a world progress enough to develop their astral or emotional body, they enter a stage where they appear to go backwards, by normal deductions, but it is really a part of spiritual evolution. As their emotional selves develop, their attention shifts to making decisions based on feeling rather than instinct. Because humanity has not yet learned the full use of the mind, the astral life is the only choice for them. Unfortunately, our emotional selves reflect true reality backwards as in a mirror; and when seeing through the eyes of emotion, truth is reflected into something illusionary that seems like truth, but, instead, creates tremendous deception and pain for humanity. This may seem an odd thing, but it serves a grand purpose. Just as with the Keys, so far you have had to learn what is not true before you can appreciate and understand what is true. Even so, humanity has had to do the same. Their long journey through emotional seeing has led them into every possible direction that does not work, until they are now forced to develop higher reasoning and thinking so they can see what does work."

"So what does this have to do with the Dark Brotherhood?"

asked Elizabeth.

"Quite a bit," said John. "As this emotional deception begins to manifest upon a world, a window of opportunity opens for the Dark Brotherhood, who have lodges on many worlds. A handful of them then come to the developing world and establish a lodge with the purpose of dominating the whole of humanity so they can extend their lives, and the lives of their superiors, by vampiring and dominating the lives of the emotional populace."

"So where is the Brotherhood of Light when this is taking place?" she said.

"The Brotherhood of Light arrives long before the Dark Brothers, and assists in initiating a self-conscious humanity. For many eons, all of the Brotherhood has been from other worlds, but after a long period of nurturing - when higher reasoning, along with the love aspect develops - they replace themselves with advanced humanity. We are now at the stage where most of the Brotherhood who work directly with humanity evolved from this world. This Brotherhood is composed of two groups. The first are the Masters of Wisdom, who concentrate on removing illusion through higher mind linked with Spirit. The second group is the Lords of Compassion, who concentrate on stimulating love in the world. Unlike the permanent inhabitants of Shamballa, who are still from other worlds, these two groups, who are advanced beings from the human race, work directly with human evolution and liberation."

John sat back, took a breath and continued, "There is one important lesson that the Great Ones, who have traveled from world to world, have learned; and that is, you cannot force people to do good. They see to it that humanity is assisted when their consciousness is ready to move ahead; but when it is not they take on the position of a Watcher and wait for windows of opportunity.

"When humanity first develops their emotional nature, the Brotherhood of Light has to either work with them in very direct ways or stand aside and wait. The emotional period is a time of opportunity for the Dark Brothers, because in many ways the hands of the Great Ones are tied, and they can only watch and wait. During this astral period of the race, the Dark Brothers are able to take full advantage and control of most of the planet. Their representatives either become gods to the people or false ministers of God. Therefore, because of emotional polarization, the Dark Brothers dominate the various worlds for many ages. For their disciples, it seems as if permanent domination is a sure thing and will continue forever, but the more advanced disciples know better. They know the odds are against them, and have preparations to leave to another young world at the time humanity becomes enlightened. But then, every once in a while, their luck holds out; the people resist the light and complete domination is achieved, as it was on Aeton. When this happens, the best of the inhabitants are moved to another world, and the dark planet is destroyed; however, sometimes just the intelligent life is destroyed and evolution begins again. So, in a word, the principle is this: the Dark Brothers generally dominate humanity at the early part of evolution, and the Brotherhood of Light dominates at the end.

"Throughout the universe this principle of Dominating Good applies. Evolutionary and constructive principles dominate over regressive, destructive ones. The heart of every seeker of truth registers this fact, and causes a hope to burn in his heart which can never be extinguished."

"So what's the fate of this earth?" I asked. "Is it in any danger of being the one-out-of-a-hundred dominated by the Dark Brothers?"

"This earth would be on a sure footing except for one thing," John answered giving me a serious look.

"What's that?" I asked, with some unsettledness.

"A little item called *weapons of mass destruction*, most notably the atomic bomb. The problem is this energy was released over a hundred years before its time. Humanity is too immature at present to handle advanced science safely. They are like a child with a loaded revolver. They are told it can kill, but this knowledge is not enough to cause them to handle it with complete safety."

"So why did we develop the bomb ahead of schedule?" asked Elizabeth.

"This was brought about through the tension of World War II. The Light Brotherhood could have prevented its appearance, but they took a chance and allowed its development by the Allies, as the ultimate insurance that Hitler would be defeated. Few realize how important this defeat was; Hitler's conquest would have put the earth in grave danger of being dominated by the Dark Brothers."

"So are we in danger of being destroyed?" I asked.

"Rather than annihilation, the greater immediate danger is the destruction of civilization to the extent that the world reverts to tyrannical rule, which could give the Dark Brothers the control they need for domination. The responsible citizens among the nations must step forward and secure, through law, the nonproliferation of today's weapons."

"Something needs to be done," I said, agreeing. "If we do nothing, the worst is bound to happen."

"You are correct. Without added intelligence to a problem, the principle of entropy creates the worst. The Brotherhood is working diligently on this problem, and we only have a few workers in place to assist us, even if they have not achieved full discipleship. We are hoping that *you* will eventually achieve some high name recognition through your writings. If so, you may be of use to us in neutralizing the danger of these weapons."

"That's something I would be happy to help with and have already done a lot of thinking about it. I can see that, unfortunately, I have little influence in my current situation."

"We must always remember that we must begin where we are, not where we wish to be, to insure ultimate success.

"One more thing," I mused. "The Dark Master said there was a way to escape karma. What was that about?"

"No one escapes cause and effect," he said. "When the strongest Dark Brothers escape to another planet, or plane, they merely delay ultimate effect. It is like missing a house payment. This does not mean you do not have to pay. Instead, you will pay later with interest. They believe they can put off karma indefinitely, but sooner or later they get trapped in their causes and, at the time of dissolution, their terror is so great that only he who experiences it can understand. All the pain and suffering they have inflicted upon others returns to them and destroys all that is left of the lower self, which is all they know."

"If they were not so deserving of their fate I would almost feel sorry for them," I said. "Does ultimate justice always prevail in the Universe?"

"Justice is merely the consummating effect of our causes. These effects can be delayed, but not escaped. Each Dark Brother thinks he will be the one to escape effects forever, but this is a mathematical impossibility, and justice always prevails in the end. Even if it were possible to live in the lower self to the end of the universe, the final consummation would destroy them; at that point, all the lower worlds will go back to their source. Within this period of pralaya is the divine rest, enjoyed by all those who have achieved union with God, but missed by those who identified with the lower nature."

"Interesting," I observed. "Now I have to ask you about the entity who owns Excalibur. He never revealed who he was."

"Do you have to be told?" John said, with a twinkle in his eye.

"What do you mean?"

"I mean, did you not recognize his vibration? Didn't his presence seem familiar?"

"Yes. It was very familiar. I just had a hard time believing it was him." Elizabeth and I exchanged glances.

John took the Bible off the table and handed it to me. "Turn to Revelations, chapter three, and read verses twenty and twenty-one.

I found the passage and read, "Behold, I stand at the door, and knock: if any man hear my voice, and open the door, I will come in to him, and will sup with him, and he with me. To him that overcometh will I grant to sit with me in my throne, even as I also overcame, and am set down with my Father in his throne."

John took a deep breath and continued, "Let's cover the meaning of this verse. What do you suppose the door is?"

"Could it be consciousness?" I guessed.

"Very good," he said. "The inner Christ, as well as the Great Master who occupies the office of Christ, stands always attuned to higher consciousness, wherein oneness lies. When any of the seekers among humanity raise their consciousness to the plane of the soul, the door appears before them. This is not a physical door, of course, but an opportunity to enter into a new realm, the kingdom of heaven.

"The instruction in the verse is to hear the voice of Christ. You, my friend, have heard his voice a number of times. Do you remember the words you projected just before you received Excalibur?"

"Yes, I do. I cannot forget them. They were *Join to the hand of the servant of the Most High.*"

"And where do you suppose those words came from?" he asked.

"It came so naturally that it seemed they came from me, yet a part of me realizes they came from somewhere else."

"You are right in that the words did come from somewhere else. The truth is that you stood at the door and heard the voice of the Master. What does the scripture say comes next?" he asked, looking at Elizabeth.

Elizabeth read over the scripture again and said, "After you hear the voice you must open the door."

"And how does one open the door?" he asked.

"I'm not sure," she said. "Does it have something to do with hearing the voice?"

"It does indeed," he smiled. "To open a door implies action. What kind of action must be taken?"

"Would that be following the voice?" she said sheepishly.

"Exactly. And when did you two follow the voice?"

"It was Excalibur that followed the voice I just mentioned," I said.

"But that's not the only time you heard the voice. How did you know that Elizabeth was your Lady of the Lake?"

"You mean it was Christ who communicated that to me?" I asked in wonderment.

"Think about it," said John. Then he looked again at Elizabeth and asked, "And when did you hear him speak?"

"When he told me he wanted me to receive the sword."

"And what happened when you obeyed this?"

"He came into me," she said.

"And what does the scripture say will happen when you open the door?"

I retrieved the Bible, studied the scripture and said, "Amazing! It says *I will come in to him, and will sup with him, and he with me.*"

"Isn't this exactly what happened?" asked John. "You both obeyed the voice and shortly thereafter he came, first into Elizabeth, and then into you, Joseph. What does it mean that you and Christ will sup, or feast, together?"

"I guess it means we are nourished."

"In what way?" he asked.

"Spiritually, I suppose," I said.

"Now think back to when he was within you. Did you feel nourished?"

"Wow! Now that you point it out, that scripture really makes sense. I felt tremendous nourishment in every part of my being."

"But there is more," said John. "Not only do you eat, but it says that Christ himself will sup, or eat, with you. In other words, the one visited is not the only one who is nourished."

"Are you saying that when Christ was in us, he got something out of the deal? I never thought of him as even needing anything from me," I said.

"We are all more interdependent than you realize. And it is a good thing that the universe is this way. The reason is simple; even the most high and holy lives would lose interest in the lower lives if they got nothing out of the help they offered. For instance, man is higher than animals, but the cow and the sheep would have little hope of sustaining their current numbers if they were not useful to us. The same is true in the vegetable world. Many vegetables that do not do well in the wild are nurtured by man because they sustain him; the weeds that get in the way are pulled out. That which is useful to the higher lives is nurtured by them."

"It sounds like selfishness is a motivation of the Brotherhood of Light as well as the Dark Brothers," observed Elizabeth.

"All lives, light or dark, good or evil, high or low are only motivated to sustain the lower over any period of time, if there is some benefit to them. If there is not some way the lower catches the attention of the higher, then the higher's attention will focus somewhere else. This is not a good or evil thing, for the higher's attention may be placed upon some noble cause while ignoring the lower. Because there are always many good causes on which to place attention, the lower must prove itself essential to the higher to cause the greater lives to take their attention from a seemingly higher good and focus on the lower."

John paused a moment in thought and continued, "For instance, what man of high thought would toil through the day growing potatoes when he could be doing something creative or teaching his child or furthering his education? Even though these seem to be more useful things to do than to grow potatoes, man is forced to divert his attention to more boring work a good percentage of the time because he must have food. Thus the lowly potato gets its share of humanity's attention and nourishing. But if it were not useful, it would be ignored and have to fend for itself."

"Surely there's a difference between the selfishness of the Brothers of Light and Darkness," I queried.

"There is indeed," he added. "The basic difference is this: The Dark Brothers only see that small part of reality which composes or nourishes the lower nature. Now, if this was all there was to existence, their attention on the little individual self as supreme would at least make sense. Think back to your life on Aeton. What was it that turned you from dark to light?"

I reflected a moment and answered, "It was when I first felt the peace of the higher worlds. As soon as I felt it I wanted more."

"And at that moment I became very valuable to you, didn't I?" John asked.

"Yes, you led me to it, and I thought you had even more to offer."

"So you turned from dark to light because of self interest, but with a difference. What was that difference?"

"I became aware of the existence of something higher than I had ever felt before."

"Yes," said John. "You were seeing a greater part of the whole than the average person sees so your motivations changed; but you still wanted what was best for you. Those who become holy are those who see the whole and are motivated by complete vision."

"But are not great lives motivated by more than self interest? Mother Teresa seemed to be only interested in helping people with no thought of self."

"Mother Teresa and other servants of the race serve with little or no thought for the lower self, but that is not all there is to self. In fact, it is such an insignificant part in the whole scheme of things that we often call this the *not self*, because it is only a reflection of our true nature. Our whole self is linked to all other selves, as expressed in the ancient mantram: *The Sons of men are one and I am one with them.* When we realize we are one with all other selves, we discover that we serve ourselves when we serve others. We then take care of our own lower needs only as required in relation to the whole. The Brothers of Light see themselves linked to the whole and are motivated by the progress of the whole. On the other hand, the Dark Brothers see themselves as separate, isolated entities, and are thus motivated for the good of the separated self only. Both Brotherhoods are motivated by how self is defined in their eyes."

"Interesting," I said. "So even a great being like Christ is motivated in part by what I can do for him. Am I then like a potato in his field that he is forced to toil for, while there are many other finer and more exciting things he could be doing?"

John chuckled, "That's one way to put it. In fact, the time he spent with you was more difficult for him than working in a potato field. The first week or so of adjusting to your vibration was quite uncomfortable, but he put aside his more interesting work because he saw this as necessary preparation."

"Did he find my body uncomfortable when he was in me?" asked Elizabeth.

"Actually, he never complained about you," he said smiling.

Elizabeth then gave me a mischievous grin.

I decided to be a wise married man and say nothing. I turned to John and said, "There's another thing that mystifies me. After the resurrection, it seems that Christ had a physical body. We are told that he appeared to the apostles and they touched him. Then he ate fish with them. Does he have a physical body today; and, if so, how can he enter into a disciple's body and commune with him as the scripture says?"

"Good question," he said. "The incident you are referring to is recorded in Luke chapter twenty-four. The eleven apostles, along with several disciples, were meeting and discussing in an enclosed room when Jesus suddenly appeared, seemingly coming right through the wall of the building. Because he came through the wall, most thought he was a spirit and were afraid until he invited us to touch him. As we touched him and felt with our own hands that he was physical, we knew for sure it was Jesus and not some deceptive spirit. Now most Bible readers will accept that the Master had a physical body at the time we touched him, but what kind of body did he have as he was passing through the wall?"

"That's an interesting thought I have never considered," I said. "Are you saying that his body could not have been physical as he went through a physical wall?"

"What do you think? Do you think that if we tried to touch him as he was passing through the wall we would have felt a physical body or would our hands have passed through him?"

"He passed through the wall as if he were a spirit, so I would guess that your hand would have also passed through him at that time. Am I right to assume that some type of change takes place in his body to allow a Master to go through a solid object or to travel large distances?"

"There is one way to illustrate." John stood up and extended his hand. "Take my hand."

I stood also and grabbed his hand.

"Would you say that my hand and body is physical?"

"I would say so," I answered.

He then let go of my hand and stepped back toward the wall. He closed his eyes for a moment as if in deep thought. Suddenly his body became transparent, and he stepped back into the wall so his body was half in and half out. Then he extended his hand again and, even though he did not speak, I knew he wanted me to attempt to grab it. I reached forward and my hand passed right through his, as if he were a spirit. Normally Elizabeth and I would have come close to passing out with surprise, but we were at the point where the miraculous was becoming a common occurrence, so we just looked on with wonder.

Even so, John managed to amaze us by backing further into the wall until he disappeared. There was then a long moment of anticipation, wondering what was going to happen next. After what seemed like an age, even though it was only a moment or two, we heard another knock on the door. We quickly ran and opened it, and, as expected, it was John. I placed my hand on his shoulder just to make sure he was physical again.

As John walked back to his chair he said, "Excuse me for leaving, but I decided to take a quick trip to my room in Tibet to retrieve a tea that I have not yet shared with you."

"You went all the way to Tibet?" exclaimed Elizabeth.

"Yes, I live there when some mission does not take me away from it. Even then I will often go to my room there for rest."

"In what part of Tibet do you have this room?" I asked.

"If I told you I'd have to kill you," he said somberly.

I was somewhat stunned and did not know how to respond. Then to my surprise John let out a hearty laugh and said, "Had you going there, didn't I?"

Elizabeth and I looked at each other and sighed with relief, "Yes, I have to admit you did. Am I right in assuming that this location is not to be published?"

"You are correct. It would be a danger to me and others to have it revealed. Now, let us continue with the lesson. When the Master was walking through the wall to visit the disciples, was he physical or in the spirit?"

"Well, as you have just demonstrated, he was not physical, so he must have been in some higher spiritual form," I said.

"Now gather your own thoughts and tell me how the Christ could have a physical body, yet co-exist within the body of a disciple."

I reflected a moment and replied, "Evidently, he can somehow alter the vibration of the body so only the higher spiritual vehicles remain, which allows him to enter the body of a disciple."

"Close enough," he said. "I'll give you more details another time, but for now, we must proceed with the lesson. Tell me your progress on the word for the Middle Way or the Second Key of Knowledge."

I sat back and said, "I've been doing a lot of thinking about it. I've also read some more about Buddhism. I've also talked it over with Elizabeth and Wayne. I've even asked the ultimate authority, the Master who was within me, but still I am not sure."

"And what did the Master tell you?" smiled John.

"I just received impressions from him on various things. The impression on the key word was that it would hinder my understanding to just give it to me, or to come between you and the lessons."

"Very wise," said John. "Kind of like the butterfly emerging from the cocoon. It is sometimes best to not help too much; else the butterfly will have no strength or beauty." He paused a moment and continued, "So. Do you have a key word for me?"

"I have one, but I am not sure of it."

"Why are you not sure?"

"It just does not register as correct within my soul. I think it may be close, but I do not think it is the one."

"So what do you think your chances are that this is not the word?"

"Probably about 90%," I replied.

"But you said the word does not register within your soul. How can you say this and still give the word a ten percent chance of being correct?"

"Maybe I'm being too generous. Perhaps I should have said one percent."

"Again – how can you say this and still give the word even a one percent chance of being correct?"

"When I think of it, I don't suppose I should give it even a one percent chance," I replied.

"Now think again. Since the word does not register with your soul, as you contemplate the matter, should you give it any chance of being correct?"

"Probably not," I confessed.

"Can we say, then, that you have eliminated this word?"

"Yes. I think we can. It feels good within my soul to eliminate it."

"Why didn't you eliminate it earlier?" he asked.

"I just wanted to make sure this was not the word before I moved on."

"But if you would have trusted your inner self you would have cleared this up before I came. You must learn to trust the impressions that come from your soul. This is the beginning of true faith that can move mountains."

John paused, pulled out a small cloth packet of tea from his pocket, and handed it to Elizabeth. "Here is the tea I removed from my room. It is one you have not tasted before. Would you make us a cup?"

"I would be happy to," said Elizabeth, rising.

As Elizabeth was heating up the water John continued, "Today you are fortunate. Since I only allow you to take one stab at the key word each lesson you have saved some time. You now know this word you have been considering is not the word so you can move on."

"Well I may have eliminated a word tonight, but I have not found another," I insisted.

"The night is not over," he said. "Now tell me this word you have considered which is not the key word for the Middle Way."

"I was thinking it was *discernment*," I replied.

"And why is this not the word?"

"Because one can discern and not act upon it. I feel that one must do more than discern the Middle Way to truly find it. I sense that the first key must be involved, that a decision must come into play."

John let out a short chuckle, "It is amazing that you know this much, yet the key word still eludes you. You're going to feel a little silly by the time the night is over."

"Are you saying that we will know the key word by the time you leave?"

"Perhaps," he said. "How's that tea coming?"

"I'm letting it steep," said Elizabeth. "Just another minute."

"You're going to enjoy this tea," he said, smiling. "It will give you a new experience."

His statement made me curious and I tried to tune into his thoughts, but I couldn't read them.

"No fair trying to read my mind," he said. "I'm entitled to surprise you now and then."

"I hope it is a pleasant surprise then," I said, growing anxious to see what was going to happen next.

CHAPTER TWENTY-THREE
Possibilities

Elizabeth finally served us the tea. As I was staring at my cup wondering what was in store for me, John said, "Are you ready?"

"I think so," I replied.

"One thing you must realize is this substance is far more valuable than Dom Pérignon."

"Well, we really enjoyed the Dom Pérignon, so this must be quite something," I added.

"You will not be disappointed," he said, and offered a toast. We all clinked our cups as he said, "To seeing the ALL."

This statement made me more curious than ever, as I wondered what he meant by the word ALL. As we drank, I figured I was in for *some* experience.

"Now we must be silent for three minutes. Contemplate on something desirable and see where it takes you."

I never realized how long three minutes of silence was. It seemed as if an hour had passed during that short time. Just at the point my mind seemed to be drifting toward some other-worldly experience, I heard Elizabeth scream. "My father! I see my father. He's right in front of me."

I turned and looked at her. "But your father's been dead for years."

"But it's him! He's holding me on his lap as a little girl. I feel like I'm actually back to when he used to do that."

"And what do you see Joseph?" asked John.

"Nothing," I said.

"Nothing?" he said, pointing toward the wall. "Look in that direction."

I looked with perplexed feelings. At first, nothing seemed to be there but a wall; then it seemed to blur, and I saw right through it to our front yard as if I was looking through empty space. Even though it was dark outside I was able to see the neighborhood as if we were in the noon day sun.

"This is fantastic," I exclaimed. "I can see right through the wall and all the details outside as if it were daytime."

"You can see much more than that. Look in the distance."

I attempted to see further and suddenly I saw a jungle, possibly in Africa, full of wild animals. "Wow! I see a lion," I exclaimed.

"Now think of seeing a city," he said.

I thought of a city and I saw what I thought was New York. I honed in on the larger buildings and when I saw the Twin Towers I was sure of the location. The Towers caught my attention for some reason. I had a sense of foreboding, but did not know what it meant at the time.

Then I thought of the Statute of Liberty and in an instant she was in my view. Next I thought of Central Park and found myself taking a tour of the famous landmark. "I see a number of places in New York," I said.

"Look upward," he said.

I looked up and saw the moon. I wondered if it would be possible to see it up close and as I thought about it, the moon started coming closer to me. It became almost frightening as I watched the moon become so great in size that it filled up my whole field of vision. It wasn't like I was traveling to the moon, but the moon was coming to me. Finally my vision approached the surface in what I guessed was the Sea of Tranquility.

This made me think of the moon landing and I wondered if I could see the landing spot of Apollo 11. Suddenly it was as if my vision were crossing the lunar landscape at over a thousand miles an hour until I arrived at a planted American Flag, looking just the way it did back in 1969. Nearby I saw numerous footprints looking as if they had just been impressed hours ago. I realized this was because of no atmosphere to wear them away.

"I see the location of the first lunar landing," I said. "I guess it was not a hoax after all."

"No. It was no hoax," said John. "Now look out into space and let your imagination take you somewhere."

I picked a fairly dim star and wondered if it would be possible to see it up close. Almost imperceptibly at first it began to get brighter, but then increased in light rapidly. I became aware that it was some distance, and several other closer star systems passed me by until I saw before me a blazing yellow sun that seemed to be surrounded by about twenty planets. I thought about viewing the one that was most like the earth and saw before me a planet about the size of earth that was completely covered with clouds. I desired to see the planet as it would look if I could see below the clouds, and I saw that the planet was like a giant greenhouse full of vegetation throughout the whole circumference, except for large lakes dotting the land. There seemed to be no oceans. The whole planet was naturally watered by the continual mist. I saw many differing kinds of animal and vegetable life, some similar to our own and some very different. I saw a fairly advanced civilization composed of humanoid types but with thick wrinkly skin. I seemed to know that this civilization had not changed or progressed much for thousands of years.

After I explained what I saw to Elizabeth and John, he stated, "I saw that planet with you and there are many like it. We on earth take the stars we see for granted, but the inhabitants of untold worlds live in misty lands and see only darkness or fuzzy gray light when they look upward at night. Then in the daylight they see a misty light, but never see the sun in its strength or the stars by night."

"I got the feeling that their civilization was very old and stable but it didn't seem to be going anywhere or making much progress," I said.

"Progress is always slow on worlds where they cannot see the stars or bask in the fullness of the sun – and there is a reason for it. You've heard the saying *reach for the stars*?"

"Yes," I replied. "It's a common saying we use when we are stretching our potential."

"Common clichés are like scripture. They come from the soul of humanity and often reflect as much or more truth than a prophet stating *thus saith the Lord*."

"I always liked *a bird in the hand is worth two in the bush*," said Elizabeth.

"That is a good one with lots of meaning," he said. "But let us consider the *reach for the stars* cliché. This tells us that there is something about seeing the distant stars at night that inspires humanity to stretch themselves, and it stimulates their imagination to attempt the impossible. Those who see the stars eventually go to the stars; on the other hand, such a journey does not even occur to one who does not know stars exist. It is true they take other journeys, yet the people of the mists never learn their full potential until the mists are cleared."

"So, will the people on this planet we saw ever see the stars?" I asked.

"Ages in their future, their skies will clear and the stars will be discovered," he said. "In the meantime, those inhabitants who advance in consciousness to the extent they are stretching their potential, will incarnate on other planets where the stars are visible, and *there* their imaginations will roam and expand."

"It's funny, but I never thought about us being lucky just because we can see the stars."

"About 99% of the life forms on the various planets never see the stars," he said. "This is also the case in our own solar system. Take Jupiter, for example. Within its gaseous body are many life forms unlike anything on the earth, and to them, the universe consists of only that small area in which they circulate. To those who see the stars, the universe is infinite."

"Interesting," I said.

"The tea stimulates the vision of the third eye, the energy center between the eyebrows. All seekers, however, will eventually develop this power, but the tea amplifies what is already there. You demonstrated how vision can be amplified to see through space, but you can also see through time as Elizabeth is doing," he said looking her direction.

"Yes," she said. "I have been looking back in time enjoying seeing my Father again."

"But you can see more than this. See yourself in your consciousness rising above the city of Boise."

"I'll try," she said. At that she closed her eyes and seemed to be concentrating. "Wow!" she exclaimed. "I can see the capitol building and most of the city."

"Now concentrate on seeing backward in time."

"OK." After a few seconds, she said, "The buildings are disappearing and being replaced with farmland and trees." After another pause, she continued, "Now the capitol building is gone and there are just a few log buildings. Now there's nothing but wilderness."

"Is there anything else you would like to see from the past?"

"I would like to see the planet Aeton that Joseph talked about."

"I will need to guide your consciousness then, for you must see through much time and space." He then took her hand, and they both closed their eyes.

After a moment I asked Elizabeth, "Do you see anything?"

"This is fantastic. I have this sense of passing through great vistas of time and space, and now I see the great planet filling up a good deal of my angle of vision. From Aeton the sun is about twice as large in the sky as ours, but the heat received is about the same because it is not as hot. It is orange instead of yellow. The inhabitants of this planet can see the stars, but they did not develop space travel. I get the sense that the battle between light and dark distracted them from advanced science."

"What does the surface look like from a distance?" I asked, realizing that my memory of the physical planet was only fragmentary.

"From space it looks much different than earth. It seems that the orange sun causes a rusty tint to the atmosphere, and instead of large oceans, the surface is mostly land – I'd say about 80% land. I'm zeroing in on the inhabitants now who are humanoid, similar to the earth, but instead of many races, there seems to be two major ones. The one has an oriental look and the other, that you and John belonged to, had features like American Indians but dressed something like ancient Romans. These two races were often at war with each other and themselves."

"It seems that the earth has more oceans than most worlds," I observed.

"Yes," said John. "Few inhabited worlds have the vast expanse of ocean the earth does, but a handful have even more. Then there are some that are completely covered in water, yet have still evolved some intelligent life forms. Nature does not waste *any* of her raw materials in the great work to supply forms for life essence."

"So, can we use this power to see into the future?" I asked.

"Yes and no," he said.

"I'm starting to get frustrated at you saying that," I said. "How can the answer be yes and no on this one?"

He smiled and replied, "Because of free will, the future is composed of many possibilities. These possibilities are divided into three categories. First there are those future events that have near 100% chance of happening. For example, the sun coming up in the morning is one of these. So is the fact that when you finish your current breath, you will soon take another. Cyclic events are very predictable and are only interrupted when something extraordinary happens.

"The second are those future events which have been decided by one who has power to consummate the goal. This can range from a cat which has captured a mouse and has predetermined the mouse's fate, to a human who decided to eat chicken for dinner, to the Ancient of Days who decides a time to sink an entire continent. When any life makes a decision of a future course of action within his sphere of power, that event will happen, with rare exceptions.

"The third category are those possibilities which are a combination of cycles, intelligent decisions, group thought, and unintelligent motion left over from decisions of the past. These possibilities can rarely be predicted with 100% accuracy. Some possibilities within this category can be seen quite clearly and others cannot. I want you to pick a future you want to examine and take a look at it."

"I'll try," I said. "What I am most concerned with is the possibility of World War III, or that we could destroy ourselves in one way or another."

John pointed to the wall and spoke authoritatively, "Look and see."

I looked at the wall and saw three images. Two were bright and clear, and one was fairly obscure. "I see three images. What does it mean?"

"These are three different future possibilities. The clearer and brighter the image, the more probable is the future it depicts. Pick one."

I decided to pick the brightest image first, and the moment I did, the image expanded into a future vision. I did not see everything, but did see images that seemed to answer my question. I saw that in the immediate future (from 1998 on) world tension seesawed back and forth. Many worried about cataclysmic events at the turn of the millennium, but nothing significant materialized.

Terrorism increased, though I couldn't see the exact time or place of the attacks. One or two of the attacks seemed particularly horrific. As the free world lead by the United States fought against terrorism and rogue nations such as Iraq, tension increased, mistakes were made, and the threats to freedom were not completely neutralized. Not only did we have to fight terrorists and worry about rogue nations, but there was great strife within the United States and between America and other normally friendly nations.

Several possibilities appeared. Pakistan and India remained a point of tension that had the possibility of exploding at ant time, but throughout the vision it just remained a powder keg that eventually lost strength. I sensed, however, that some unforeseen stimulation could make this the hot spot of the world. I saw North Korea continued to develop its nuclear program and begin to rattle its nuclear saber. In this scenario there was a strong possibility it would launch several nuclear weapons at South Korea and Japan, and make a list of demands upon the United States and the world. It would also go on a crash program to perfect missiles which could reach the United States. I then saw the United States launch several nuclear weapons in return; however that response was not 100% sure. This action was determined by who was president at the time and the advisors surrounding him. Even so, the retaliation with nuclear weapons was the most probable response. After this, China threatened a nuclear response in return, but did not act. They did not dare to as they feared for their own survival.

South Korea, with the support of the United States, Britain, most of Europe and Japan attacked North Korea and overthrew the government. North Korea eventually became reunited with the South as one country, similar to what happened to East and West Germany, but the link seemed a little looser.

After the dust settled from the nuclear exchange, the alarmed nations of the world called a general conference, and declared by international law that the proliferation of nuclear weapons was strictly illegal; and any further nuclear development would be met with a physical attack. Many wanted the current holders of the weapons to disarm, but there was not enough agreement or trust to comply.

Several from various nations worked relentlessly for a ban on all nuclear and other weapons of mass destruction in all the individual nations; and they grew steadily in their influence.

Many nations singled out Israel as one that should disarm, whereas a few did not. This caused tension between Israel and many other nations. I saw that several nations and peoples had designs to destroy Israel with weapons of mass destruction and there was around a fifty percent chance that there would be an attempt during the next several decades. If opposing forces stay vigilant, this catastrophe can be avoided.

The most probable outcome in the Middle East was that the discord and enmity will slowly erode. This will be stimulated by a much improved government in Iraq after Saddam Hussein is removed. More Islamic people will integrate within the boundaries of Israel, causing the motive to attack Israel by the more radical of Islam to be neutralized. It will be some time before the majority of Moslems and Jews accept each other, but the rising generation will learn to peacefully co-exist if a major war can be avoided.

I then saw that this problem became a catalyst that suppressed the rogue nations and terrorists from using atomic weapons. They lashed out with other weapons and poisons, but it did not cause a cataclysmic event comparable to a nuclear explosion.

I then saw that during the next one hundred-fifty to two hundred years, the nations of the earth achieved relative stability and seemed to be guided into a much better and peaceful age as they controlled and overcame their problems. This journey was not without additional difficulties such as economic problems, natural disasters, famine, a plague, and diseases that took millions of lives.

I then removed my sight from the first vision and focused on the second. The second was better than the first. The freedom lovers of the world became so alarmed at the threat of terrorism and nuclear weapons from rogue nations, that they were able to take the measures necessary to enter into the new age without a nuclear attack.

In this scenario, North Korea, China and the Middle East were contained through creating enough union of thought among the free nations that they did not dare strike first. The wise use of humanitarian aid coupled with the threat of force neutralized some enemies until a new generation of less aggressive leaders came into play. In this probability, we entered into the New Age at about the same pace, but with less pain and fewer economic problems because a nuclear confrontation was avoided.

I withdrew from this vision and looked at the third and darker alternative.

The most alarming thing about this alternative were terrorists smuggling various atomic and biological weapons across the U.S. and European borders and releasing them. This caused a stock market crash and the U.S. economy came to a standstill, with the nation in fear and chaos. The economy of the world then followed suit. North Korea launched nuclear weapons at its neighbors and the United States was too weakened and distracted to counter with enough force to stop the aggression. China supported Iran as well as Korea and also attacked Taiwan. In addition Pakistan and India attacked each other. All this was the beginning of the unthinkable World War III.

The war was complicated by the divisions of radical Islam against Christianity and Western civilization as a whole. They added their support to every totalitarian regime that would be an enemy to the Allies. In addition to this, radical Moslems living in Europe and the United States caused so many problems that there was serious talk of rounding them up in camps. This type of talk divided many non-Moslems and only made matters worse.

From this, I saw two probable endings. The first ended with a victory by the democratic nations. The war was a great setback to civilization, but new commitments were created and within 50 years civilization was back on track with strong commitments to peaceful co-existence. In the other alternative freedom was extinguished and darkness ruled the earth for a thousand years. I saw this was a slim possibility, but a real one that shook me to the core and made me want to do all in my power to avoid it.

I withdrew my vision and thought of the three paths as a whole and a kaleidoscope of probabilities crossed my mind and boggled my imagination. There are indeed more future possibilities than the hand of man can write. I did not realize how much of the future is predicated upon our free will, or the First Key of Decision. Another thing I saw was that there are wild cards in the future, and every once in a while, an event can materialize through an odd turn of happenings and create great changes through a domino effect.

As I explained what I saw to Elizabeth, John injected his thoughts. "What you have seen explains the reason there has not been one person, who has been well recorded, who has been an accurate prophet, especially in modern days. In simpler times it was much easier for a prophet to make accurate predictions, but the more developed civilizations add many more variables.

"I could take what you have seen and add it to my more extensive visions of the future and make predictions for the next 100 years with a 90% probability of accuracy. With your lesser experience, your accuracy would be less than 80% and not too accurate on the timeline. The principle here is the future operates on a different principle than the past, even though many teachers tell us that the past and future are the same. The past represents decisions made and the future represents decisions to be made. A decision made is one; whereas a decision *to be made* is one of many possibilities. The past is etched in stone, the future is malleable. The two are only one in that they interplay to create the present wherein lies all consciousness."

"Interesting," I said. "From my experience, I think I can see why many people have visions of the future they feel is infallible revelation from God, yet few of them come true."

"Excellent conclusion," said John. "When a visionary enters the mystic state, he usually does so with the mindset that the future is fixed by God and there is only one time track to see. Whereas, you saw three paths because you are open to probabilities, the mystic usually sees only one, and that one follows the trend of his preconceived notions. If he has a belief that the world will end soon he may see a vision of very low probability that will match his belief system. The vision will be so real he would swear on his life that the future of doom will happen. Little does he realize the earth only has about a one percent chance of complete apocalyptic destruction during the next 100 years. His bias thus causes him to see the one percent probability rather than the high probabilities of better times. The sad thing is the mystics often see the worst probabilities of destruction rather than the high probabilities of progress."

"One thing I saw that roused my interest was the existence of wild cards, or unexpected events in the future timeline. Can you tell us more about them?"

John thoughtfully replied, "Wild cards usually have a short-term effect, with the future returning to its probable course. Then there are a few times that a permanent change occurs.

"The assassination of John Lennon was a wild card that did not have to happen. The timeline adjusted to it, but it did create some ripples that will yet affect us for some time to come.

"The prevention of disastrous wild cards is the main work I am involved in right now. We have already prevented several unwanted transfers of nuclear weapons and possible detonations. We have also deterred terrorists from several heinous acts toward New York, Washington, London and Paris.

"This is a difficult job for us and it is only a matter of time before one comes along that we cannot prevent, or higher will does not allow intervention. One odd way to look at it is the future will always contain a few wild cards we should be able to prevent, but will not be able to. So, from this angle, a small number of wild cards materializing are, overall, a sure thing. They are just difficult to plan for, even for the masters."

"So, if I read about some explosion in a major city in the near future, I'll know the Masters were working on it, but were unable to prevent it?"

"It's only a matter of time," he sighed. "We are limited in numbers and there is only so much we can do to protect civilization from itself. In the whole scheme of things, a few wild cards will play their hand, but even the Higher Lives with whom I work have difficulty in accepting some inevitables which spell temporary disaster."

"This conversation would seem kind of odd to standard believers," noted Elizabeth. "They have the belief that God knows everything, and nothing unexpected happens."

"God is a body of which all of us are a part," he said. "Overall, your body is omniscient as far as it is concerned. There is nothing that happens in the body that some part of the body does not know about. But there are many things that happen in the body of which the individual parts are unaware. The conscious self is unaware of the activity of the various organs, and the various organs only have a vague sensation of the activity of other organs.

"Even though the body is aware of all things that happen within the body, it is often unaware of specific future events that will affect the whole of the body. There are some future events that are possible to predict, but others that are not. A lack of understanding of this truth has caused much of humanity to relinquish its responsibility to create its own future and place all responsibility in the hands of God.

What this does is to give power into the hands of the real decision-makers. The trouble is that the decision maker with power over people's future could be a Hitler or a Jesus. Humanity must take back its power and not give it over to chance, but pave its own path with focused intelligence.

After a pause, Elizabeth spoke, "My vision has returned to normal. I can't see the past, the future or in the distance."

"The effect of the tea is wearing off," said John. "It's time to return to our lesson."

CHAPTER TWENTY-FOUR
Right Use of Mind

"Before we begin the lesson there is one question I must ask," I said. "It seems that every religion believes that God, or whoever they worship, knows everything in the future that can ever be. Are they all wrong?"

"Not completely," said John. "The Life, "I am the Alpha and Omega," that is God sees the end and the beginning of all things, but that which happens in the middle is up to the lesser lives. The decisions made by these lesser lives sometimes move events toward the end God sees and sometimes not."

He paused and continued, "A great painter may envision very precisely how the final image is to appear, but could not predict every brush stroke, nor would he want to. There are certain ends decreed by the will of God that none can stop, yet that which happens in the middle is not completely predictable by any life in the universe. If it were so we would have no free will."

"How is that so?" asked Elizabeth.

"Think of a number between one and ten," he said.

Elizabeth looked to the ceiling a moment and then said, "OK, I have one."

"Now I have developed some telepathic powers and know that you first thought of the number seven, but then you decided that may be the number I would expect so you changed your selection to six. Is that correct?"

"Wow! That's amazing," she exclaimed.

"It's not amazing when you learn how to do it," he said. "But the point I wish to make is that a few moments ago I could not have predicted your selection. Furthermore, before I came here tonight I could not have guessed that we would have been talking about this exact subject. Your free will brought this about. But let us suppose that some cosmic plan had within it the fact that you picked the number six. Would you truly have had any free will to pick any other number?"

"I think I see what you're saying," I added. "If all of our decisions are predetermined, we have no free will and are not really making decisions, but are just puppets following the dots in some predetermined picture."

John added, "And if we are mere puppets, then our essence could not be the first Key of decision for there would be no real choice. There can be no decision where the future is one hundred percent predictable. As a case in point, you have no free will deciding whether or not the sun will rise in the morning, for that is predetermined. If you decide that the sun will not come up you will have no effect. But you can use your power of decision in choosing what you will do in the sun according to your sphere of power. For instance, you can decide whether or not to get a tan. There has to be some unpredictability before decision can exist.

"We are guided from one point of the Plan of God to another. Because time does not try the patience of God, it matters not whether the steps toward the plan take a long or short time. It does matter to our consciousness, and we often give ourselves much grief in delaying the manifestation of the Will of God. For example, peace on earth will definitely be achieved, but it is up to our free will whether this event takes place within fifty years or a thousand, or more. The manifestation of the Plan in between is not set and thus accomplished through the power of decision. Because we have free will many mistakes are made. But one thing that is predictable is that human intelligence will see its mistakes and eventually correct them by free will. The tendency of all intelligence to eventually select the good, the beautiful and the true gives God the power to use us to consummate his ideas and plans. The will of God is always accomplished, but because of free will, the time factor involved can be long or short."

"So if it's in the plan that we have peace on earth, good will to men, this does not mean it will happen at a set time. I take it we could delay it for another thousand years if we make the wrong choices and have a major nuclear war," I concluded.

"You are basically right. Free will gives us the ability to postpone the inevitable and play around with the details in the process. This process winds up giving us an understanding as to why the destined end is that which must be. This is a fascinating subject and I'm sure your free choice will lead us into more questions, but for now we must continue to pursue the Second Key of Knowledge. Now gather your notes and research and tell me the sixth directive of the Eightfold Path of the Buddha."

I gathered my notes and papers and sat back down. "From my studies, I gather that the last three directives concern mental focus or concentration. The first of these is generally called *Right Effort*. Sometimes it is translated into English as *Right Endeavor, Striving* or *Exertion*, but *Right Effort* seems to be the popular one. According to my notes our Right Effort should master four categories which are *the effort to avoid, the effort to overcome, the effort to develop,* and *the effort to maintain*."

After listening intently, John spoke. "Very good, but what we need to do is get to the core meaning behind each of these directives, and the core principle behind Right Effort touches very closely to the Second Key. The fact that there is such a thing as right effort reveals that there is also a wrong or incorrect effort. In each work we attempt to accomplish, there arise numerous decisions to be made. Each fork in the road reveals at least two choices. Because no two choices produce equal results, this means that one will be superior to the other. To master right effort we must learn to make the right choices which will most speedily take us toward the goal. The first category you mentioned was the effort to avoid. What is the meaning behind this?"

"I think most Buddhists believe this means they are to avoid being controlled by the lower sensual nature. This frees them up to enjoy the fruits of the Spirit."

"This is true," he said, "but the basic principle has a much wider application. In every work we do there are things to avoid. It is a mistake to only view a spiritual enterprise, or quest, as being the field where these principles are applied. Every work we do where a service is rendered is spiritual from a certain angle of vision. For instance, even building a house has a spiritual dimension. Correspondingly, you want to avoid a weak foundation, a leaky roof or hitting your thumb with a hammer. Success in any endeavor is greatly enhanced by avoiding all pitfalls."

"It seems like the thing the world needs to avoid is a nuclear war," added Elizabeth.

"Excellent point," said John. "Now the second category is the effort to overcome. What is the meaning here?"

"In Buddhist teachings one overcomes that which he cannot avoid - which tempts him toward the carnal life," I responded.

"Yes," said John. "You avoid many problems and pitfalls, and in this there is wisdom. Unfortunately, there are many problems and temptations we cannot avoid. Instead, we must face and overcome them. Let us go back to the example of building a house. You can make sure many potential problems do not occur by getting the financing in order, choosing a good contractor, finding a design you like, picking your colors and many other items. Even after doing everything possible, there will still be problems to face that couldn't be anticipated. Maybe the building inspector will find something wrong with the wiring and demand some work be done over. Maybe there will be a crack in the foundation that will need repaired. Maybe you will be short on a special order of floor tiles and it takes a month to get some more in. But even then, after the house is complete, maybe your wife does not like the color of the carpet and you have to get a new one."

"Now that's something that could indeed happen," I exclaimed looking in Elizabeth's direction.

"What's more likely is that the man would pick up the wrong carpet and install it before he knows he made a mistake," she shot back with a grin.

John smiled, "The point is that Murphy's Law prevails, and there are always many problems to overcome in any worthwhile project; and though we can avoid many of them, we cannot plan on avoiding them all. If we expand on Elizabeth's point, we could say that the peaceful nations could do everything in their power to avoid war and conflict, but still there will be a number of terrorists who will not be able to be stopped and will commit destructive acts. Now what was the third effort you mentioned?"

"The effort to develop," I replied.

"Again I ask, what is the meaning of this?"

I thought a moment and replied, "From a Buddhist point of

view, I would assume it means that when we have avoided all temptations possible and then overcome the ones we couldn't avoid, we develop a higher consciousness and experience new spiritual joys."

"In other words, after we overcome, we enjoy the fruits of our labors and develop a higher quality of life from them. And how would this apply to the house analogy?" he asked, turning to Elizabeth.

She reflected a moment and said, "Well, after we actually get the house built we move in and enjoy it. Perhaps the effort to develop applies here by the fact that we then fine tune the details so we can enjoy the new house more than the old. We'll make sure the final colors are to our liking and do some extra landscaping, plant extra trees, and put a barbecue in the back yard and so on."

"That is true," he said. "But even after you get the house just the way you want, there is one more thing. You actually develop a relationship with your home in that you learn how to make use of it so your living enjoyment can be maximized. Now give me the final category."

"It looks like the final one is *to maintain*. I suppose you want me to expand on this."

"Indeed," he said.

"Speaking from the spiritual angle, I would suppose it would mean that merely attaining a higher consciousness is not enough. Many people seem to attain a spiritual high and then lose it. The first three steps are in vain if one is not able to maintain the spiritual consciousness."

"Good answer," said John, "but there is an important key to maintaining that state which must be realized by the disciple. Have you noticed that after a spiritual experience, the physical brain will remember that you had the experience, but it will not properly recollect the actual feeling?"

"I'm not sure," I said.

"Let me put it this way. Have you had a spiritual experience that impressed you so deeply, it seemed that nothing could ever deter you from the path, but then, after a few days passed, life returned to normal, and your motivation switched to material things and the cares of the world?"

"Yes," I replied. "I think I see what you are getting at. In fact, I have noticed that a few days after a spiritual experience people often succumb to a negative energy and the spiritual high seems an eternity away."

"Yes, this is a normal thing. Because of the Law of Oscillating Polarities a high is usually followed by a low, and the negative energy that comes in during the low will often make the last state of the seeker worse than the first. This principle was taught by Jesus. Elizabeth, would you turn to Matthew Twelve and read verses 43-45."

Elizabeth found the passage and read: "When the unclean spirit is gone out of a man, he walketh through dry places, seeking rest, and findeth none. Then he saith, I will return into my house from whence I came out; and when he is come, he findeth it empty, swept, and garnished. Then goeth he, and taketh with himself seven other spirits more wicked than himself, and they enter in and dwell there: and the last state of that man is worse than the first. Even so shall it be also unto this wicked generation."

"To speak to our modern age, try substituting the word *energy* for *spirit* and *negative* for *unclean* or *wicked* and tell me what you glean from the scripture."

Elizabeth stared at the page for a moment and answered, "When a negative energy leaves a person it seeks a place to abide. As it circulates, it gathers in strength about sevenfold and returns to its original abode. This original person is overwhelmed and becomes more negative than he was before."

"Actually, the figure is eightfold," he said. "There are seven spirits plus himself. This figure symbolizes the eighth sphere of darkness."

"This is beginning to make sense," I said. "Spiritual experience casts out negativity, but a short time later the negative comes back with a vengeance. I have seen this happen."

"But does it have to happen?" John asked. "Can a person withstand the temptation to relinquish the spiritual state?"

"I would think so," said Elizabeth.

"Yes, we all inwardly know it is possible to stand no matter what storms may arise, but the *how* part is the difficulty for many. The key is given in the Buddhist teachings around detachment. When the disciple is not drawn to heaven or hell, happiness or misery, but is willing to stand in his spiritual being, no matter what experience is revolving around him, then, and only then, can he endure the light of a thousand suns or the attack of the lowest hell. He will then discover that the attack of what seemed to be overwhelming negative energy has no effect on him. It becomes as if it never was."

"Does this apply to spiritual feelings also?" I asked

"True spiritual feelings touch the life of God, which have no opposite. There are many positive and negative feelings which begin and end, yet the life of the One God is endless and all that proceeds from It is also endless. True joy is higher than normal human happiness because it gives a glimpse of the Eternal. Joy does not end, but we can withdraw from it for a time. Because it comes from God we are always drawn back to it. Joy is our destiny."

He paused and continued, "Now tell me Elizabeth, how would you use the analogy of the house to explain the principle of maintaining?"

She thought a moment and stated, "Even after the house is completed, and we have all the things the way we want, we still have to keep it up. We, or should I say I, have to keep it clean."

"Hey, I do a few things," I said feigning hurt feelings.

She put her hand on my shoulder and said, "You do OK for a guy, sweetie."

"So what else do you have to do to keep the house up?" he asked.

"Well, you have to mow the lawn, weatherproof it in the winter, do repairs on the roof, plumbing, etc," I said. "Then you have to repaint once in a while."

"Achieving a goal such as the ownership of a home or the possession of a spiritual state is only half the battle," he said. "You have seen those who have gained possessions, by inheritance or gift, who do not value or maintain them. If attention is not placed on the merit of a possession, it will not be long until it is worthless. A home or a car neglected is soon desired by none. Even so, the seeker must see and understand the value of the spiritual state and then by the power of right effort force his attention on keeping himself centered on the light of his last spiritual manifestation. By the force of will, he must exert this effort to remind himself daily to maintain the highest consciousness he has received. Then, too, he must follow the highest he has received. If he does not do these two things, the light he has attained will slip from him, and his attention will be swept away by forces eight times the power of those that first stood at the door of progress."

"So if he is overcome by eight times the original inertia, one would wonder if such a person could ever progress into spiritual consciousness," I noted.

"Fortunately, the human spirit cannot be defeated," he said. "When one has descended so far into negativity to the extent that the pain becomes unbearable, the pilgrim reaches a point where he feels he must conquer or die. An alcoholic at the end of his rope is a case in point. It is over eight times as difficult for him to pull himself up and rise above his problem at the end rather than the beginning of his problem. But when the reality of his mistake stares him in the face, he will often find reserves of strength he did not know he had and overcome his addiction once and for all."

"But many alcoholics die without overcoming their problem," said Elizabeth.

"And these will come back in a future life and face their eight devils once more. This will happen again and again until the entity is victorious. But the point to realize here is that all this wasted time and pain and suffering can be bypassed by following the Noble Eightfold Path, particularly by making right effort as we have been discussing. And the key ingredient in right effort is to learn to center oneself in the light and sustain the highest we know."

John then sat back in his chair and took a deep breath.

"I take it your pause means you are changing the subject," I observed.

"You are correct, grasshopper," he said, smiling. "It's time to move on to the seventh directive. Tell us what you have there."

"The seventh is Right Mindfulness," I said. "It is sometimes translated as Right Thoughts or Recollection, but mindfulness is most common."

"And what do you suppose is meant by this injunction?" he asked.

"From my reading, I gather that it supports the teaching you just gave us. We are to examine and understand our mind and thoughts so we can put them in the right perspective, and not allow them to distract us from the spiritual path."

"Correct," he said. "Perhaps a short parable will aid with the understanding."

He seemed to formulate a thought and began, "There was once a man who had a great love of beauty, pleasure and comfort. He spent his whole life in pursuit of these until after years of hard work he attained success. He not only had money, but also free time to enjoy the good life, and for several years he had all the enjoyments needed to gladden his heart.

"Then one day, as he was sitting in his den, sipping a glass of wine, admiring a valuable painting he had just acquired, he received a phone call. It was a kidnapper telling him that he had taken his only son and would kill him unless he did exactly as he was told. First he was to go to the bank and withdraw $100,000. Next he was to go to three different locations and find hidden clues. Upon finding the third, he would know where to deliver the money and recover his boy.

"The man was alarmed and immediately his attention was taken off of his treasures, his wine and comforts, and placed upon redeeming his son.

"First he went to the bank and withdrew $100,000 in cash. As he put the money in a bag he had no thought about what it could buy or no lust for its value, but only the thought of redeeming his son.

"The place of the first clue was an art gallery containing many valuable works the man desired. Normally, he would have enjoyed spending hours looking at the works of beauty, but this time he sought only the clue until it was found. Then, he did not stop to look at the art, but immediately moved on to the next location.

"The next place was a country club, where he had a membership. Normally when he visited there, he enjoyed a round of golf, or relaxed sipping quality wine with his friends, or a dozen other pleasurable activities. But this time was different. The golf, the wine, the pleasure was still there, yet he paid no attention to anything except finding the second clue. Finally, after a concentrated search, he found the clue and moved on to the third location which was an exotic night club.

"He entered the club, and to his view were beautiful girls doing striptease acts that would have normally caught his full attention. This time it did not. Even though he could see the beautiful girls in full view, they had no attraction for him, for his complete attention was on finding the next clue. As he searched for the next twenty minutes, he ignored the girls, the comedy acts, the available drinks, and several old friends in attendance.

"Finally, he found the last clue and put the three together. He then discovered that his boy was back home in his room. *Could the kidnapper be so bold as to hold my boy ransom in my own home?* he wondered. For a moment, he was afraid to go home because the kidnapper may kill him as well as his boy, but he cancelled out the fear and departed. He soon burst in the house, then to the boy's bedroom and found him alone playing games on his computer, seemingly without a care in the world.

"*What's going on*? demanded the Father. *I thought you were kidnapped!*"

"*No*, said the boy, *I've been fine all along. The problem is that you've been ignoring me for years in pursuit of your various interests and pleasures, and I wanted to see what was most important to you. Do you care more for me or your comforts you so cherish?*"

"The father was upset at first, but then when he assessed the experience, he realized he had been overlooking some things of real importance. He gave the boy a hug with the promise that he would now make him a higher priority than the passing pleasures of life."

John paused again in thought and asked, "Now tell me what you learned from this parable."

"Since we're taking about Right Mindfulness, I assume that the only son represents the priority that we should have, and the pleasures the man enjoyed represents the distractions that take us away from what's really important," I said.

"And what is that important thing the boy represents?" he asked, looking at Elizabeth.

"I would think it would be the spiritual life," she responded. "We do not realize how important it is until some crises shakes us to our senses, like my past illness did with us."

"Very good," he replied. "When the crisis occurred, for the father right mindfulness became the total dedication of his thoughts toward finding his son. Any attention paid to the drink, the pleasure and the beauty would have been wrong mindfulness. To find his son, he did not have to deny the existence of pleasure or the senses, but to merely put them in their right place and obtain the power to completely ignore them when the situation required it. Now tell me how to apply this principle in the spiritual quest we all have at one time or another."

I decided to answer and said, "We all go through a long series of lives when we take the path of least resistance, where pleasing the senses seems to be the most important thing. Then, one day, we get a wake-up call, and we realize that we are missing the better things of the Spirit. When this realization comes, we must then go on a quest to find the clues that will take us to higher consciousness."

"And, to find the clues, we must do what?" he asked.

"We must learn to completely ignore the pull of the pleasures of the senses and look for communications from our higher self, so, in the end we can find the full revelation. If we let the pleasures of life distract us, we miss the clues and miss the spiritual life."

"But we had some Dom Pérignon earlier," noted Elizabeth. "This was a pleasurable activity. Was it wrong minded for us to drink that?"

"One of the most profound scriptures given was written by Solomon, wherein he said that there is a time and a place for everything. This is also a good seed thought for you to contemplate in finding the Second Key.

"Contrary to some current Buddhist thinking, right mindfulness does not mean you have to ignore pleasure all the time. The key, instead, is to prioritize your attention so the spiritual world always takes precedent over the world of the senses. The disciple must attain the mental frame of mind which will give him power to never let the pleasures of the world distract him from his spiritual focus. He must be willing to drop everything that connects him to the sensory world at the drop of a hat, even to living in poverty, suffering or death. He who overcomes is willing to sacrifice all he has that connects him to the physical world.

"Some Hindus realized this before the time of Buddha. They felt the only way to liberation was abject poverty and complete denial of pleasure. Some lived naked in the woods and starved themselves to death.

"The Buddha, Siddhartha, almost fell into this trap and was down to surviving on a couple of grains of rice a day when he had his revelation on the Middle Way. After the revelation, he taught that neither starvation nor gluttony, complete deprivation or indulgence was the correct path, but instead a course that runs somewhere through the middle.

"In our modern era, however, current Buddhists read their masters' teachings on the control of pleasure and the senses, and interpret them in a black and white manner that denies followers to indulge themselves at any time. By comparison, this is the same mistake the ancient Hindus made. The true Middle Way is not black or white and changes with the circumstance. The keynote for finding this middle is the phrase, *a time and place for all things*.

"After your victory it was the time and place for our sharing of the Dom Pérignon. To have done anything less would have not been following the Middle Way."

"That's good to know," I said. "Sometimes it just seems right within my soul to indulge a little or to spoil myself. It doesn't seem right to deny ourselves just for the sake of denial. After listening to you, I can see that this attitude was the mistake the Buddha made before his enlightenment."

He smiled and replied, "It sounds like you are achieving enlightenment yourself. Now let us move ahead. I see by your notes you have listed the *cattaro satipatthana*."

"The what?" I asked.

"The Four Foundations of Mindfulness," he said.

"Yes, I suppose I do, but I think English is the Middle Way when teaching us."

John chuckled and replied, "Yes, I suppose you got me on that one, my friend. As soon as Elizabeth takes her bathroom break, we shall finish that and then to the last directive."

I could tell that Elizabeth was a little uncomfortable with John reading her mind again, but she let it pass and went upstairs to the bathroom.

CHAPTER TWENTY-FIVE
Approaching the Key

It wasn't long before we again sat around the table and John continued the lesson. "Now tell me the Four Foundations of Mindfulness."

I checked my notes again and replied, "The first is mindful contemplation of the body; the second, of the feelings; the third concerns states of mind; and the fourth, phenomena.

"Again, we will start at the beginning. What is meant by *mindful contemplation of the body*?" he said

"Apparently the teaching is that the Buddhist is supposed to pay attention to everything that happens in the body beginning with your breathing and then to other bodily happenings such as walking, standing, sitting and lying down. This is then extended to other happenings in the body such as dressing, bathing, eating, drinking, defecating, falling asleep, waking up and then to the various actions and activities the body takes during the day. We are to become mindful of the cause of all the actions the body takes. Then this teaching takes us in a direction that doesn't seem right to me."

"And what is that?" said John.

"It tells us that we are to take the body, which we consider beautiful, and break it down into unattractive parts like the liver, intestines, sweat and so on so we can free ourselves from being attracted to it. I guess that if a person sees another with warts he is supposed to meditate on this to diffuse the sexual attraction so the appeal will be lost."

"And why don't you like this idea?"

"Well, I think the human body is the most beautiful creation in existence, and to reduce it to its least attractive parts would be like taking the Mona Lisa and tearing it to shreds and then seeing nothing but trash. This idea does not do much for me."

"Point taken," he said. "Anything else on this first foundation?"

"The teachings tell us to then see the body as separated into the four behavior modes of matter, which is solidity, fluidity, heat and oscillation. Then we are to visualize the decaying body after death. Seeing the decaying corpse is supposed to help us attain the ultimate detachment toward the body."

John listened and responded, "One of the problems with Buddhism, as well as Christianity and other religions, is that many of their teachings were designed for an ancient people and have not been updated to capture the attention of modern consciousness."

"And why do I get the feeling you're going to do some updating?" I said.

"Probably because I am," he said, smiling. "The thing to look for in any teaching is the core principle behind it. What are they attempting to teach?"

"It seems to me that the principle goes back to one of the first things you taught me. We are not our bodies. This idea of meditating on the body in such a way that it loses its attractiveness appears to be preparing the student for this teaching. It seems to me we can come to this realization without denigrating physical beauty."

"So you think we can appreciate physical beauty, yet be detached from it?"

"I would think so," I said.

"And how can you be detached from something so beautiful and with so much value?"

"Yes, I'd like to hear how you feel you could detach yourself from me," Elizabeth said with a mischievous smile.

"It looks like I backed myself into another corner," I laughed, looking at John.

"Don't look to me for help," he mused.

"OK, here's my answer," I said, "and I don't think Elizabeth will be offended. In the traditional Buddhist teaching, detachment from the carnal pull of the body is obtained by destroying its beauty in the student's mind. My approach would be, instead of destroying beauty by dissecting it to its ugly parts, one should see beyond the body to something with more beauty still. By seeing our spiritual essence, we see a beauty far greater than the body, and the beauty of the higher gives us power of detachment from the lower."

"So you're saying that even though you can detach yourself from my outer beauty, you will still see my inner beauty?" asked Elizabeth.

"Close enough," I said.

Elizabeth looked at me suspiciously. "Why do I get the feeling you're getting out of something?"

"Maybe he's learning more wisdom than I thought," John laughed. "Actually, both views are necessary. We need to realize that things of physical beauty are merely transient elements made of numerous parts which will someday have an end to their organization. Even so, we can appreciate the beauty of the creation and avoid attachment by realizing that a more permanent and glorious beauty lies ahead in the higher worlds."

"Glad to hear you say that," I said. "I thought the Buddhist teaching put way too much emphasis on the negative."

"You must also realize that there are many versions of Buddhism, just as there is Christianity," he said. "Some schools of thought are adjusting the teachings with a more positive slant. Now let us move on to the next contemplation. Tell us what you have learned."

I checked my notes again and replied, "The second contemplation, or Foundation of Mindfulness, is that of feeling. By feeling, they seem to mean the various feelings and sensations we receive through the six senses. Feeling arises when the consciousness perceives the outside world through touch, sight, hearing, taste, smell and mind. These feelings can be pleasurable, painful or neutral."

"And what does the teaching say about the negative results of these feelings?" he asked.

"Our attachment to these feelings, and the pleasure and pain they give, causes many of the vices we have. Too much attachment to the physical feeling of pleasure can cause sexual misconduct. Other pleasant feelings produce greed and selfishness. Pain and unpleasant feelings create hate, fear and jealously. Even neutral feelings can have a bad effect by creating a false sense of security and delusion."

"And what is the solution to detaching ourselves from the hold of these negative pulls?" he asked.

"The solution again falls back to Right Mindfulness. Instead of just letting the current of these sensations lead us to some dead end, we are supposed to observe them and never let one go by us unnoticed. The teaching is that if we do not pay attention to these feelings, they will dominate us. By applying the principle of mindfulness, paying attention and dismissing the feelings as not a part of our real self, they will have no hold on us."

"You've done your homework well," he said. "Now let us pick a negative feeling to see how mindfulness can diffuse it. Have you ever been jealous about Elizabeth?"

"I suppose," I said. "Right after we got married she was working in a job where this guy in her department seemed to idolize her. He was always doing little things for her and giving her gifts. At first he about drove me crazy."

"So did you pretend the feeling did not exist, or run it by your consciousness and analyze it?"

"I'm not one for sweeping things under the rug," I said. "I analyzed it a lot."

"And what did you come up with?"

"As I analyzed my feelings, I realized that if I did nothing they would not go away, but perhaps grow into something that would separate us. I shared my feelings with Elizabeth and she assured me that I had nothing to worry about."

"And how did you respond when she told you there was nothing to worry about?"

"At first it did not help, because I thought that would be the response I would receive even if there *was* something to worry about."

"So did you just leave the feeling hanging like that in your consciousness?"

"No," I responded. "I ran all my feelings and the facts of the situation by my consciousness many times."

"And what did you conclude?"

"The answer she gave me was more than words. There was something about the way she spoke about there being nothing to worry about that made me trust her."

"And what was that?" he asked.

"Several things," I said. "I analyzed the sound and tone of her voice. I considered that she had never lied to me. My feelings were also soothed by the fact that she did not overreact the way a guilty person often does. She was patient in explaining the situation. I added all the facts up and mentally concluded that Elizabeth would be faithful to me even though this guy at work adored her."

"So were you at peace after this?"

"Basically," I said. "Even though I managed my feelings so they did not interfere with the relationship, I still stayed tuned in to the guy, just in case and asked Elizabeth questions about her work so I could get a feel as to the temptations she may be having."

"And here I thought you were just interested in my work," said Elizabeth, reaching over to squeeze my arm.

"That too," I added, injecting damage control. "I also checked him out at work functions and parties that I attended. I was a little disturbed by how he fawned over you and looked at you with syrupy eyes."

"He was just sweet," said Elizabeth. "But you had nothing to worry about." She took my hand and squeezed it. "He had none of the qualities that attracted me to you."

"So can we say this," continued John, "that by running all the feelings and details by your consciousness and objectively analyzing them, you diffused the negativity and made the relationship work?"

"I suppose that would be a correct statement," I replied. "Some of my friends thought I should just drop my feelings or pretend they did not exist."

"And what would have happened if you had ignored your feelings?"

"I think they would have resurfaced in a destructive way so I would have subtly sabotaged the relationship."

"You speak correctly," he said. "Negative feelings create an inward pressure like steam in a teapot. If there is no release valve, the pot looks like it is handling the pressure just fine; but if the pressure becomes too great, the whole thing will explode, causing much destruction. On the other hand, the release valve, which lets off excess steam, keeps the pot in functioning condition for a long time to come. By sharing your feelings with Elizabeth, and then analyzing the situation to make sure your negative feelings did not build up, you made your relationship work, and avoided the explosion that would have occurred if you had merely held everything in or went into a state of denial."

"So I take it that this harmonized with the teaching of the Buddha that we learn to cease identifying with feelings by being aware of them and where they originate?"

"Exactly," said John. "The average person creates many problems for himself by identifying too strongly with his physical nature and his feelings. Instead, he must take the viewpoint of the observer, and by observing, understand where sensation and feeling originate. When he realizes they are not a part of his true self, he can then construct release valves that place them under his control."

He then sat back in his chair, raised his arms and stretched. "So what is the third contemplation?"

I looked at my notes again and said, "It is the Contemplation of the State of Mind."

"Which means…?"

"Some of what I read on this is a little confusing. The basic idea seems to be we associate our identity with our state of mind, which could be happiness or unhappiness. Our state could be determined by our education, or status in the world, the money we make, the family and friends we have and so on. We are to examine our various states of mind until we realize that the mind is a vehicle we *use* and not a part of our true reality."

"Yes," John said. "The same principle we have been discussing applies here. Again, we must examine our states of mind until we realize these are mere ingredients to our temporary makeup. All states of mind experience change, and all that changes has a beginning *and* an end. Now what is the final contemplation?"

"The fourth is the Contemplation of Phenomena. Apparently, we are supposed to examine all that has or gives appearance, and contemplate the reason behind it."

"Yes," said John. "All that appears real is merely an effect of an underlying cause. When one is finally able to not be distracted by that which is not real, and place his attention on the real, he has achieved a one-pointed concentration necessary to any advance in consciousness. This finally brings us to the eighth directive of the Noble Eightfold Path. Tell us what you have on this."

I took another look at my notes and after a moment I responded, "The eighth is called *samma samadhi,* which is usually translated as *Right Concentration.* Samadhi literally means *to direct towards,* so the word *concentration* seems to fit the bill. It is interesting that all three last directives are under the category of Concentration and the very last directive also bears this name."

"And how is *samma samadhi*, or Right Concentration, attained?" he asked.

"It seems to be the culmination of many exercises ending with the seeker being able to concentrate on an object and become one with it, to tuning out all thoughts and entering a state of bliss, or Nirvana. A lot of details are written on this. The yogi seems to achieve complete self mastery and the highest state of union to the extent that worldly ideas and passions have no hold upon him. Someone wrote that it is *the state of being aware of one's existence without thinking*."

"Yes," said John reflectively. "There are many details written that are supposed to aid along the path to *samma samadhi* and books have been written on it, but what we want to explore tonight is the core principle behind it. What do you think it is?"

"I've been thinking on this also; the more I read the more confused I get. All I can do is guess that the core principle has something to do with self mastery, or mastery of thought which leads to union with the Spirit."

"It does involve mastery of thought to the extent that the mind can take a thought and concentrate on it with one-pointedness," he said. "But this is the process and not the principle. Now think. What is a word that describes the process of focusing your thoughts in a concentrated manner upon one image, thought or idea?"

As I was pausing in thought, Elizabeth joined in, "I would say the word would be contemplation."

"I would say you are correct," said John. He looked at Elizabeth and continued, "and what have you two been contemplating since you met me?"

"I suppose that would be the Keys of Knowledge," she said.

"Yes, and you are currently in the process of contemplating

the second key, which will be discovered by Right Concentration, or we could say Right Contemplation. Have you ever had a problem or question that bothered you, and you thought and thought about the answer over some period of time, and then suddenly out of the blue, in a flash, the whole answer comes to you?"

"Yes," I exclaimed. "I've had that happen to me a number of times. It is a wonderful experience."

"That is the true end product of Eightfold Path, and the real beginning of experiencing Nirvana."

"I never thought of getting a flash of inspiration as being Nirvana," I said.

"And just where is Nirvana?" he asked.

"A world or state beyond any form," I replied.

"And where does an inspired idea or principle come from?" he asked. "Does it come from a world of form?"

"It doesn't seem to," I said. "When I contemplate and receive an inspired answer, it seems to come out of nowhere."

"All true inspiration and understanding of principles comes from Nirvana, or the formless worlds," he injected.

"Interesting," I said. "I would have never made that connection."

"All the disciplines and exercises of the Buddhists are elementary preparations for true Right Concentration. If you have power in current time to contemplate and receive the flashing forth of light, then you have already completed these disciplines in one form or another in past lives. He who has mastered Right Concentration has the power to focus his mind with one intent upon a thought or an assortment of data in search for greater light. Once the thought has been sufficiently focused, it develops a life of its own and hangs in the background of the thinker's mind. Then one day, at a certain moment, the veil between heaven and earth is broken and instant enlightenment comes."

"From some of my readings it sounds as if the end of *samma samadhi* is to attain a type of consciousness that transcends thinking and brings some type of union with the divine."

"Here is a key to keep in your consciousness," said John. "Every step the seeker makes in true progress toward the divine will bring him greater power and usefulness within that sphere wherein his labor will lie. If you see a man who claims unspeakable transcendence with God, yet is of little use to God or man in the world, then the mastery of the encounter has yet to be won.

"It is true that many have spent numerous lifetimes as monks, nuns and holy men withdrawing from the world. Yet, if they are not producing useful service, or good fruits from their activities, we know the intended lesson for them is not complete. Withdrawal and focus is only the first half of the equation. The second half is to link heaven and earth, and bring down ideas from above that are usable for humanity. Many of our great scientists, inventors and creative thinkers have spent a dozen or more lifetimes in religious orders where they went through techniques similar to those in Buddhism to learn right concentration.

"Scientists and inspired thinkers have a reputation for being absent-minded. Einstein and Edison are two notable examples. When Einstein went for a walk, he was sometimes so absorbed in thought that he lost track of where he was, and had to catch his bearing to find his way back home. This absent-mindedness which is so common among thinkers has been seen as a nuisance to those who have it, and often an extreme aggravation to those in relationship with the person. In reality, it is often caused by a mind so focused that the lower mind is tuned out and the higher consciousness tuned in. Such a person in contemplation is often unknowingly in this state of Samadhi."

"I've always been absent-minded and sometimes thought it was a curse."

"John," spoke Elizabeth "don't encourage this man. If he thinks he's in Nirvana when he forgets things because he is not paying attention, he will become unbearable. He tries my patience the way it is."

"That's just the price to pay for being married to a visionary," smiled John. "When Joseph seems to be off in another world, he sometimes is. The intuitive world is a very pleasant place to be and makes it difficult to pay attention to general physical reality."

"Make a note, Elizabeth, that John called me a visionary." I said grinning. "That's the first good word that has ever been said about my lack of attention toward the real world, as people call it."

Elizabeth frowned, "I'm just worried that your attention span on things, such as chores around the house, will get even worse now that John has given you a compliment."

"I don't think he will get any worse," John smiled. "At his age, he already has a number of routine chores and actions on automatic pilot, and these will continue to serve him."

"Automatic pilot," said Elizabeth thoughtfully. "That's a good description of his driving also. I'll sometimes send him to the store and he'll wind up at the office because he set the wrong auto pilot in his mind. He often does not catch his error because his mind is off in another world."

"I kind of kick myself over the time I waste though," I replied. "I am somewhat relieved that you put this in a positive light for me."

"At least we have placed Right Concentration in a context that many people will understand. We have now finished the eight directives of the Noble Eightfold Path. There is much more that could be said about them, as well as hundreds of books touching upon them, but we have met the goal of summarizing them in a way that will relate to the Western mind."

"So what's next?" I asked. "Are you going to give us any more hints concerning the second key word to the Middle Way Principle?"

John grabbed my hand across the table and squeezed it. "My friend, do you not realize that each time I have taught you about one of the ingredients of the Eightfold Path, I have been giving you hints aplenty?"

"I wish I had realized that. Maybe I would have paid more attention, or should I say a more selective attention."

"Pick at random one of the paths," he directed.

I looked at my list and said *Right Speech.*

"A powerful hint indeed," he said, shaking his head. You cannot arrive at Right Speech without the second Key."

"How about *Right Action* then?"

"Another powerful hint, if you think about it. What do you need to do before you can take a right action?"

"I guess you need to make a decision."

"But what must precede the decision?"

"Thought."

"And what comes between thought and the decision?"

"Contemplation."

"And what comes between contemplation and the decision?"

"Hmmmm," I thought to myself. "Let me think about this a moment."

John sat back in his chair and said, "Have you heard the story of the blind men and the elephant?"

"Yes!" Elizabeth exclaimed. "I *love* that parable."

"What you may not know is that it was created by the Buddha and demonstrates the value of the Second Key. He knew the Second Key would be lost, but this story would never die. Since that time long ago, it has circulated in many forms, but always carrying with it a poignant teaching."

"Interesting," I said.

"Would you like to hear how he teaches the parable today?"

"The Buddha still teaches today?"

"You don't think he spends all his time slumbering in Nirvana, do you?"

"I never thought about it."

"His consciousness is, of course, in Nirvana, or the kingdom of God, but this does not keep him from teaching exchange students in the halls of Shamballa, or the lodges of the Masters."

"I would like to hear the parable as he teaches it today," injected Elizabeth.

"And you shall have it," John added.

"Wait and let me go get my tape recorder. Would you mind?" asked Joseph.

"As long as you don't share the recording with others it will be fine," warned John.

"If I'm going to be writing this into a book, I want to get it perfect." Joseph excused himself and retrieved the recorder and set it up. "Okay, I'm ready."

After taking a moment to get comfortable in his chair, John began.

Three Blind Men and the Elephant

In a mountainous village in India, there once lived three blind men named Amol, Gayathie and Shahi, each belonging to a different family. At least once a week their families met in the Village to shop, and left the three men together to share tea and stories at a bench near the market.

Young boys would often play with them, have them hold various object in their hands, and guess what they were. Sometimes the blind men would guess accurately, but other times they were so far off it would make the boys laugh.

Then one day a man came into the village on an elephant. Now in this particular location, it was a special occasion for an elephant to be passing through, so its presence created a lot of excitement, especially for the boys and young people.

The three blind men sensed the excitement and became very curious about the elephant. Finally, several of the young boys came to sit beside them. "Tell us about the elephant," said Amol.

"Has no one ever explained to you about the elephant?" said the boy.

"We know the elephant is a big animal but no one has ever described it to us," said Gayathie. "Our families just tell us that we would have to see one to understand."

"I've got an idea," said one of the boys. "The elephant is tied up a short distance from us. Let us escort these three men to the elephant and have them touch and feel it and see what they come up with."

"Excellent idea," said another boy. "We can even take bets on how close they get."

The three blind men were happy to oblige and allowed the boys to lead them to the elephant. As they approached, it was patiently standing, awaiting the return of its owner.

"You go first," said one of the boys to Amol.

"Just point me in the right direction," he said. This the boys did and Amol walked fearlessly toward the elephant. After several steps he bumped into a back leg. He then steadied himself and put his arms around the leg. Then he ran his hand up and down the leg, feeling the length and texture of it.

Amol withdrew and stated, "OK. I am ready to describe the elephant."

The boys laughed amongst themselves, wondering what kind of description Amol would come up with by feeling the leg only. "So, give us your description," challenged one of the boys.

Amol stared with wonderment in his blind eyes and said, "The elephant is like a great tree that stretches into the sky. It must indeed be unlike any other animal on the earth."

Upon hearing this, Gayathie spoke out and said, "Let me also touch the elephant."

But the clever boys did not point him to the same part of the elephant, but toward the front part. As Gayathie approached the elephant, his hands grabbed on to the trunk. As he began to grasp it tightly the elephant became alarmed and with a mighty sweep threw Gayathie to the side, roughing him up a bit. As he stood up and composed himself, the boys asked, "Tell us, our friend. How would you describe the elephant?"

"It is clear to me that Amol did not understand the elephant," he said. "Perhaps it was asleep when he touched it. The elephant must be the greatest of snakes for I felt its powerful snake body, which tossed me like a leaf. People need to be warned to stay away from these creatures."

Upon hearing these two differing descriptions Shahi became very curious and said, "I too must touch the elephant so I can judge for myself. Guide me toward the elephant."

Now the boys were getting a good laugh out of the two deceptive descriptions and decided to add even more fun to their game. "Take my hand," said one of the boys, "and I will guide you to the elephant."

A second boy built a crude ladder out of several boxes, placed Shahi on the top, and laid the ear of the elephant in his hands. Shahi carefully felt the shape and texture of the ear and exclaimed, "It is enough. I have solved the mystery. Neither of my friends was correct. The elephant is neither like a tree or a snake, but is like a living carpet."

Upon hearing this, the boys chuckled amongst themselves, but Amol and Gayathie began to stridently disagree with Shahi. The boys, feeling satisfied they had pulled off a clever trick, left the three blind men arguing amongst themselves.

Now their arguing did not cease. For the next several weeks, each time they met, they spent the whole time arguing about the truth of the elephant. Those who passed by listened with amusement, but no one wanted to spoil the fun and tell them the truth. In fact, the three were so dogmatic in their views that they did not *want* to hear any contradiction.

One day a holy man with higher spiritual vision came into town and began to teach people to see with the inner eye. Then one of his students said to him, "You've got to go to the market and listen to the three blind men argue about the elephant."

The holy man was curious, approached the blind men and stood beside them for a few minutes.

"I tell you the elephant is like a tree. I felt it with my own two hands," said Amol.

"You are wrong. It is like a snake," said Gayathie.

"You are both confused, for I felt a living carpet within my two hands," said Shahi.

And thus did the conversation seem to continue endlessly. Finally, the holy man spoke, "My friends, do you not realize that you have been feeling in the dark, and because of the darkness you may all be incorrect? I have come to bring true inner vision, and in finding this your outer vision can also be restored."

"Are you saying that our sight can be restored?" asked Shahi. "How could this be?"

"The inner precedes the outer," said the man. "Right now, you are not only physically blind, but you also talk as blind men, refusing to even see the other's point of view. Do you think your other two friends are lying to you? I tell you the answer is no. Learn to see the truth in what your friends are saying and then your vision can return. I shall come back to you in three days to see if you have accomplished this."

After the holy man left Amol asked, "Is it truly possible that our vision could return?"

"I do not know for sure," said Gayathie, "but I have heard that this holy man has performed miracles before."

"Then it is worth it to follow his advice," said Shahi. "What have we got to lose?"

For the first time the three men started working in cooperation. Amol said, "The holy man told us that none of us are lying. This means that I did feel something that was like a tree, Gayathie felt something that was like a snake, and Shahi touched something that was like a living carpet. If we truly all felt correctly and are telling the truth, then what is the explanation?"

Suddenly a light went on in Shahi's head. "There can only be one explanation," he said. "None of us felt the whole elephant, but only parts of it. Do you not remember the mischievous boys laughing when we told them our description? They were seeing the whole elephant, so our description of the parts seemed amusing to them."

"I think you are correct," said Gayathie. "Why, those boys deserve a good spanking!"

"Forget about the boys," said Shahi. "Do you not realize what this means? It means that the true elephant may be unlike anything we have pictured, but it will have all the parts we felt. Now Amol felt something that was like a tree, but perhaps this was merely a giant leg."

"That's possible," said Amol, "but what part would Gayathie's snake have been?"

"Perhaps the elephant has many tentacles, like sea monsters we have heard of," said Gayathie. "But what part could something that feels like a carpet be?"

"It could have been some type of protective covering, or even a large ear," said Shahi."

"Do you know what just occurred to me?" said Amol excitedly. "It is entirely possible that the elephant has many parts that we were unable to touch. Could it be that a complete vision of the elephant would reveal an animal totally different than anything we have imagined?"

"Yes, that is possible," said Gayathie, "but the interesting thing is that even if the picture of the whole is different than we have imagined, that part we have touched and perceived will be accurate.

"An interesting thought indeed," said Shahi.

And thus did the conversation of the three blind men turn friendly and cooperative. During the next three days, they received much enjoyment and stimulation by comparing notes and making different guesses as to the true nature of the elephant.

Finally, the holy man returned and questioned them. He was pleased with their progress and stated, "Before, each of you were only concerned with being right. You wanted to be the one who described the true elephant. But now you trust each other and evaluate one another's experience, and have developed a true desire to see-more than the desire to be right. Tell me. If your vision is restored, are you willing to drop all preconceived notions and accept the true shape of the elephant, no matter how wrong you have been in your guesswork?"

They all agreed to this.

"Behold, an elephant is in the market today. Let us go forth and see him."

The holy man then led the three blind men to the market and stood them before the elephant. From his robe he withdrew a small container of holy salve and rubbed it on their eyes. "Now clear your eyes - look and see!" he declared.

The men blinked, rubbed their eyes, and to their amazement they saw light followed by forms. Amol was the first to see the elephant. "What on earth is this strange creature?" he asked.

"That's your elephant," laughed the holy man.

"But it cannot be," said Gayathie. "Where are the snake-like tentacles?"

"Touch its trunk," said the man.

Gayathie touched its trunk and exclaimed. "Yes. That is what I felt. This animal's strange nose is what I perceived as a snake or tentacle."

"And we were right that the part that was like a tree is merely a large leg," said Amol.

"But where is the carpet?" asked Shahi.

"That giant ear has to be your carpet," said Amol. "Remember how the boys lifted you up on boxes?"

"Yes. Yes," said Shahi. "That must be it."

As they were marveling among themselves, the holy man pulled them aside and pointed in the distance. "There is much more to see and discover besides the elephant. A whole world awaits your exploration."

Thus the three previously blind men went forth, transformed into men of vision: to see, to explore, and to serve their brethren.

CHAPTER TWENTY-SIX
The Key Word

"That's a beautiful parable," I said as I turned off the recorder. "I would like to be able to write something like that."

"What makes you think you can't?" he said.

"I guess I've never thought about writing in that direction," I said. "I've always had great respect for parables and to think of writing one is like attempting to write new scripture. It almost seems like sacrilege to try."

John smiled and said, "You don't need any authority from God or man to write parables or *any* truth as you see it. A parable, written correctly, transmits the truth as well as any scripture and the points of truth contained therein are almost impossible to refute. The writer of accurate parables must touch the soul, and, when he does, he will write that which lies beyond his normal intelligence. Therefore, I give you a new assignment. Use the principle of Right Contemplation and write parables."

"But what am I to write about?"

"Just meditate on the idea of writing parables and at the right time the material will come. You have the proven ability. Trust me."

"Thanks for the vote of confidence," I said. "I'll see what I can do."

"Meanwhile, are we ever going to get to the key word?" injected Elizabeth.

"I'll work with you," said John, "but you must make an effort to discover it. Have you figured out what comes between contemplation and a decision?"

"It could be a couple of things." I said. "What happens if we guess incorrectly?"

"Then you'll have to wait until the next lesson to try again."

"I'm also getting impatient and want to get this over with. Can I ask a couple of questions?" I said.

"Go ahead."

"You said there are major hints in the eight directives we have been discussing. Is this correct?"

"Yes."

"Now, you specifically said there was a major hint in the two I named, which was Right Speech and Right Action. Is this correct?"

"Yes again."

"Is the major hint in the explanation you gave us of the directives, or the directives themselves?"

"Both," he smiled.

"So this means there is a major hint in the wording of the directives themselves?"

"Correct."

"Well, there are only four words in the two I just quoted – Right Speech and Right Action. I don't see the words *speech* and *action* as much of a hint. Could it have something to do with the word *right*?"

"What do you think?" replied John.

"That's it, isn't it? Why didn't I think of it before? Each one of the eight directives begins with the word *right*! This has to be the major clue. In fact, if I remember correctly, you placed special emphasis on this word and discussed the translation."

"And do you remember what I said?"

"Let me think," I replied in an attempt to recall his words. "I remember you said there is not agreement among Buddhists as to how the Pali word *samma* was to be translated. They think the word *right* implies dualism, which they wish to dismiss. They have come up with some less dualistic translations. What did you say they were?"

"I mentioned holistic, wise, high and perfect."

"Then I asked you which of the translations was the closest."

"And he said the word *right* is the most accurate," added Elizabeth.

"Yes," I noted. "When faced with a decision, whether it is an action, speech or any of the other directives, we are faced with a choice between two or more alternatives or paths. One of the paths will be the right one and the others will be wrong, or perhaps I should say, not so right."

"That's not a popular line of thinking," said John. "Many Buddhists do not believe in right or wrong in the Western sense, and this concept, that there is no wrong decision, is gaining in popularity in the West."

"Yet, each directive in the Eightfold Path, as embraced by all Buddhists, begins with the word *right*. If there is a right action or thought, this means there has to be a wrong action or thought also. It is becoming clear to me why many Buddhists do not like this word *right,* especially if they see themselves as being beyond the dualities. Yet the funny thing is that almost every English translation used this word for all the directives."

"And why do you suppose that is?" asked John

"I suppose it is because the word is the most accurate, as you told us."

"Think on this," said John. "Many Buddhists see the truths in the Eightfold Path as being beyond duality. Many also see their consciousness as beyond duality. Now if the major hint of the lost Key lies in the word *right*, a word that can only have meaning in duality, what does this tell you?"

"It tells me that the key to the Middle Way was lost because the key lies hidden in duality. Because the Buddhists put so much energy in looking beyond duality they have also looked beyond the key and lost it."

"That would be almost as astounding as Christianity losing the meaning of the word *love*," said Elizabeth.

"Christianity is struggling today to find their key word, which is indeed love," he replied, "but many times in the past 2000 years has its meaning been lost. Today a small number with sincere hearts are rediscovering it. But you are right. Just as the standard Christian consciousness looked beyond their key word, so have the Buddhists. Any more questions?"

"OK. So I am at a crossroads, faced with the choice of a right action. I can either take the road on the left or the right. I gather the details, contemplate, and just before I make the decision, I use the key. Is this correct?"

"Basically."

"Now my thought goes back to the story of the moment that Buddha was said to receive enlightenment on the Middle Way. When he was seeking enlightenment through starving himself to death he heard a song that inspired him. The words he heard spoken were something to the effect that if you tightened the strings of a harp too tight, they will break, but if you do not tighten them enough they will not make a good sound. They have to be tightened just right to produce pleasing music. Here we have this word *right* showing up again. The Buddha was inspired by these words and concluded that our minds are like strings that must have right adjustment to function correctly."

"Have you ever tuned a stringed instrument?" asked John.

"I've tuned a guitar," I said.

"And how do you know a string is in tune?"

"You harmonize it with another note from a piano or another string which you know is in tune."

"Is the original note ever exactly in tune?"

"You use an original note that is so in tune that the human ear cannot detect any disharmony, but because there are technically millions of gradations in sound, there would be no way to declare that any particular note is exactly in tune." I said.

"And when you tune a new string to be in harmony with the first, do you think you ever achieve an exact harmony in vibration? In other words, do both strings vibrate at exactly the same number of repetitions per second?"

"As I said, the vibrations will be close enough that it sounds the same to the human ear, but it may not be exact."

"So when you tune a string, you adjust the sound up and down and then stop when it seems to make the same sound as the original tuning note. Is this correct?"

"Yes," I said.

"So, as you are moving the sound of the string up and down the scale, what inherit ability do you use to decide exactly where you are going to stop?"

My eyes lit up. "I think I finally have the key word. There is only one thing it could be. I can see now that when I am faced with a decision, especially a difficult one, I must use this key to insure that my decisions are wise."

"I think I see the key also," said Elizabeth. "The only thing that makes me doubt is seeing how it relates to the parable of the Three Blind Men."

"Good point," said John. "Why were the three blind men so deceived at first?"

"Because they only felt one piece if the elephant," she said.

"They only felt one piece of the elephant, but how many pieces should they have had knowledge of?"

"I suppose it should have been three pieces, because the three blind men shared their perceptions."

"Yet even though they had information on three pieces to the puzzle, each insisted on using just only his own piece. Why?"

"I suppose they didn't trust each other," she replied.

"The answer goes beyond trust. Think again."

"I think they were just mentally lazy," I ventured. "It's human nature to want to just touch or see one thing and have *it* be the answer. They do not want to go to the trouble to put pieces together and then assess a more complete answer."

"Exactly," said John. "The moment they ceased their mental laziness and started comparing notes was the time they began using the second key. You'll note that the use of the key did not immediately give them a complete picture of the elephant, but it did immediately increase their knowledge and take them in the direction of full vision."

"I can see how the word I have fits now," said Elizabeth.

"Are you ready to give it to me?"

"Just a moment," I said. "I want to confer with my partner here."

I pulled Elizabeth aside and asked her what key word she came up with. She whispered it in my ear and I was pleased to hear she came up with the same one I did. We sat back at the table and I said. "We're pretty confident that we have it, we both came up with the same word."

"And you both could be wrong."

"That's true," I said, sounding a little downcast.

"And what do you sense from within?" he asked.

"I feel confident the word is correct."

"Even though it is one of the most maligned words in human

speech?

"Now I know we have the correct word; it certainly is a word which has fallen into disrepute."

"So, what are you waiting for? Give me the word."

"Judgment," I replied.

"And why was it so difficult for you to come up with this word?"

"Well, for one thing, most Buddhists writings I have read teach that judgment is a negative quality that needs to be overcome. I had a difficult time believing this could be the missing key of the Buddha when most of them teach against using it."

"Christians are also teaching not to judge," added Elizabeth.

"Not to mention most new age and metaphysical groups," I added.

"Correct," he said, "but you would be amazed if you realized how often the majority are wrong on a point of philosophy. Jesus talked about the wide gate where the many would go and the straight one that few would find. The true reality of a teaching is always seen by the few and the illusion seen by the many. This will slowly change as the balance on the earth shifts from darkness to light in the minds of humanity, but the rule still holds sway. The truth of the keyword should have been easily discernable from the story connected with Buddha's enlightenment. When a string is tuned correctly it is neither too loose nor too tight, but just right to make a pleasant sound. To achieve a fine tuning the musician must tighten and loosen the string until his judgment tells him it sounds right. Think of it. There is no exact tightness through some black and white formula; a judgment call must be made, and the higher the quality of judgment, the more finely tuned will be the instrument."

"That makes sense," I said. "You're right, I do feel kind of silly not seeing this, but I think it is the negative attitude that so many have toward this word that made me overlook it."

"And this point is perhaps as important a lesson as the key word itself. Misleading thoughts in the minds of the masses can create a pull that can distort the interplay between the seeker and his soul. This is why Jesus told us we must become like a little child to see the kingdom of heaven. If you had sought with the freshness of a child, you would have had no preconceived notions about this word and would have seen it much earlier. As it was, your adult mind, which is full of distracting data, shifted your vision away from your soul and the truth."

"I indeed feel within my soul that you are correct here. I am committing myself to not let preconceived notions mislead me again."

"Recommit yourself each time this happens to any degree, and you will know the truth and the truth shall make you free," he said.

"But how do you explain the fact that Jesus told us not to judge?" asked Elizabeth.

"But did he?" replied John.

"Yes. I'm sure he did," she said, not sounding too confident.

"And where did he say such a thing?" he asked.

"I think I can find the passage you are talking about," I said, and opened the Bible to Matthew chapter seven and read the first five verses:

"*Judge not, that ye be not judged. For with what judgment ye judge, ye shall be judged: and with what measure ye mete, it shall be measured to you again. And why beholdest thou the mote that is in thy brother's eye, but considerest not the beam that is in thine own eye? Or how wilt thou say to thy brother, Let me pull out the mote out of thine eye; and, behold, a beam is in thine own eye? Thou hypocrite, first cast out the beam out of thine own eye; and then shalt thou see clearly to cast out the mote out of thy brother's eye.*"

"See. He's telling us not to judge," said Elizabeth.

"He's not telling us not to judge," said John, "but how to judge. There is a big difference. Instead of telling us not to judge, he is warning us against making a bad judgment. What does he say happens to us when we make a judgment?"

"He says that the type of judgment we give out will come back to us," I said.

"And if you make a condemning judgment, what will then come back?"

"It sounds like you'll be condemned in return," I said.

"And what would come back to you if you made an accurate positive judgment that inspired someone to change his life for good?" he asked, looking at Elizabeth.

"I suppose you would be judged positively in return," she

replied.

"Read verse two again," he said.

I read, "*For with what judgment ye judge, ye shall be judged: and with what measure ye mete, it shall be measured to you again.*"

"And what meaning do you get from this verse?"

"It's not telling us to not judge," I said, "but how our judgment will affect us. It's basically the law of karma. Both good and bad judgment will come back to us. He seems to be warning us against bad judgment."

"Exactly," said John, "and this is how we understood him and we sat at his feet. Now read again verses three and four."

I read, "*And why beholdest thou the mote that is in thy brother's eye, but considerest not the beam that is in thine own eye? Or how wilt thou say to thy brother, Let me pull out the mote out of thine eye; and, behold, a beam is in thine own eye?*"

"Here he gives the reason for bad judgment. What is it?"

"We can't see to pull a tiny sliver out of our neighbor's eye when we have a beam obscuring our own vision," I said. "In other words, we cannot judge or correct the fault of another when our own faults may be much worse."

"Correct. Now, verse five tells us how to make correct judgments."

I continued reading, "*Thou hypocrite, first cast out the beam out of thine own eye; and then shalt thou see clearly to cast out the mote out of thy brother's eye.*"

"So what is the key to good judgment?" he asked, looking at Elizabeth.

Elizabeth reflected a moment and spoke, "I suppose we must work on our own faults first. Then when become proficient in a certain area, we can see how we can judge and assist our neighbor."

"Have you noticed that most critical and overly judgmental people seem to have faults to a greater degree than those whom they are judging?" he asked.

"It really seems that way to me," I said. "I know I have faults, but I find it very annoying to be critically judged by someone who is in worse shape than I am."

"And why do you suppose this happens so often?" he asked.

"I think people see a reflection, or perhaps a projection, of their own faults," added Elizabeth. "Sometimes judgmental people tend to describe themselves with pinpoint accuracy when they criticize others."

"You are describing the principle here. If one has a beam in his own eye, he can only see a blur and will not have a clue about the particle in the eye of his neighbor. Now we have established that Jesus was condemning judgment of a condemning nature, especially judgment which is obscured by our own faults. On the other hand, he does encourage good judgment in the scriptures. Now turn to, John 7:24."

I opened the Bible and read, "*Judge not according to the appearance, but judge righteous judgment.*"

"Is he telling us here to not judge at all?"

"No," I replied. "He seems to be telling us to not judge by appearances, but to look deeper to judge correctly."

"Jesus explained why he could make a righteous judgment. You can read this in John 5:30."

"I notice we are reading a lot of the scriptures you wrote," I observed.

"Maybe I'm a little biased," he smiled.

I then read the following, "*I can of mine own self do nothing: as I hear, I judge: and my judgment is just; because I seek not mine own will, but the will of the Father which hath sent me.*"

"And why could Jesus judge correctly?" he asked.

"It seems to have something to do with following the will of God," I said.

"It has a lot to do with it," he said. "Until we receive a degree of the enlightenment that Buddha spoke of, we see through the eyes of the lower nature, which distorts reality and spiritual vision. But then when we seek to be one with he who is higher than ourselves, we see through the eyes of a higher angle of vision. This allows us to judge accurately without interference from our preconceived notions. In between living in the lower nature and enlightenment we must learn to use our minds and exercise the wisdom of common sense. Buddha spoke of this. Hand me your printout of the Dhammapada."

I found my copy of the Dhammapada, which contained some teachings of Buddha. John thumbed through them and pointed to a paragraph on page 256 and told me to read, which I did.

"To pass judgment hurriedly doesn't mean you're a judge. The wise one who weighs the right judgment & wrong, the intelligent one who judges others impartially, unhurriedly, in line with the Dhamma, guarding the Dhamma, guarded by Dhamma: he's called a judge."

John listened and responded, "Dhamma, or Dharma, is used in a number of different contexts today. Most associate it specifically with the teachings that Buddha produced, but the meaning goes beyond this. Just as the path and the truths that the Buddha discovered were his Dharma, even so do we discover Dharma of our own.

"Just as Buddha went on a search for enlightenment, even so does each one of us eventually make the quest. Our quest may not be so intense or cause a change in world teachings, but our discovery will dramatically change our own world. When the seeking pilgrim discovers a new realm of truth that is his soul destiny to absorb, and clearly sees the path he is to tread, he has discovered his dharma. It may not be the same dharma as found by the Buddha, but it will be specially designed by your soul for your own spiritual progress.

"In addition to this soul dharma, there is a lesser dharma for the lower personality. Each life has a lesson to learn for each incarnating soul. This lower personality lesson is a lesser dharma that each entity must solve in an incarnation. Now keeping this in mind, see if you can interpret the phrase quoted by Buddha. First, what does it mean to judge *others impartially, unhurriedly, in line with the Dharma?*"

I reflected a moment and replied, "To judge others in line with Dharma, as you explained the word, would mean that we must make judgments in harmony with the highest truth we have revealed to us. This should not deviate from the highest path we see we must tread."

"In other words, our judgments must be in alignment with our own soul knowledge," he said. "Now what about the next phrase, *guarding the Dharma*?"

"I would suppose this would mean that we must be careful how we judge so bad judgment does not take us away from our path."

"Excellent," said John. "Now the final one – *guarded by*

Dharma."

"This would mean the reverse is true. We not only guard against bad judgment taking us off the path, but we must be guided by our highest spiritual knowledge to insure good judgment."

"You speak, my friend, through the Oneness Principle, and answer as I would answer. Continue to meditate on this principle, for you will need to use it when you teach others as I teach you."

He paused a moment in thought and continued, "As a final spiritual confirmation, you might check the word *judgment* as it is used throughout the Old Testament. It is almost always used in a positive sense there, but one of its most interesting uses is in reference to those who were placed as judges over the people of Israel. Now turn to Exodus 22:6 and read the first line."

I turned to the verse and read, "*Then his master shall bring him unto the judges...*"

"Now get your concordance and look up the word judges."

I retrieved my Strong's Concordance and found the verse. "It says here the word *judges* comes from word number 430."

"Now look up word number 430," he said.

I looked it up and was stunned. "It says here word 430 is ELOHIYM. This is the same word that is translated as the God who created heaven and earth in the first verse of Genesis. Why would the judges in Israel be called ELOHIYM, and why was ELOHIYM translated as judges?"

"Why do you think?"

"I have a number of thoughts racing through my mind, but I am not sure."

"First let me illustrate that this use was not a one time fluke. Now read Exodus 22:8-89."

I found the reference and read, "*If the thief be not found, then the master of the house shall be brought unto the judges (ELOHIYM - gods), to see whether he have put his hand unto his neighbor's goods. For all manner of trespass, whether it be of ox for ass, for sheep, for raiment, or for any manner of lost thing, which another challengeth to be his, the cause of both parties shall come before the judges (gods); and the judges (gods) shall condemn, he shall pay double unto his neighbor*."

"Notice here that the word *judge* is used three times. Check your concordance again and tell me the originating Hebrew word."

I checked and exclaimed, "Again it is ELOHIYM!"

"And what does this tell you."

"Since Elohiym is the Hebrew word for God, this tells me that the ancient judges in Israel were called Gods."

"Very good," he said. "Even most modern versions mistranslate this, but the word is translated correctly a few sentences later in your King James. Read verse 28."

I read, "Thou shalt not revile the gods, nor curse the ruler of the people."

"This is another reference to the judges, but here the word Elohiym is correctly translated as Gods. Another enlightening scripture is found in Psalms 82:1. Elizabeth, it's your turn to read."

We found the verse and Elizabeth read, "*God standeth in the congregation of the mighty; he judgeth among the gods*."

"So who are the gods that the Big Guy judges among?"

"Could it be the judges?" she replied.

"Read the next sentence," he said.

She read, "*How long will ye judge unjustly*?"

"Does this sound like he is speaking to Israelites who judge and are also called Elohiym or gods?"

"It does sound like it," she said.

"In this chapter, God is chastising the judges, who are called gods, for not living up to their Elohiym title. Even though they did not live up to expectations, he acknowledged again their station. Read verse six in Psalms 82."

Elizabeth read, "I have said, *Ye are gods; and all of you children of the most high*."

"Notice he says *I have said*. When did god call judges Gods?"

"In the verse we just read in Exodus from the time of Moses."

"As further affirmation, Jesus makes a reference to Psalms 82:6. Turn to John chapter ten verses 34-36 and read."

Elizabeth turned to the verse and read, "*Jesus answered them, Is it not written in your law, I said, Ye are gods? If he called them gods, unto whom the word of God came, and the scripture cannot be broken; Say ye of him, whom the Father hath sanctified, and sent into the world, Thou blasphemest; because I said, I am the Son of God*?"

"What did Jesus say the law called the ancient Israelites?"

"Gods."

"And why did he quote this scripture from Psalms?"

"He seems to be saying that it should be no big deal that he would be called the Son of God when the ancient judges were called Gods."

"Now the master question is why were the judges, those who exercised judgment among the people, called Gods? In other words, is there a relationship between the second key word of judgment and the power or life of God?"

"That's a fascinating question," I said. "The first key word was Decision, which directs us to who we are, which is the power that makes the decisions. I would guess that this power is common among all self-conscious lives, whether they are gods or men. The second key word is Judgment. A judgment must precede any wise decision. Could it be that the power of judgment must be used to manifest the power from God which is within us?"

"Very close," he said. "It is interesting that the word *judgment* is perhaps the most maligned word in the language, yet it is indeed the key to manifesting the powers of God among humanity. Now turn to Genesis 3:22."

I turned to the verse and read, "*And the Lord God said, Behold, the man is to become as one of us, to know good from evil.*"

"So after Adam and Eve partook of the tree knowledge of good and evil, what did he say would be their fate?" he asked.

"He says they would become *as one of us*, or as the gods, I suppose. Wow! You sure don't learn this stuff in Sunday School."

"Yes," said Elizabeth, "Any minister I know would have a cow if we showed him these things."

"They'd have a cow if they knew you were talking with me," he smiled. "Now look at verse 22 again. What did they have to know to become as one of the gods?"

"If they knew good from evil, they would become as one of US, or gods."

"And how does one know good from evil?" he asked.

"I suppose you have to make a judgment."

"It seems simple, doesn't it?" replied John. "But perhaps making a correct judgment of good and evil is not as simple as you learned in Sunday School. Now read Isaiah 5:20."

I turned and read, "*Woe unto them that call evil good, and good evil; that put darkness for light, and light for darkness; that put bitter for sweet, and sweet for bitter!*"

"So what was the problem among the people Isaiah was trying to teach?" he asked.

"It looks like the people were seeing everything as if it were upside down. They called good, evil; darkness, light; and the sweet, bitter. They must have been a confused bunch," I observed.

"No more confused than the people of this age," he said. "Discerning and making a correct judgment today is almost as difficult for the masses as ever. Now, to see how pervasive this error was in Old Testament times, turn to Psalms 14:1-4."

I handed the Bible to Elizabeth and she read, "*The fool hath said in his heart, There is no God. They are corrupt, they have done abominable works, there is none that doeth good. The LORD looked down from heaven upon the children of men, to see if there were any that did understand, and seek God. They are all gone aside, they are all together become filthy: there is none that doeth good, no, not one. Have all the workers of iniquity no knowledge? Who eat up my people as they eat bread, and call not upon the LORD.*"

"How many in the days of this scripture had knowledge of good?" he asked.

She reflected and replied, "It says that there was not one that did good, or understood, so perhaps no one at that time had the ability to judge good and evil."

"So let us contemplate what the prophets have told us. The peoples' understanding is often upside down; they call evil good and good evil, and there are times that not even one among the people has the knowledge to do good. Why do you suppose it is so difficult to correctly judge good from evil?" he asked.

"One reason in this age is that it seems that everyone, religious or non religious, seem to teach us not to judge. It is a very politically incorrect word to use," I said.

"The principle of judgment has been maligned in every age, for the powers of darkness seek to hide the powers of godliness from mankind," he said. "If mankind will learn to judge wisely, and use their power of decision, then unjust powers and authorities will no longer hold humanity imprisoned. Tell me, if people refuse to judge good from evil, will they ever know good from evil?"

"Perhaps not," I said.

"Yes. Perhaps not," he affirmed shaking his head. "Now let us take another short break and then we will finish up for the night."

CHAPTER TWENTY-SEVEN
Understanding the Key

It was becoming a ritual to gather around the table after our breaks John so thoughtfully gave us to keep us alert. "Could you clarify for me why the second key word is *judgment* rather than *discernment, perception* or some other word?" I asked.

John looked at me thoughtfully and replied, "Perhaps we should go back to the first key and expand from there. The first key word was *Decision*. This is the word that best describes the key, but is not the key itself. The key of who we are is that life essence within us which has the power to make decisions. Now this power can be used with randomness or through intelligent application. In the beginning of the evolution of a soul, decision is made with randomness, or by pure reaction; and intelligence, which existed as a mere seed, is developed through trial and error. An example of an average person using random decision-making is through the flipping of a coin. What do you suppose is an example of intelligent decision-making?"

"There are quite a number of things most people do not want to leave to the flip of a coin," I said. "For instance, what we do for a living, who we marry, where we will live and so on."

"You mean that if you were single and had to decide between marrying Elizabeth or some other female; you wouldn't just toss a coin?"

"Absolutely not," I replied emphatically.

"Would you use perception?"

"I suppose."

"How?"

"Well.... I'd take in how she looks, how she acts and how she responds, among other things."

"And all this data could be entered into a computer, couldn't it?" he asked.

"Yes."

"After you perceive data on the two, you then discern their qualities and note their differences. Correct?"

"I think so."

"But a computer program could make differentiations between various data, could it not?"

"Probably."

"But after the wise seeker perceives and discerns, he contemplates and makes a judgment. Can a computer do this?"

"I'm not sure."

"Let us suppose this," he continued. "We put the data concerning Elizabeth and another female into the computer. We place information on their looks, intelligence, sense of humor, height, weight, personality and any other items you can think of. After the data is entered, how could the computer be programmed to make a choice? For instance, would it pick the most attractive one?"

"I wouldn't imagine a computer program picking the least attractive one."

"Suppose the other female was a Hollywood starlet, more attractive than Elizabeth. Would you automatically pick her?"

"Hey, don't give him any ideas!" injected Elizabeth.

I smiled and answered, "No, but a computer could be programmed to give points to a number of alternatives and then make a decision on the one who scored the highest."

"So let us suppose that we found a female who could score more points than Elizabeth. Would you let a computer pick her over Elizabeth?"

"Of course not!"

"Why?"

"I would take everything into consideration, contemplate the two and, like you say, make a judgment."

"And do you think your judgment would always be predictable?"

"Some of my judgments may be, but many of them would not be. I don't think anyone could have predicted all the judgments I made in relation to Elizabeth throughout our relationship."

"Have you ever had a friend who you thought would marry a certain type of person, and he winds up picking someone who completely surprises you?"

"That has occurred a number of times. Right now I'm thinking of a jock-type friend who could have married any girl he wanted and he married a frumpy librarian type."

"Do you think a computer could have predicted this choice?"

"I don't think so," I said. "My computer brain certainly missed it."

"So what does this tell you about judgment?"

"It tells me that judgment is not predictable."

"Why is that?"

"I'm not sure. It seems to be closely linked to free will or the power of Decision," I said.

"Very good," said John. "When a person approaches a fork in the road, he first examines all the nuances of both paths. Secondly, he weighs all the benefits of the two. Thirdly, he makes a judgment as to which path is best for him. Finally, he uses his life essence that has power of decision and chooses a path. This choice usually follows his judgment."

"But not always?" I asked.

"You've heard the phrase *against my better judgment*?" he responded. "We usually choose according to our judgment, but sometimes we refuse to trust our judgment and decide contrary to it. Even though a judgment is tied to free will, the final decision is the ultimate act. A larger problem, however, is that many refuse to even make a judgment. This is partially due to the negative connotation associated with the word, as well as self-doubt and unrecognized fear that many people have. So what kind of decision would be made if judgment is either ignored or avoided?" he asked, looking at Elizabeth.

"It would be like depending on the flip of a coin," she said.

"That would sometimes be the case," he said, "but there is more to it than that for average humanity. If you are driving down the road and a child runs in front of you, what makes you decide to immediately stop? Is this a random choice like the flip of a coin?"

"Indeed, it is not the flip of a coin," affirmed Elizabeth.

"Do you make time to take in all the facts, contemplate and then make a judgment?"

"If I did that, the child would be dead," she said.

"What, then, makes you immediately slam on the breaks?"

"It's just a built-in reaction," she said.

"Caused by what?"

"I suppose it would be from my training when I first learned to drive," she said.

"Would you then agree that many choices which we call decisions are really mere reactions to internal programming?"

"Yes," she responded, "but would such a reaction even be a decision?"

"It is and it isn't," he replied. "It *is* in the aspect that you still have the free will to either put on the brakes or not. But your reaction to put on the brakes is based on an earlier decision made by you and your teachers concerning what you should do. Because your decision to be harmless is already made, you do not have to decide again in an emergency situation. There are many choices which we think are decisions, which are not; they are mere reactions to past programming and are void of judgment. Can you give me examples of this?"

"I think this applies to the way many vote," she said. "Instead of deciding a vote by weighing the issues and making a judgment, many either react or vote as programmed. Maybe they vote a certain party because their parents or friends vote that way."

"I would say that those who react are like the three blind men. They only react to what is in front of them instead of taking all the pieces of information, putting them together and making a judgment," I added.

"So we have two categories of people," he said. "There are those who make a random or reactionary choice and those who use judgment followed by the real power of decision."

"But don't people who use judgment also react at times?" asked Elizabeth.

"Of course," he said. "Even the most powerful decision maker will use reaction when a new decision is not necessary, but those who *depend* on reaction rarely use their real power of decision.

This is an important point. As I said, judgment is the key to releasing the higher powers of the soul and spirit in humankind, yet it is hidden from the many because of ignorance or fear of its use. The highest path is always found by *the few*, and when they do find it, *the many* attempt to convince them they are in error."

"That's interesting," I replied. "I can't remember how many times someone has preached to me not to judge. I think the average person hears this so much that judgment spooks him."

"Those who are on the cutting edge of truth are always opposed by those still trapped in the veil of illusion," he said.

"On the other hand, it seems that those who tell us not to judge have a point. Some critical judgments can be very hurtful and do seem wrong to me," I noted.

"You are right, of course, and this was my emphasis a while back when I told you that Jesus was attempting to warn us against bad judgment rather than judgment itself. To make sure you understand, let us examine the two categories. Elizabeth, give me three examples of good judgment."

Elizabeth reflected a moment and said, "I believe I used good judgment when I agreed to marry my husband."

"I will not argue with that one," said John. "Now another example."

"Young people who go to college are making a good judgment," she said.

John put his hand to his mouth, thinking, and replied, "In most cases, this is an example of good judgment, but this is also an area where there could be an exception to the rule. Maybe the student would do better in life working in a trade or some other activity that does not require college, and the best judgment for him would be to choose another path."

"I suppose that would be true," she replied.

"And this is one of the interesting points to take in about the power of judgment. Judgment finds an exception to every rule. He who uses judgment may seem to be predictable for a period of time, but will eventually reach a fork in the road where his judgment will tell him to take the road least traveled. When this happens, his friends will often be alarmed and even upset. Now give me one more example."

Elizabeth thought another moment and said, "All kinds of

judgments seem to be called for in relationships. There have been many times in my life where I did not know if various friends were telling me the truth or not, so what I did was examine all the facts that I did know and try to ascertain the truth. If it turned out that I could not know the truth for sure, I attempted to give them the benefit of the doubt and judged them positively rather than negatively."

"And what if you found some facts that revealed a friend was lying?'

"Then no judgment would be necessary," she said. "I would know I was lied to and the only judgment necessary would be how to deal with the situation."

"Excellent observation," said John. "You have revealed an essential ingredient that makes judgment necessary. We judge when we are faced with multiple possibilities. The uncertainty caused by free will facing many paths may be great or may be small, but in either case it calls for the courage necessary to make a judgment. Even God does not know what his decisions will be until he makes them, and must use judgment as each decision is faced. You are created in the image of God, and as a reflection of the Divine, you must do the same to manifest God in you."

"That's interesting," I said. "The scriptures call God a righteous judge and praise his judgment. But since judgment precedes a decision, this would indicate that God still makes them like we do, and it would be impossible to know a decision until it was made."

"Glad you see the point," he said. "Now, Joseph, name for me three negative judgments that should be avoided."

I thought a moment and replied, "One thing that has always bothered me is ultra-religious people who judge others as being on the road to hell because they do not follow a particular brand of religion."

"This was a great problem in the days of Jesus, and he was strongly criticized for working with the non-religious people. Do you think that the judgment you mentioned is accurate?"

"Not really. Some of these non-religious people have a lot more kindness in their heart than the church-goers, and I believe God looks upon the heart more than outward appearance."

"And what caused their inaccurate judgment?" he asked.

"I would say a faulty understanding?"

"Do you believe that any of them have seen heaven, hell or understand the heart of God?" he asked.

"I doubt it," I said.

"So they are judging that which they do not know?"

"Yes, I suppose they are."

"If these people were to base their judgment on what they do know, then what kind of judgment should they make?"

"Since they do not have sure knowledge of life after death, or the mind of God, they should refrain from making a negative judgment on the non-believers. They may be worse off in the eyes of God than the person they are judging." I replied.

"Correct," he said. "Now let us take another situation. Let us say you are a teacher and discover a student covered with black and blue marks. You investigate and he tells you his father beats him regularly. Now how will you use your power of judgment?"

"Well, in this case, I have some information that I know for sure. I know the boy is being abused and his word gives evidence it is his father. My judgment would tell me that I could be deceived, but the evidence is powerful enough to have strong suspicions of the father, and, I would investigate or call the authorities."

"So we learn here that good judgment should be based on more than mere belief, but on knowledge of which one is reasonably sure."

"That makes sense," I said, "but what if you do not have any good data, and have to rely on belief? What then?"

"In this case, you only make a judgment when there is no alternative. The religious person, giving a condemning judgment to another with an alternative belief system, represents the bad judgment Jesus warned against. Such a judgment, based entirely on belief, and not facts, is not necessary and is harmful. Whereas this type of religious judgment is not necessary and should be avoided, individual spiritual judgment based on belief is a necessity for the beginning seeker. As an individual, one may not know if there is life after death, but it is actually helpful for him to make a judgment based on not much more than his opinion of the truth on the matter. The individual may have never seen God or higher life forms, but there is nothing wrong with him gathering his thoughts and making a judgment about it. Almost every belief system is based on a series of judgments. Many accept a belief system with no judgment involved because of accepting their parent's beliefs, or indoctrination, and this creates a mindset that must be destroyed. On the other hand, a belief system composed of a series of judgments is very powerful, and can lead to discovery and the uncovering of much truth. The key is to always be open to letting old judgments go and new ones form."

"I never thought about it in that light," I said. "The typical member of a religion just accepts a whole package of beliefs, but the individual seeker examines and makes a judgment on his beliefs item by item. The independent individual makes many judgments, but a church member makes one judgment that causes him to accept a whole package of beliefs."

"Good observation," he said. "And to accept a whole package of beliefs instantly eliminates the opportunity to judge the parts. This is an important defect because even the best belief system is composed of faulty parts that should be analyzed and judged. If members of the various religions would judge the parts instead of making a package acceptance, they would improve the quality of their religion, rather than allowing it to crystallize and fall behind the progress of civilization as a whole."

"I *have* noticed that religion falls behind the progress of civilization," I added. "For instance, the Catholic Church refused to accept the discoveries of Galileo and other scientists. When I was a child, many religious people told me we would never go to the moon."

"True spiritual science should be ahead of civilization instead of falling behind," he said. "Now give me a second example of bad judgment."

I reflected a few seconds and said, "Elizabeth gave our marriage as an example of good judgment, but I have noticed that many relationships are formed through bad judgment, or perhaps no judgment. Many times, a person will fall in love with someone completely unsuited for them. Instead of analyzing the qualities of the person with their mind and making a good judgment, they go with their heart, or lower energy, and make a disastrous judgment."

"Important point," said John. "You just brought up a crucial ingredient of good judgment."

"Would that be the use of the mind?" I asked.

"Correct," he said. "The emotions are very powerful for the average person, but they will often lead to very unwanted results. Good judgments require the discerning power of the mind and a decision to allow common sense to prevail over common emotion. Now give me a third example of bad judgment."

"I would say that it is bad judgment to make a blanket negative judgment toward those who use judgment."

John smiled, "Clever observation. You are correct that those who condemn others for using their power of judgment are indeed making a negative judgment themselves, and are guilty of what they accuse others of doing."

I reflected a moment and said, "There is one thing that bothers me about this key word. Not only do many Buddhist writings teach about judgment as a negative trait, but numerous other intelligent writers have also. The most notable of recent date is *A Course in Miracles*. Now this book claims to be a revelation from Jesus and the intelligence in it does seem to be far beyond a regular human. It tells us outright that we must cease making all judgments and even perceptions that lead to judgment. It says that a judgment implies that there is more than the oneness of God; and a rejection of one thing over the other leads to a rejection of the one truth or the oneness of God. How would you respond to this?"

"First, let me tell you that you must question, analyze and judge all things, teachings and people. One of the worst things one can do in his spiritual progression is to believe a teaching without question because such teachings seem to come from God, an angel, or even Jesus, as in the case of *A Course in Miracles*. You should not even believe *me* without judgment coming into play. And to your credit, you do not do this as evidenced by your question. You give my words great weight because you realize that I have a wider knowledge than you, yet when the second key word did not seem to fit with all that you have learned, you question, seeking to understand the full truth. This is as it should be."

"So why does *A Course in Miracles* teach us not to judge? Is the book a fabrication?"

"I will rarely give you my thoughts on the validity of a teaching," he replied. "This is especially true when you will be writing my words for others to read. The reason is quite simple. There are many people in the world who are on a sincere quest for truth, and in their quest, they find a teaching that seems to speak to them. Let us suppose that you were just beginning to search outside of mainstream religion, and discovered a writing that claimed to be a revelation from God. You find some things that speak to you and become overjoyed that you have found new knowledge. Now another comes along and reveals to you that the book is a deception and proves it. How will you feel?"

"I may feel rather discouraged, and may cease my search for a while for fear of being deceived again."

"Exactly," he replied. "Most books claiming to be inspired are full of error. Even so, they still have morsels of truth spliced amidst the mistakes. As the light dawns upon the mind of the seeker, the darkness of error is dispelled and only the truth remains. It is better to have one continue in his search for truth, and wade through the good and the bad, than to stand still and do nothing. Always remember the first parable I gave you that revealed that true hell is indecision, standing still, and being afraid to move forward."

"So I take it, then, that you do not want to reveal to the world how close to the truth the various spiritual books are, as this would do more harm than good?"

"Yes," he replied. "A seeker must learn to use his judgment. The various teachings, mere classes in the college of life, must be examined and graded. Eventually, each sincere seeker will come to the same conclusions at the end of the grand course in which we all participate.

"Let me ask you this," he continued. "When you were younger, did you find a teaching or book that impressed or inspired you, yet now, on reflection, you see that the teachings are not so reliable after all?"

I thought a moment and replied, "I think I can see your point. Back in my younger days the books that filled me with enthusiasm, on reflection, don't seem to be that great."

"And aren't you glad that no one was able to dampen your enthusiasm as you began your quest?"

"I have to agree," I said.

Elizabeth joined in. "I remember some teachings that I *thought* were based on fact, really encouraged me, but I later found out they were entirely fiction. Even so, there were truths mixed in with the fiction that stay with me to this day. I'm glad I was able to digest them *before* I found out the experiences in the book were fabricated."

"Yes" said John. "I can perceive the teachings you speak of, and some of the principles discussed are true. It is good that you pondered them."

"But it does seem as if you are saying that *A Course in Miracles* is not correct in its teachings on judgment," I challenged.

"Not exactly," he said. "When the seeker comes across any teaching that seems to be revealed by more than human intelligence, he must not relinquish his power of judgment and accept at face value with black and white reception. Very little light will be added to the mind if this is the case. Instead, he must examine it closely and attempt two things. First, to see the truth behind the words, and secondly, to look into the mind of the writer and see the point he is trying to make. Take the Apostle Paul for example. Many misunderstand him because they interpret his words with no judgment. They take everything he said literally and often miss his point on his teachings on faith.

"In his day, the great emphasis was on the power of works and strict obedience to the law of Moses. The people were literally extremists in following the literalness of the law and were slaves to it. To push the people toward the other end of the spectrum, Paul realized that he had to emphasize the extreme in the other direction. Therefore, he downplayed works and over-emphasized faith. But this created another problem. Instead of moving to the middle ground, many shifted away from a belief in works altogether and accepted faith only. To this day, many religions think that all you have to do to be forever saved is to express a belief in Jesus. This was not the end game in the mind of Paul. He wanted to take the people away from being enslaved by the law, but did not want them to go to the extreme belief in faith without works.

"Now this same problem manifests in teachings given out in our day. A teacher may want to emphasis a particular truth that humanity needs to absorb and, in doing so, the students may not correctly read the intent of the author and may take the teachings to an extreme."

"I think I see the point," Elizabeth added. "*A Course in Miracles* seems to put emphasis on the avoidance of negative judgment and, seems to be teaching us to not use judgment at all."

"I can see that to a degree," I said, "but in some places it does seem to be telling us to not judge period. It tells us that judgment involves acceptance and rejection. This rejection involved in judgment causes us to focus on the negative in others, and to reject the whole truth of God, or something to that effect."

John listened intently and said, "The whole truth is the key to understanding, especially when seeking to understand judgment. Now, let us see how closely you read the book. According to the Course, what is the source of negative or incorrect judgment?"

"The ego, I suppose."

"And what does it say the ego is?"

"It seems to be what some writings call the lower self, that part of us that is not eternal, or real."

"And when the ego judges, what kind of judgment does it make?"

"I don't know. A bad one I suppose."

John smiled and said, "Please get us your copy of the Course."

I went to the bookcase and retrieved the three volumes of the set and laid them on the table. John grabbed Vol. 1, opened it, and pointed to a passage. "Read these two lines," he said.

I took the book and read, "Any thought system that confuses God and the body must be insane. Yet this confusion is essential to the ego, which judges only in terms of threat or non-threat to itself."

"And when you began learning from me, what was the first thing you learned you were not?" he asked.

"We are not our bodies," I said.

"Yes," he said, "and those who identify with the body also identify with the ego *which judges only in terms of threat or non-threat to itself*." He then took the book and opened to another page and handed it to Elizabeth. "Now read here."

Elizabeth took the book and read, "I told you that the ego is aware of threat to its existence, but makes no distinctions between these two very different kinds of threat. Its profound sense of vulnerability renders it incapable of judgment except in terms of attack. When the ego experiences threat, its only decision is whether to attack now or to withdraw to attack later."

"Now the Course teaches that the important decision we have is to identify with the ego or the Holy Spirit. If you identify with the ego, how then will you judge?"

"It sounds like the only judgment will be in some form of attack," she said. "I like how it says *to attack now or to withdraw to attack later.* I have certainly seen people do that before. If they can't get the best of you now, they'll scheme as to how to do it in the future."

"And how does that make you feel?" said John.

"It makes me want to attack back." Elizabeth paused seeming to reflect on her answer. "I try to not do that though."

"I'm sure you do," he smiled. He looked at me and asked, "What does the Course say is an accepted judgment you can make while in your lower nature?"

"I'm not sure. It seems like it tells us not to make any," I said.

John turned to another page and pointed to a passage. "Read this," he said.

Elizabeth read, "Your mind and mine can unite in shining your ego away, releasing the strength of God into everything you think and do. Do not settle for anything less than this, and refuse to accept anything but this as your goal. Watch your mind carefully for any beliefs that hinder its accomplishment, and step away from them. Judge how well you have done this by your own feelings, for this is the one right use of judgment. Judgment, like any other defense, can be used to attack or protect; to hurt or to heal. The ego should be brought to judgment and found wanting there."

"So what is the right use of judgment?" he asked.

"It is to judge our own minds and feelings about our progress in moving toward God."

"Excellent," he said. "And judgment can be used for what?"

Elizabeth read the passage again to herself and replied, "It *can be used to attack or protect; to hurt or to heal.*"

"Here we are told that judgment is not limited to attack and hurt but for what else?"

"To protect and to heal," she said.

"Correct use of judgment can protect and heal, even while in the lower nature," he said. "Now who is it that always judges correctly?'

"I'm not sure," she said.

John then turned to another page and pointed to some text. "Now read here."

Elizabeth read as follows, "When we have overcome fear—not by hiding it, not by minimizing it, and not by denying its full import in any way—this is what you will really see. You cannot lay aside the obstacles to real vision without looking upon them, for to lay aside means to judge against. If you will look, the Holy Spirit will judge, and He will judge truly."

"Who judges truly?" he asked.

"The Holy Spirit," she replied.

"And how can you judge truly?" he asked.

"By having the Holy Spirit," she said.

John looked at me and asked, "If you receive a communication from the Holy Spirit, will it be true and reliable?"

"I have faith it would be," I said.

"And if you know a thing is true, is any judgment necessary?" he asked.

"I would think not," he said.

"And this is the true teaching on judgment one should acquire from the Course," he said. "While living in the lower nature, judgment, particularly of others, is usually wrong and should be avoided if knowledge is incomplete. The path to complete knowledge is to become one with God and establish a communion with the Holy Spirit. Because the Holy Spirit's judgment is true, then our judgment will also be true. When this communion occurs, we will perceive and understand the judgment of the Spirit because we discover that our true mind is one with the mind of God. Now I'll have you read one more passage."

I picked up the book and read the text he pointed to: "The miracle joins in the Atonement by placing the mind in the service of the Holy Spirit. This establishes the proper function of the mind and corrects its errors, which are merely lacks of love."

"So how are the errors of the judgments of the mind corrected?" quizzed John.

"By placing it in the service of the Holy Spirit."

"And here's the interesting point. There are many judgments to be made as we go through life. Some are made by us and some are made by the Holy Spirit, of which our true self is a part. Whether the judgments are made with or without the Holy Spirit, they are still judgments, for judgment is essential to moving forward and precedes the appearance of all things in creation. Anything that is created is preceded by a judgment from some intelligence. Now, there are several uses of judgment not discussed in the Course. When you receive knowledge or judgment from the Holy Spirit, what are you supposed to do with it?"

"Whatever the Holy Spirit indicates," I said.

"And have you received direction or information from the Holy Spirit before?" he asked.

"Yes, a number of times," I replied.

"And when you received these things, did you automatically know in every detail what you were supposed to do with it?"

"You have a point," I replied. "I can think of several times that I received some great inspiration, but seemed to be left to my own devices as to how to make the best use of it."

"In other words, you were left to your own judgment."

"Yes, I suppose I was," I replied. "Was I correct, then, in using my own judgment?"

"As long as you follow the highest you know," he said. "If you are in doubt and follow the highest you know, the time will eventually come that your highest judgment will lead you to a sure knowledge of the judgment of the Spirit. And this is why the judges in ancient Israel were called Gods. Judging by the highest we know, and being true to our highest light, leads to discovering the judgment of God and being one with God."

CHAPTER TWENTY-EIGHT
The Pendulum and the Key

"We will finish tonight by discussing the core principle of the lost Key to the Middle Way. We must clarify what the Middle Way is and is not. As we said earlier, the Middle Way is often associated with moderation. But, is this what it is?"

"I believe we ruled that out," I said.

"And tell me in your own words why the answer could not be moderation."

I reflected a moment and replied, "The Middle Way is supposed to be the Path of Liberation, or a doorway to the Kingdom of God. Those who have tread the Middle Way have been the great teachers of humanity such as Buddha, Christ, Krishna, Moses and others. Now I can't think of any of the great teachers who were consistent examples of moderation. We already talked about several incidents from Buddha's life, but I'd also say that Jesus did not exemplify the normal definition of the Middle Way either. He was not exactly showing us moderation when he fasted for forty days, or chased the money changers out of the temple. Anyone who would willingly allow himself to be crucified could not be called moderate by any measure."

"Then there was John the Baptist," added Elizabeth. "He lived in the wilderness eating only locusts and honey. Anyone who did that today would not be called moderate, but a wild man."

John smiled and replied, "Many thought he was a wild man, even in that age." He paused and added, "Consider this. Moderation is generally considered a place in the middle, between two extremes of action. Yet, as you point out, the greatest sages of the ages do not stay at that point in the illusionary middle, which could be called moderation. In fact, they have seemed to go to the extreme at times. If this is so, then why would the path they trod be called the Middle Way?"

"That's an interesting question," I replied. "But if the Middle Way is not in the middle, why would it be called the Middle Way? It would seem that it should be called by some other name."

"Perhaps not," he said. "Perhaps the Middle Way is as good a name as any. Perhaps one needs to consider exactly what the mid-way point is in the middle of. Are the two points on each side of the middle always at the same location?"

Elizabeth's eyes widened as she said, "I told you two a while back that the Middle Way was a moving target! If the two points on each side of the middle shift, then maybe I was right."

"So could it be that Elizabeth was correct and the points do shift?" I asked.

"What do you think?" he asked in return.

"I sense that she is right, that the Middle Way is a moving target, but I do not understand completely," I said.

John sat back in his chair and continued, "Let us return again to the moment that inspired Buddha to discover the Middle Way. What was it again?"

"It was the words about the tuning of the strings of a harp. This story made me realize that the key word was judgment, for good judgment must be used to tune an instrument."

"This is correct," he said, "but also consider this. Each string has a different note which is its correct adjustment between the two extreme points. Let us go back to your guitar again. How many strings are on it?"

"Six, I believe."

"And how many midway notes are there after the strings are tuned?"

"You can produce many different notes, but you use one for each string for tuning purposes," I said.

"That means you have six notes which are midway points for tuning purposes. Would you agree?"

"Yes," I acknowledged.

"Now, other instruments, like the piano, have many more strings to tune to their midway point, but let us stay with the guitar. Let us call each of these six notes a midway point of truth. Why is it that when we move up the scale, the point of truth, or the true note at the middle way, changes?"

"I can see that when you adjust the string to play higher notes that you are moving further away from the natural note at the natural midway point. Then as you move up the scale the midway point seems to get further away." I paused and said, "I suppose that you cannot play a tune with one natural note. Thus, a musical instrument must have numerous strings, with each of them tuned to a different note. In other words you have six midway points on a guitar."

"Exactly," he said. "The unfortunate thing is that many want to live their life by one note. Just as you cannot play a melody with one note, neither can life be lived in fullness by searching for and finding that one *be-all* or *end-all* to religion or philosophy. The seeker cannot find the Middle Way that leads to the heart of God by merely examining the extremes and always choosing the exact middle point. As he moves up and down the scales of life, the midway point changes, for the notes change, thus causing the extremes to change. With all these changes going on around him, he cannot be forever seeking to hit the same note. If he does, no music will be made and the magical work of creation will not take place."

"That's a profound thought," I said. "Elizabeth was more correct than we realized. The truth at the Middle Way seems to change as circumstances change. Does this mean that truth changes?"

"Just as middle C does not change, truth is ever consistent, but circumstances do change. One time you have to play the C note, and in another you play G sharp. In one circumstance you need one effect and in another a different effect is called for. A flexible attitude and an open mind is the key to finding the Middle Way."

"Could you give us a real world example of finding the Middle Way?" asked Elizabeth.

"Yes, but before I do, you need to realize that every time a decision is required, an opportunity to find the Middle Way arises. For example, each young person has to decide what he will do for a living. If he follows the Path of the Middle Way, he will study different vocations from which he can choose, and make a judgment for the one that will most likely be best for him. If he avoids the Middle Way, he will avoid judgment. Instead of using his power of decision, he will allow someone else, or circumstances, to make the decision for him."

John continued, "If one is a member of a religion that does his thinking for him, he cannot find the Middle Way. *But* if he can live his religion while reserving many judgments to himself about his own beliefs and directions, then the true path opens before him.

"If one is a member of a political party and uses no judgment, following the direction of the party without making any decision on his own, he is missing the Middle Way. On the other hand, he who treads the midway path will always be judging the direction of his party, and when good judgment dictates, he may decide on a direction contrary to his party."

"So, it sounds like the mystery of the Middle Way can be reduced to something as simple as using good judgment," I observed.

"It seems simple enough when viewed in that light," he said, "but discovering what to judge and then making good judgment has enough mystery behind it, so all but a few miss the principle. Let me give you evidence of this. Many laws come before the vote of the U.S. House of Representatives with 435 members, several hundred on each side. How often is the vote almost 100 percent along party lines?"

"Quite often," I noted. "Sometimes I think they are a bunch of sheep on both sides, just voting the wishes of the party bosses."

"So, instead of making a judgment and deciding, most in Congress relinquish their real power of judgment and merely vote as they are told to vote for the party, and not the good of the country. Now, the interesting thing is that the representatives are voted in because they are seen by the people as being more intelligent than the average citizen. If these individuals, who are deemed the most intelligent, cannot use *their* judgment, then how can we expect to find it among the rank and file?"

"Interesting point," I agreed. "Everyone talks about good judgment like it is used by all, but if even the most intelligent among us go out of their way to avoid it, then perhaps judgment is a rare commodity."

"It is a rare commodity indeed," John agreed. "Let me assure you that when those times arise that every Republican or Democrat votes along party lines, each will see himself as making a true judgment. This is because he will go through the motions of making a true choice, but he is deluding himself. In all but a few occasions, his choice is already predetermined by party dictates."

"So why is true judgment so rare?" I asked.

"It is rare because it is the natural disposition of people to be mentally lazy," he replied. "The method of decision-making for the majority is really non-decision making. What they desire is a few facts, or some voice of authority, that seem to make the choice so black and white that no decision or judgment is really required. People on a jury, for instance, desire to be presented with evidence so clear that they will know their decision is correct. When the evidence is not clear, the jury will often sweat and strain for many hours, or even days, before a judgment can be made. They only make a judgment because it is forced upon them. But in everyday life, human nature seeks to step around all judgment. To avoid judgment people will adopt a mindset, a dogma, a religion, a party, or a set of rules that takes away judgment and makes their decisions for them. They want lots of *thou-shalts* and *thou-shalt-nots,* so true judgment can be avoided."

"But aren't the *thou-shalt-nots* like the Ten Commandments a good thing for society?" I asked.

"Basic laws are necessary for every group and organization," John said. "He who treads the Path will be very cooperative in most cases, but that which truly governs him will be something higher than words and rules written in stone. Open the Bible again and turn to Jeremiah 31:33-34."

Elizabeth found the verses and read:

"But this shall be the covenant that I will make with the house of Israel; After those days, saith the LORD, I will put my law in their inward parts, and write it in their hearts; and will be their God, and they shall be my people.

"And they shall teach no more every man his neighbor, and every man his brother, saying, Know the LORD: for they shall all know me, from the least of them unto the greatest of them, saith the LORD: for I will forgive their iniquity, and I will remember their sin no more."

"Tell me," he said "where will the laws of God be written?"

"In our hearts," she responded.

"Now turn to Ecclesiastes 3:1-8."

Elizabeth found the chapter and read:
"To every thing there is a season, and a time to every purpose under the heaven:
"A time to be born, and a time to die; a time to plant, and a time to pluck up that which is planted;
"A time to kill, and a time to heal; a time to break down, and a time to build up;
"A time to weep, and a time to laugh; a time to mourn, and a time to dance;
"A time to cast away stones, and a time to gather stones together; a time to embrace, and a time to refrain from embracing;
"A time to get, and a time to lose; a time to keep, and a time to cast away;
"A time to rend, and a time to sew; a time to keep silence, and a time to speak;
"A time to love, and a time to hate; a time of war, and a time of peace."

"Outward laws and commandments are necessary for humankind in their current state of evolution," he said. "But no matter how just they are, even if they are given by the finger of God, they cannot apply to all situations in all times. There is a time and place to break every rule, every law, and every norm of mankind. For example, Jesus went out of his way to technically break the Jewish Sabbath to illustrate to the people the fallacy of rigid black-and-white interpretation."

"But he did obey the spirit of the law, didn't he?" asked Elizabeth.

"He did indeed. The Master had the law written in his heart and instinctively knew how to fulfill its true intent. He knew the time and place to break the law as was understood in his time. He knew the true Middle Way, as did the Buddha. This scripture we just read, however, gives the underlying principle of the Middle Way in profound simplicity. Read verse one again."

Elizabeth read, "*To every thing there is a season, and a time to every purpose under the heaven.* Those are words to one of my favorite songs," she smiled.

"Now study the verses that follow and tell me of some things for which there is a time that most would think would never be approved by God."

Elizabeth studied for a moment and replied, "It says there is a time to kill, a time to hate, and even a time to go to war."

"Yet the scriptures of the world are replete with commands to not kill, to love instead of hate, and to seek peace instead of war. How do you explain this apparent contradiction?" he asked.

"I think all the great teachers and leaders desired the positive things like peace and love instead of hate and war," I said, "but I can see what you are getting at. There is an exception to all rules and admonitions. All but a few would agree that World War II was a time to go to war, rather than lie down and let Hitler take over the world."

"Indeed," he agreed. "Progress does demand that we encounter a few thorns before we can pick the roses. Before we proceed though, there is one point I wish to make clear. The last thing a disciple does is to rebel for rebellion's sake, merely to affirm he is not one with the group. This type of rebellion is done by one who has not yet learned even the basic lessons in life. Overall, the disciple will work for the unity of his group or country. He will only take a position of rebellion when the right season has come. One such season was in Nazi Germany, where there were a handful of Germans who sought the overthrow of Hitler. There has to be a greater good to justify extreme measures. The fact that you do not like a law does not give you justification in breaking it. The laws of the land are flawed indeed, but the alternative of anarchy would mean the end of civilization. Therefore, the disciple cooperates in obeying the laws of the land unless wise judgment tells him otherwise."

"And when does judgment tell otherwise?" I asked.

"And here, my friend, you have just put a finger on the reason the second key of judgment is not seen, except by a very few."

"I did?" I said with surprise in my voice. "How did I do that?"

"By demanding what all but the few on the razor-edged path demand," he said.

"I don't understand," I replied.

"You don't understand what you just asked? Then repeat the question," he said firmly.

I examined my memory and replied, "All I asked was *when does judgment tell us otherwise*? In other words, how are we to know when to break the rules?"

"And if I gave you rules about breaking rules, then where would judgment be found?"

"I think I see," I said with some relief. "If we live our lives strictly by black-and-white rules, no judgment is ever necessary. Then, if we have rules telling us when to break rules, again there is no room for judgment. Instead, there are only layers of rules."

"Exactly," said John, who looked glad he was finally making some progress. "Sooner or later in life, the pilgrim comes to a dead end, where no law or rule tends to apply. When this happens, he can do one of three things. He can do nothing and be overtaken by the tide of events that may force him with the current against his will. Secondly, he can cling to some rule that does not work and may spell disaster. Finally, there is a third alternative. What do you suppose that would be?"

"He would have to gather all possible facts about the situation and make a judgment. After this, he should make a decision to proceed in harmony with that judgment."

"Yes," said John. "When we approach a dead end, or darkness falls upon the Path so vision is impaired, the First and Second Keys of Knowledge must be used. If they are not used, the traveler will be at the mercy of forces over which he will have no control, leading him to a destination that he would never have chosen."

"Interesting," I said. "I can see where someone like me would have to use judgment, but how about you and the Masters above you, or even the Ancient of Days? Surely a point is eventually reached where judgment is no longer necessary. Surely the Masters have no doubt of their next step upon the Path."

"This type of thinking is perhaps one of the most prevalent illusions among the seekers of knowledge. This much is true, however. After judgment and decision are made upon a matter which is obscure, and the seeker moves ever onward, the time will soon come that the daystar will arise and vision will be clarified. When this happens, judgment will no longer be necessary about this particular point on the path. But when judgment becomes unnecessary for one location, the disciple must merely look ahead. When he does, he will realize that there are bends, clouds and obstacles on the path ahead that will always require additional judgment."

"Could you give me examples in the lives of Buddha and Jesus where they had to use judgment?" I asked.

"I could give you many, but here is one," he said. "Buddha told his disciples to not perform miracles, but Jesus encouraged his to do so. Do you suppose that one teacher was right and the other wrong?"

"I'd be hard pressed to disagree with either one of these great men," I said. "Why do I get the feeling that you are going to tell me that neither of them was wrong?"

"Because, your feeling in this case comes from the soul," he smiled. "Now, if neither of them were wrong, tell us how is it that they could both be correct when making opposing decisions."

"I think I know," injected Elizabeth. "It's like the scripture says, there is a time and a place for all things. Buddha lived in a time and circumstance that was best to focus on common sense; Jesus was in a time and place that required faith and miracles."

"Very well put," said John. "Both Buddha and the Christ assessed their situations and projected in their minds the effect that miracles would have upon their disciples and the masses. After assessing all things at their disposal, Buddha made a judgment to discourage miracles and Jesus made one to encourage them. There was no rule book for either of them that designated the course of action. Therefore, they each had to make a judgment."

John paused a moment and added, "You wish to know some black-and-white rules of correct judgment. Such rules do not exist. Judgment is necessary when some of the results are not completely predictable because of free will or unseen circumstances. The basic requirement of good judgment is to acquire all knowledge possible on both sides of the issue and then weigh them with wisdom. Again, we need to go back to the tuning of a guitar string. You adjust the sound up and down the scale until the right note is hit. Then you use your best judgment to stop as close to the perfect note as possible. When the instrument is tuned, you test all the strings again. After the test you may discover some additional fine tuning is necessary.

"The interesting thing is that even though Buddha discouraged miracles, he still performed a few near the end of his life; even though Christ encouraged miracles he attempted, after the resurrection, to guide the church toward the more practical aspects of the teachings. In other words, they both did some fine tuning on their judgments, and as they did, they reached a more common ground.

"Unfortunately, much of that fine tuning has been lost to history, but on the fortunate side nothing is lost forever. All the teachings that are in harmony with the Spirit are registered forever in the hearts of those who received them. Indeed, there are many people who have come into incarnation in the world today, having the truths of the past in their hearts, with intent for them to flower forth with greater fullness than ever before.

"As the parable of the sower indicates, the past masters were merely planters of the seeds of truth. After a seed is planted, you have a period of time passing where there is only barren ground and nothing seems to be happening. But this is only temporary, for soon the plant bursts forth into sunlight and later bears fruit. Even so, a true teaching only appears to be lost when speech is suppressed and manuscripts burned. But the real truth is that it is only sprouting below the surface, waiting to burst forth into the light of day. We are now approaching that great age where the lost teachings of all the ages past will flower forth in oneness within the great field of the entire world."

That's a beautiful thought," I said. "You've always encouraged me to see the principle behind your teachings, and I sense there is more you can tell us about the principle behind judgment. For instance, you acknowledged that Elizabeth was correct in stating that the Second Key involved a moving target. Could you elaborate on this?"

John stretched out his arms to relax as he said, "Could I elaborate? Yes. I suppose I could. Let me see how I can word this so you can understand. Visualize a pendulum swinging back and forth while on a forward moving train. Even though it may seem to a passenger that the only motion is the back and forth swing there is a larger motion transpiring. What is it?"

"You would have the motion of the train which is moving the entire pendulum forward," I replied.

"Yes," he said. "Because the passenger is moving with the pendulum it seems as if the location of the actual pendulum is not moving when it is moving. This is just one example of the many illusions of the pendulum. Now we will examine additional problems within the pendulum itself. Bring me a pen and some paper."

After I laid several sheets of paper and a pen in front of him he quickly drew five images. "What do you see here?" he asked.

"It looks like five pendulums," I replied.

"And how are they different?" he asked

"Their swing is each in a different position," I noted.

"Name the positions."

I looked at the drawings and replied, "The drawings seem to depict the swing of a pendulum. The first image appears to represent the pendulum at the midway point as it would be if stationary. Then we have a swing at the far right, the center right, the center left and then the far left."

"Now what would you say is the desired result of making a judgment?"

"I would say that it is an attempt to find the most perfect course of action or purest truth," I replied.

"Yes," he stated. "For instance, as you attempt to steer your car a block down the road you use your best judgment to guide it as correctly as possible. But what happens when you let go of the steering wheel?"

"You run off the road," I noted.

"So no matter how closely you fine tune your initial steering, it is never good enough to reach the goal without correction. Is this not true?"

"You are correct," I agreed. "I don't think that I could even go one block without correcting my steering."

"Now imagine this," John said, with a knowing look in his eyes. "Visualize the possibility of creating a perfect aim with your steering so you could let go and travel, not only a block but for miles, in a straight line with no correction. We will call this perfect aim the point of purest action. This point is represented by my first drawing of the pendulum still at the midway point between the two extremes. Now when the pendulum is not in motion the point of truth is obvious. But this is not the case when it is in motion.

"To illustrate, visualize the still pendulum growing in size until it is as large as a ride at the carnival. You note there is a seat for you right at the midway resting point attached to the blade of the large pendulum. Now see yourself taking a seat there. You have a red highlighter in your hand, and you reach down and draw an X on the floor under your seat at the midway point of your rest. This marks the midway point of truth. In addition make a mark exactly above this X on the blade to which you are attached. Now, in this existence of stillness the midway point of truth is black and white. All you have to do is look under your seat and X marks the spot."

"OK so far," I said.

"Now here is where it gets interesting," he added. "You see the pendulum ride beginning to move until it has a large swing back and forth. You are now way over to the far right or at the point in my second drawing. Where is the point of truth now that was marked with the X?"

"Now the two marks are no longer lined up." I said. "The X on the floor is back where I made it but the X on the pendulum has moved with me.

"Which X now corresponds to the point of truth?"

"It would be the one back at the point of origin on the floor which is now some distance away," I said.

"But what about the second X that you made on the pendulum itself?"

"This X has moved with me."

"Yes, this X on the pendulum moved with you and you can realize this because you are looking at the whole picture. But see yourself as one taking the ride and then tell me which X seems to be moving?"

I reflected a moment and replied, "As the ride starts it would appear that the X under the seat is moving and the X on the pendulum is still."

"And this reflects the illusion of the Middle Way and reveals the grand key to understanding. As we travel through life we want to hold the truth close to us and we assume the X that marks the spot on the moving pendulum is the truth that does not change. When the pendulum moves this second X moves with us, but the real point of truth, represented by the first X on the floor, seems to be moving. In reality it is the rider who is moving away from the initial point. Because of the illusion that the initial point is moving away, the person assumes this initial point of truth is now distant and wrong. He thus sees that which is in motion as still, and that which is still as in motion."

"In other words, he sees changeable error as the truth and unchangeable truth as error," I observed with satisfaction.

"So let us be clear, where is the point of truth?" he asked.

From this I concluded that the point was not at the obvious place where the X was marked. I reflected a moment and answered, "The only other place it could be would be the point which was on the floor where the pendulum rested when it was still, but is now in the distance."

"Correct," he said. "When the pendulum moved, the rider assumed the point moved with him. Now, relative to your body, the second X on the blade is in the same location, but relative to the whole, the midway point did not move, but was left behind. From an upside down point of view, the midway point seemed to move, but what really moved?"

"I moved away from the midway point. This is getting interesting," I said.

"This is an extremely important point in understanding the Second Key," he said. "All points of truth are consistent and unchanging. All that really changes is our location in relation to the truth. The truth thus seems to be relative and changing, but instead, it is the observer who changes. Now, for another important point. Where is the location of the originating point of truth?"

I reflected and replied, "By one reckoning, the point is between the two extremes of the swing of the pendulum, but by another it merely exists as a point with no dimensions."

"Yes, in reality the point is formless, with a true existence outside of time and space," he said. "This is why Jesus identified the path to the truth as *narrow*, for to arrive at the point of truth without dimension requires a narrow path indeed.

"Now see yourself swinging to all the four locations in my drawings. First the far right, then the center right, then over the point of truth to the center left and then to the far left. Is the midway point moving or are you moving?"

"I am moving and the X at midway is still," I replied.

"But when you look back on your originating point, does this point seem to be moving or standing still?"

"I think I see what you are getting at," I said. "I have read a little about relativity, and from that teaching the question would be, *am I moving away from the point or is it moving away from me?* The answer is that it depends on how you look at it."

"Exactly right," said John, looking pleased. "And this is what keeps the true power of judgment away from the grasp of the many.

The many see the point of truth as being in motion when, instead, it is them swinging back and forth away from reality. True judgment can only come to the individual when he realizes that it is he who is moving away from truth, and, until he perceives this motion and adjusts for it, the truth can never be found or even approximated."

"This illusion you are talking about kind of reminds me of ancient man's deception that the sun went around the earth rather than the earth going around the sun," I added.

"Yes, he nodded. "The deception is very similar. Because the earth turns on its axis, it appeared to the ancients that the earth was the center of the universe and that the sun and all the stars moved around us at the center. Then, after the telescope was invented and the science of astronomy was developed, a larger picture was obtained. We then discovered that the central point of truth for us was not here on earth, but that our permanent center was the sun. Many today are still deceived about what the central point of truth is as it applies to their own lives. They think they are standing still on the truth when, in reality, there is motion everywhere around a central point that must be understood or their vision of reality will be greatly distorted. The direction of the true point of truth must be sensed before the power of correct judgment can even be exercised."

"Could you give us a real world example?" asked Elizabeth. "My head is starting to spin."

"Perhaps the best example is in the world of politics," he said. "Let us say that the conservative view is represented by the swing of the pendulum to the right and the liberal view is the swing to the left. However, both the swings to the left and the right are far away from the midway point of truth. For instance, after World War II, the world, particularly the United States, went through a conservative period. Censorship was everywhere and overdone. On TV and in the movies actors had to have twin beds and not show any passion or scenes that would even indicate the existence of sex. Words spoken, pictures printed, and articles written were censored and often very sterile. Conservative politics acquiesced to the dominant religions of the time and did not challenge them nor offer any criticism. Women, blacks and minorities were judged by the conservative values of the past, civil rights were suppressed, and many were denied civil rights. It was *my country right or wrong* epitomized by the conservative era. The thought of going to the moon seemed like fantasy and science fiction. The music was dull and unimaginative. Then a change occurred, and the pendulum shifted from the right to the left, achieving its greatest momentum in the Sixties and Seventies. Both of you, in your younger years, witnessed the changes that took place. How about naming a few?"

Elizabeth replied, "I'll take a stab at it. For one thing, music became much more exciting with the advent of rock-and-roll. Censorship was all but eliminated—to the point that almost anything goes. Few movies are complete without explicit sex today. We've bent over backwards so much for minorities that the civil rights of the majority are at risk. It seems strange today that we females are called a minority when we are greater in number than the male, and control more wealth. It seems that instead of *my country right or wrong,* the motto of today is *my country is always wrong*. Instead of supporting traditional religion it seems to be attacked at every opportunity. In my youth a minister or priest was often the good guy in the movie or book. It seems that today every religious person who appears in a movie is either the villain or is crazy as a loon."

"Great observations," said John. "Now, have you noticed a change in the liberals since the swing of the Sixties and Seventies?"

"I certainly have," I said. "I have great respect for the liberals who worked for change in the early days like JFK and his brother Bobby, Martin Luther King, all the great musicians who changed the world of music, NASA and supporters who took us to the moon, the innovative movie makers who challenged censorship, and the liberal comics who loosened us up. The trouble is that they did not leave good enough alone. They seemed to think that if some liberalism is good, more is better, and today the admonitions of the liberals seem to be extreme in most areas, and the conservatives seem to be the voice of reason. The tables are now reversed from the early Fifties. Does this mean that the conservative pull will cause the pendulum to swing the other direction?"

"Yes," he replied. "The pendulum always returns to center and then swings to an opposing extreme again. But here is an important Key to enhancing your power of judgment. When the pendulum swings back again to the right, we will not have an exact repetition of the last conservative cycle. With each swing of the pendulum, the force to the left or right is slightly reduced by the friction of the times. This means that the next conservative cycle will not be as oppressive as the one before, and the future liberal cycle will not be as unrestrained as the one we are in now."

"I have an interesting question," I said. "I take it that some time between the Fifties and Sixties the pendulum swung over the midway point of truth. Can you tell me when this occurred?"

"I can tell you the exact day," smiled John. "It was October 28th, 1956. I'm sure you remember the day"

"That's earlier than I would have thought," I said. "The date does not ring a bell with me."

"That was the date Elvis Presley appeared on the Ed Sullivan Show," he said with a grin.

"I certainly remember that date," said Elizabeth, her eyes lighting up. "I was very excited, but my mom and dad seemed to think he was possessed by the devil or something."

"That's interesting that a musician marked the turning point," I observed. "I would have guessed the launching of the Sputnik, the election of Kennedy, or something of more orthodox significance would have been the point."

"But there's nothing more powerful than music or the arts to loosen people up to prepare them for a liberal cycle," he said. "Because it was known to the Brotherhood that Elvis was to mark a turning point, I was sent to him shortly before he became famous to give him some advice and encourage him."

"Wow, really? Did he know who you were?" I asked, my jaw dropping.

"No," he smiled. "Few who have met me know who I am."

"What did you do to influence him?" I asked incredulously.

John appeared to reflect deeply and responded, "We knew that he was the most probable and best suited person to change the direction of music, so to help his destiny along I paid him a visit one Sunday at his church in Tupelo, Mississippi in 1945. He was only ten years old at the time. I befriended him and mentioned to him after the church meeting that I heard him sing and thought he had a lovely voice. I then mentioned to him a singing contest at the upcoming Mississippi-Alabama fair and that I thought he should enter. I told him I had a feeling that he was a person of destiny and that he would change the world of music."

"Did he enter the contest?" asked Elizabeth.

"Yes, he did. He won second prize singing a song called *Old Shep*. I attended the event and accosted him afterwards. He remembered me with fondness and was very encouraged even though he won second prize instead of first. I again planted a positive thought in his mind by telling him that even though the fair did not give him first prize that the world soon would. I sensed that my words took effect as his deep eyes met mine. He had the impression I was some sort of messenger, or angel from God. I decided to solidify this in his mind and when he turned because of an approaching friend, I quickly disappeared into the crowd. He turned to speak to me again and I was gone, but the impression that he had a destiny took hold."

"How about the Beatles? Did you also meet them?" asked Elizabeth.

"No," he said. "They didn't need any encouragement and they were not part of any assignment. I was sent to meet John, though, several days before he was killed. As I told you before, his assassination was not expected, but we did pick up the appearance of the wild card assassin on the prowl shortly before his death. I was dispatched to warn him, but had a terrible time meeting him in private without revealing who I was. Finally, I found him alone, unrecognized, sitting on a park bench. I sat down next to him and started some small talk. He was quite conversational until I gave him the warning. I warned him that his life was in danger and he should avoid appearing in public for at least two weeks. He then looked at me with a most perplexing look in his eyes and said, *I don't know if you're friend or foe, but if someone wants to take my life that will be his decision.* He then got up and walked away. A few days later he was killed by Mark Chapman, who was motivated by thoughts planted by the Dark Brothers. This was a sad day in more ways than people realize, for John was going through a transformation that would have been complete by now, and he would have been of great use to the Brotherhood in furthering some of their plans and preparations."

"So is the Will of God sometimes frustrated?" I asked incredulously.

"The will of God is always fulfilled, but, because of free will, the time factor for accomplishing that will is variable. That which John was supposed to accomplish will be done by others, and maybe a little later than some of us want, but the task will be completed."

"What was it he was going to do?"

"Believe it or not, he was going to assist in the next swing of the wheel in the conservative direction."

"That is kind of difficult to believe," I said.

"The person with the most correct judgment is often one who has seen both sides. He would have been a valuable tool in assisting the swing toward conservatism in its positive aspects. Each swing toward the conservative or liberal side is usually progressive, and, in time, increases the momentum of the positive onward motion while it drops some of the negative resistance. Of course, the opposing view never feels this way."

"You say that each swing is *usually progressive*. Are there exceptions then?"

"Indeed," he replied. "There are exceptions to all things. Evolution always goes forward like the forward moving train I gave as an example, but sometimes it is by moving two steps ahead and one step back. The workers in the light always do their best to see that the next swing of the pendulum is for the better, but there are setbacks now and then."

"So, am I right in saying that the Brotherhood of Light is neither conservative nor liberal, but works with both sides to insure that they progress?" I asked.

"Basically," he said. "Now, to illustrate how difficult correct judgment is, the disciple must consider that there are greater and lesser cycles. What appears to be a liberal cycle of thirty years may be swinging within a greater conservative cycle of several hundred years, and yet have within it a lesser cycle of three years. The one who has good judgment must gather all the details he can and obtain an inward sense of the true picture. He will never have all the details and must, in the end, also rely on his intuition.

"Keep it simple by visualizing the swinging pendulum ride as we were discussing. As the ride starts you swing to the right. If you are the average person you see the truth as the X marked on the pendulum moving with you and are deceived into thinking you have the truth also moving with you. Therefore, when you are on the far conservative side you think you are being moderate when your X moving with you is really a far distance from the stationary X on the floor, the real originating point of truth. To see the truth, you must not look at where you are now, but toward the real center. Because you are in motion, the center appears to be a moving target and you have to use your best judgment with a little guesswork to determine a fairly accurate view. Even though the center seems to be moving, you will be much more accurate in finding it than those who are looking at the position of the X on the swing rather than the midway point.

"Then, when the pendulum swings back to the left, the same problem occurs. It seems as if the truth is in liberal values, and he who is deceived will be attached to all things liberal, again losing sight of the truth in the middle. Not only does society switch back and forth between the extremes, but so does the individual. This sometimes occurs within one lifetime, but is more apparent if several lifetimes are seen. In one life the entity may be a religious fanatic, and in the next he may be a party animal.

"But the plan of dominating good is that we swing from one extreme to the other, and in the extremes we learn a lesson or two. When we return to the left or right on the next swing, we will not be so extreme. This continues with each swing until each of us eventually finds the truth in the middle. In the meantime, disciples live in a world of extremes where few see the middle. Those who realize the truth is in the middle have to go against popular thought to pursue it. Let me ask a key question to see if I have made my point. Elizabeth, can you tell me why a person who pursues the point in the middle is often not seen as a moderate, but as an extremist?

Elizabeth thought for a moment and replied, "I know the midway point appears to be a moving target, but I am not positive how one who follows the middle can be seen as an extremist."

"Joseph, let's have your answer."

"I think we have to go back to the picture of the pendulum carnival ride to understand," I replied. "If I am on the ride, and on a swing to the left, then the majority of those around me will be thinking left, like the ancient Romans who ate drank, and made merry as the kingdom was falling. Someone who advised spending restraints on social activities and an increase in defense would have been seen as an extremist. Yet that was what was needed to preserve the empire. On the other extreme, in medieval Britain, anyone who advocated that we not burn heretics at the stake was seen as an extremist. In our time it is easy to see that letting a heretic live is not extreme, but back then the real truth was seen as the extreme."

"Very good," said John. "Elizabeth, can you see that if you were on the ride, were on the extreme of the swing, and had the belief that the moderate view was the X on the pendulum, the real midway point would seem to be a long way off, and appear to be the extreme?"

"Yes. I think I am finally getting the picture."

"So why was Elvis, who was at the midway point and seen as a moderate in music today, viewed by his generation as an extreme agent of the devil himself?"

Elizabeth put her finger to her temple, thinking for a moment and replied, "I think the adults at that time were stuck in a time warp. Even though Elvis was at the midway point, their thinking was stuck where the pendulum was a generation in the past."

"Excellent!" said John. "You have redeemed yourself from your last answer. I think I have given you food for contemplation here, even though we could spend much longer on this Key. This is not the end of the teaching on this or the first Key. We will be discussing additional insights periodically as we proceed with the various teachings you will be presented. All the Twelve Keys of Knowledge, as well as the Keys of Wisdom and Eternal Life are synthetic and interplay with one another. To see one with perfect clarity you have to see them all."

"So, are you going to start us on the next key?" I asked.

John got up from his chair and paced back and forth as if in deep thought. "I suppose it is about time to move on, isn't it?"

"Will all the Keys take as much time to get as the first two?"

"That's up to you," he said. "Some will go faster than others." He then stopped, looked at me and continued, "The name of the Third Key is *Communion*. Communion exists on many levels. Humans can commune with lives lower than themselves, with each other and with lives higher than themselves. The goal of the true seeker is, of course, to obtain higher communion through the soul and spirit. To obtain the higher communion, we must master this principle as it applies to us in the present and move upward. Have you ever played the game where a group gathers in a circle and the first person whispers an unknown phrase into the ear of the one next to him, then that person passes the message on until the message is whispered throughout the circle until it gets to the last person?"

"Yes, I have played that before," I said with a chuckle. "The results are often amusing, because when the last person to get the message states what he received, it is often completely different from the original phrase."

"Contemplate the reason for this," he said, "for it is a hint to the truth of the Third Key. This is a key to achieving communion through the soul, and this key is linked to the first two keys. Consider what this may be, and we shall discuss it further when we meet again."

"How long will it be before we see you again?" I asked.

"When you have sufficiently digested what you have been given so far," he said. "Do not concern yourself with the time between the lessons, or when I shall or shall not appear. Concern yourself instead with the lessons. If you like, we can say the Song of the 144,000 together before I depart."

To this gesture, Elizabeth and I both nodded in agreement. We held hands and said it together, and as we did, it felt like we were transported to the New Jerusalem enjoying the presence of gods and angels. When we finished Elizabeth grabbed John and gave him an enduring hug. I noticed a tear running down her face. Then I gave him a hug and it felt for a moment like we were both taken out of our bodies to become one soul. It was a great feeling.

John headed toward the door and opened it. As he was about to step out, Elizabeth touched his arm and said, “You don’t have to walk away. You can just do your thing and dematerialize yourself or whatever you do.”

John turned and smiled, “That which humanity call miracles must be manifested with purpose. There is no reason for me not to walk. Besides, I like to walk. May the peace of God be with you both.”

“There’s just one more question that has bothered me over the years that I just have to ask before you leave,” said Elizabeth.

“Ask away,” smiled John.

“Some say that Elvis faked his death and may still be alive. Could you tell me the truth about this mystery?”

I got the impression that John was about to tell Elizabeth the whole story, but changed the course of his thought and replied, “We all need a few mysteries in life to keep our wheels greased.” He kissed her on the forehead and said, “Now I must go.”

He then walked out to the driveway, turned on the sidewalk, and headed toward the city. We both went to the edge of the driveway, watching him until we could see him no more. We both knew what the other was thinking. How far did he go until another miracle occurred?

THE SWING OF THE PENDULUM

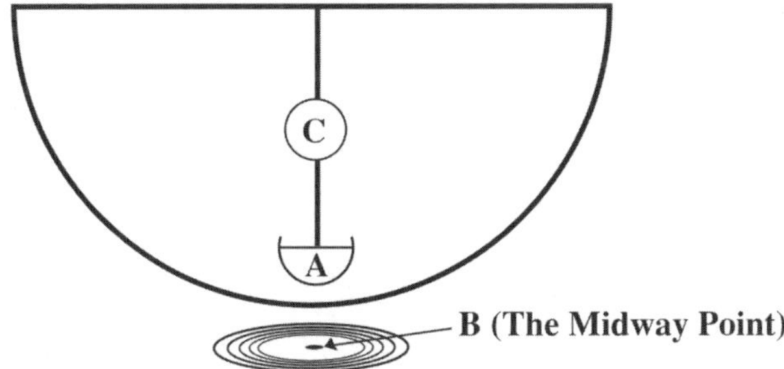

A Represents the seat at the end of the pendulum. B represents the point of truth at the immovable midway point. C represents the arm of the pendulum.

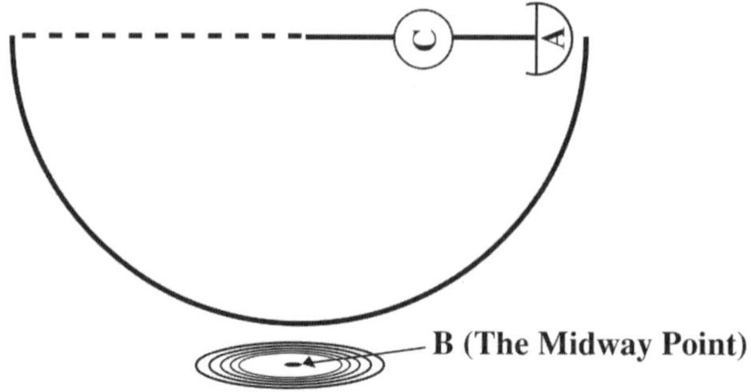

The rider swings on the pendulum to the extreme right and the point A has moved with him. The illusion now appears that the far right is correct, logical and most reasonable, yet the point of truth (B) is still where it has always been - at the Midway Point. But to the one who is now on the far right, the Midway Point seems to be an extreme left position.

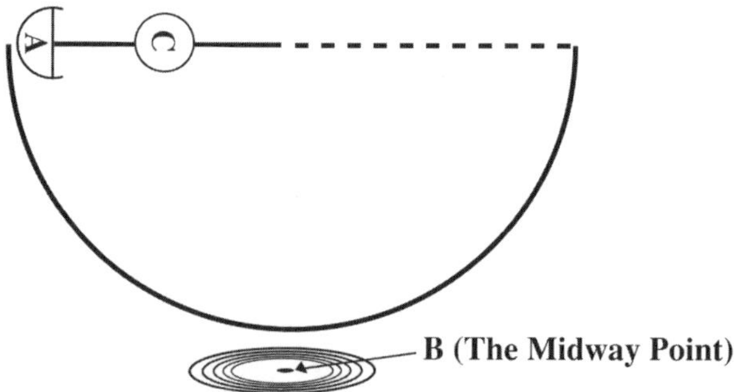

The rider now swings on the pendulum to the extreme left and the point A has again moved with him. The illusion is now reversed in that the far left seems correct, logical and most reasonable, yet the point of truth (B) ever remains in the Midway Point. The one who is now on the far left sees the Midway Point as an extreme right position.

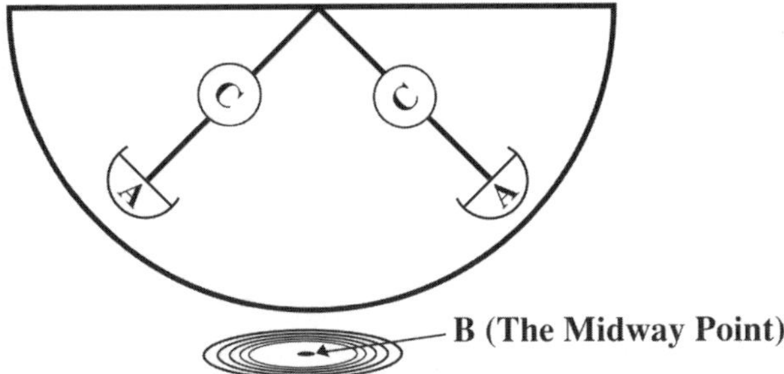

In this diagram the rider in motion is at the moderate left and later the moderate right. In these cases the real truth is seen not as an extreme, but definitely "off base," or off center.

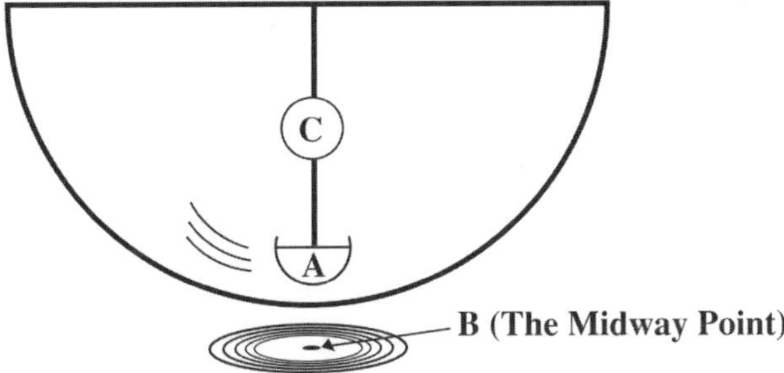

It is only when the pendulum swing takes the rider over the Midway Point again that the real point of truth is briefly seen as reasonable. But to him who understands the Second Key, this point is always known, even when the pendulum swings to the extreme.

IF YOU ENJOYED THIS BOOK

and want to be on our mailing list for announcements of future books in this series, newsletters, seminars etc., send your name, address and e-mail address (if any) to:

Great Ad-Ventures
P. O. Box 8011
Boise, Idaho 83707
or e-mail to:
book@freeread.com

This is the third in **The Immortal** series of twelve books. For a free digital copy of Book I go to www.freeread.com.

Books I and II of this series are sold as one volume and can be ordered from any bookstore or from the publisher for $19.95.

To order, inquire at your bookstore or call:

1-800-390-5687

Additional copies of this book: $19.95 each. Ask about quantity discounted pricing.

Price includes shipping and handling in the USA. Idaho residents add 6% sales tax. Foreign orders add $5.00 per book.

Send check, money order or charge card information. We accept MC/VISA/Discover and American Express.

For information for a free study class on the internet, e-mail to book@freeread.com.

Call 1-800-390-5687 for additional writings by J J Dewey:

The Molecular Relationship - $19.95
The Gathering of Lights - $19.95
The Gods of the Bible - $14.95
The Keys of Knowledge - Teachings of J J Dewey
Volumes 1-4 - $19.95 each.